Special Educational Needs and the Law

Special Educational Needs and the Law

Simon Oliver, LLB (Hons)
Barrister, part-time chair of Special Educational Needs Tribunals

Lesley Austen, LLB (Hons)
Solicitor, lecturer at the University of Exeter

JORDANS
1996

Published by
Jordan Publishing Limited
21 St Thomas Street
Bristol BS1 6JS

© Jordan Publishing Limited 1996
Reprinted May 1997

British Library Cataloguing-in-Publication Data
A catalogue record for this book is available from the British Library.

ISBN 0 85308 310 X

Typeset by Mendip Communications Ltd, Frome
Printed in Great Britain by Biddles Ltd, Guildford and King's Lynn

FOREWORD

A child with special educational needs normally requires some special educational provision, and about 20% of children are likely to have such needs at some time during their school career. This demonstrates the importance of the machinery which matches their education to those needs. Delay is clearly undesirable, and it can be avoided by a clear understanding of the procedure.

The Education Act 1993 shook up the statutory provisions which aim to ensure that children with special needs receive the education they need. It took initiatives in two directions which some might regard as contradictory: on the one hand, it emphasised the need for partnership between the parents, the school and the education authority, and, on the other hand, it gave parents new access to the law through the Special Educational Needs Tribunal appeal system.

The Tribunal opened its doors on 1 September 1994 and has already dealt with many appeals from parents. It aims to be informal so that its procedures do not intimidate those who are not familiar with legal processes. Nevertheless, it has had the effect of bringing into direct contact with the law many people who have not previously had that experience. This applies not only to parents, but also to the many professionals in this sphere: teachers, educational administrators, doctors, psychologists and therapists.

For everyone coming fresh to the law, as well as for lawyers of whom only a few are fully familiar with this area of practice, the concise but comprehensive statement of the rules and procedure in this book will be extremely helpful. It rightly starts by examining the position before there is any dispute for the Tribunal to resolve: only a small proportion of cases will ever get that far. However, the intrinsic importance of appeals to the Tribunal justifies a detailed examination of the way it works and the possibilities open to the parties. This book helpfully draws on the early experience of the Tribunal, which has enabled the authors to examine the impact of Tribunal decisions.

Ultimately, everyone benefits when disputes in this field are avoided. Because the statute was designed to promote partnership, a ready understanding of the law is likely to promote harmony, rather than provoke discord. I welcome the contribution which this book will make to that understanding.

Trevor Aldridge QC
President, Special Educational Needs Tribunal

PREFACE

The Code of Practice on the Identification and Assessment of Special Educational Needs introduced from 1 September 1994 has altered the perception of special educational needs even more than the Education Act 1981 did in its time.

The Code of Practice places the school and, particularly, the governors and special needs co-ordinators in the front line of assessment and help. This is a great responsibility and so, in Part I, we set out, for the help of those involved in the delivery of a school curriculum, their obligations and responsibilities. In addition, parents of children with special needs are often unclear about what ought to happen or what is happening. By discussing the various stages of the Code of Practice and examining what should happen, for example, when there is to be a statutory assessment of a child, we hope that those parents who did not previously know what to expect will be able to ensure that what is required is done.

Previously, there was criticism that if a parent was dissatisfied with a decision taken by a Local Education Authority (LEA), the only organisation to whom he or she could appeal was a committee of the same LEA. However, the creation of the wholly independent Special Educational Needs Tribunal has removed that perceived bias, and its growing popularity is evidenced by the ever-increasing number of appeals with which it has to deal.

Although there are both many groups with highly organised support networks and skilled advocates who ensure that a parent's case is fully represented at all stages of the appeal for those parents who can afford legal representation at the Tribunal, the majority of parents who appeal do so on their own. In Part II of the book, we hope to help such parents through the maze of procedure and regulation and, by giving examples of previous decisions of the Tribunal, enable them to present a case to the Tribunal which will completely cover all they want to say.

For lawyers, education law is a growing area. The recent decision of the House of Lords in *X v Bedfordshire County Council* is only one example where boundaries and limits are constantly being tested and extended. Under the 1981 Act, there were an increasing number of judicial review cases. Although the creation of the Tribunal means that there will not be so many in the future, the availability of Green Form advice and assistance means that it will be important for lawyers to have the procedure quickly and easily to hand. In addition, if the financial constraints placed on authorities mean that they are unable or unwilling to implement Tribunal decisions, an understanding of the next steps to take will be crucial.

We hope that this book achieves all these objectives.

We are grateful to the following people for their help and assistance in various stages of the preparation of this book: Trevor Aldridge QC, Dr Peter Smith, Christine Pearce, Maureen Long, Samantha Leigh, Jessica Saraga, Sue Collins, Alison Henry,

Melanie Hooper, Bruce Barton, Bill Willoughby, Melanie Oliver, and all members of the Tribunal staff.

Simon Oliver is particularly grateful for the patience and understanding of his wife, Melanie, and sons, Ben and Edward, without whom this book would not have been completed and to whom Part II is dedicated.

The law is stated as at April 1996, although it has been possible to incorporate some later information. The views expressed in this book are our own and do not reflect or purport to be the views of the Department for Education and Employment, or the President or members of the Special Educational Needs Tribunal. The errors are, of course, entirely ours.

SIMON OLIVER
Guildford
LESLEY AUSTEN
Exeter

June 1996

CONTENTS

TABLE OF CASES

TABLE OF STATUTES

TABLE OF STATUTORY INSTRUMENTS

References are to paragraph numbers.

TABLE OF CODES AND CIRCULARS

References are to paragraph numbers.

PART I

STATEMENTING

Chapter 1

SCHOOLS' OBLIGATIONS

1.1 GOVERNING BODY'S DUTIES

1.1.1 The Code of Practice

The Education Act 1993 imposes important responsibilities on the governing bodies of all maintained schools towards children with special educational needs. These build on the principles and practice first set out in the Education Act 1981 and extend to pupils who do not require statements of special educational needs as well as to those with statements. The 1993 Act requires the Secretary of State to issue, and from time to time to revise, a Code of Practice giving practical advice on such responsibilities, and the governing body must have regard to this Code of Practice[1] when carrying out its duties towards all pupils with special educational needs.[2]

The purpose of the Code of Practice is to provide 'practical guidance' and, 'taken together with the regulations made under the Bill and the Bill's primary provisions', to 'set the framework for special education in the future'.[3] The detailed guidance to be found in the Code is subject to the principles, practices and procedures set out in the introduction to the Code.

1.1.2 The principles of the Code

The fundamental principles set out at para 1:2 of the Code are the following.

(1) The needs of all pupils who may have special educational needs either throughout, or at any time during, their school careers must be addressed; the Code acknowledges what it describes as a continuum of needs to be found across the range of ability and recommends that this be reflected in a continuum of provision, which may be made in a wide variety of forms.

(2) Children with special educational needs require the greatest possible access to a broad and balanced education, including the National Curriculum.

(3) The needs of most pupils will be met in the mainstream, and without a statutory assessment or statement of special educational needs. Children with special educational needs, including children with statements of special educational needs, should, where appropriate and taking into account the wishes of their parents, be educated alongside their peers in mainstream schools.

---

1 The Code of Practice on the Identification and Assessment of Special Educational Needs (DFE, 1994), approved by Parliament under s 158 of the Education Act 1993, to which the Education (Special Educational Needs) Regulations 1994 (SI 1994/1047) are appended.

2 Education Act 1993, s 157.

3 HL Deb, vol 545, cols 478–486, per Baroness Blatch, Minister of State.

(4)　Even before reaching compulsory school age, a child may have special educational needs requiring intervention by the local education authority and the health services.

(5)　The knowledge, views and experience of parents are of vital importance. Effective assessment and provision are made where the parents, their children and schools, the local education authority and any other agencies involved work in partnership.[4]

1.1.3　The practices and procedures

The practices and procedures essential in the pursuit of these principles are described in para 1:3 of the Code:

(1)　All children with special educational needs should be identified and assessed as early as possible and as quickly as is consistent with thoroughness.

(2)　Provision for all children with special educational needs should be made by the most appropriate agency. In most cases, this will be the child's mainstream school, working in partnership with the child's parents; no statutory assessment will be necessary.

(3)　Where needed, local education authorities must make assessments and statements in accordance with the prescribed time-limits; must write clear and thorough statements setting out the child's needs, both educational and non-educational, the objectives to be secured, the provision to be made and the arrangements set up for monitoring and review; and must ensure the annual review of the special educational provision arranged for the child and the updating and monitoring of educational targets.

(4)　Special educational provision will be most effective when those responsible take into account the ascertainable wishes of the child concerned, considered in the light of his or her age and understanding.

(5)　There must be close co-operation between all the agencies concerned and a multi-disciplinary approach to the resolution of issues.[5]

The legal obligation to have regard to the Code led to the requirement for the Code to be laid before Parliament,[6] and was referred to by the Minister as 'no light duty':

> 'By law, those who must have regard to the Code cannot ignore it. If they do so, they will be in breach of a duty. They do not, however, have to follow the Code to the letter and in every particular. But any departure from the Code will be challenged, require justification to parents in the first instance and then, depending on the circumstances, to the Secretary of State if the matter at issue is the subject of an appeal. In justifying their actions, those to whom the Code applies will have to show that the alternative action produced results which were at least as beneficial as those which would have resulted from their following the Code.'[7]

Thus, with effect from 1 September 1994, schools' governing bodies and head teachers were required to consider the way in which their schools identify, assess

---

4　Code of Practice, para 1:2.
5　Code of Practice, para 1:3.
6　Education Act 1993, s 158(3).
7　HL Deb, vol 545, col 487.

and provide for pupils with special educational needs in the light of the Code. Whilst it was not expected that all schools would by then have in place the procedures described in the Code, all plans for future provision were to be made having regard to the Code.

1.1.4 Statutory duties

Under s 161 of the 1993 Act, governing bodies of a maintained mainstream school must:

(1) use their best endeavours to secure that the necessary provision is made for any pupil who has special educational needs (s 161(1)(a));
(2) secure that, where the 'responsible person', being the head teacher or the appropriate governor, has been informed by the local educational authority that a pupil has special educational needs, all who are likely to teach him or her are made aware of those needs (s 161(1)(b) and (2));
(3) secure that teachers in the school are aware of the importance of identifying, and providing for, those pupils who have special educational needs (s 161(1)(c));
(4) consult the local education authority; as appropriate, the Funding Agency for Schools (FAS), which was established under the 1993 Act and is responsible for calculating and paying grant to grant-maintained schools including special schools; and the governing bodies of other schools, when it seems to them necessary or desirable in the interests of co-ordinating the special educational provision in the area (s 161(3));
(5) ensure, wherever reasonably practicable and compatible with the child receiving the necessary special educational provision, the efficient education of other children in the school and the efficient use of resources, that the child engages in the activities of the school together with children who do not have special educational needs (s 161(4))[8];
(6) report annually to parents on their policy for pupils with special educational needs (s 161(5)).

1.1.5 The duty to consult

The object of consultation should always be to enhance the provision for pupils with special educational needs in the area by securing its effective co-ordination and guarding against duplication of effort or the emergence of gaps in the system.

Particular matters in relation to which governing bodies are likely to need to consult other schools, the local education authority and the FAS, will include the following.

Schools' SEN policies
When first drawing up or considering significant revision of its SEN policy, a school may wish to consult other schools in the area, the local education authority and, as appropriate, the Funding Agency. The annual report will present an opportunity to review the school's effectiveness in meeting the special educational needs of its

---

8 The substance of this duty was previously set out in the Education Act 1981.

pupils in consultation with other schools and the support services used by the schools, and, if appropriate, to consider revision of its policies.

Maximising the use of expertise and equipment
In the interests of cost-efficiency, a school may wish to consult neighbouring schools on the use of expensive specialist equipment or expertise.

Developing a specialism
Where a school is considering developing a specialism, for example, in providing for children with specific learning difficulties, it may wish to consult other schools in the area, to draw on the expertise available, and the local education authority, to agree the level of support services which may be required.

Utilising support services
Schools should be aware of the range and cost of support services available.

Buildings adaptations
Schools should always consult the local education authority or the FAS, as appropriate, when considering adaptations to buildings, for example to facilitate access for disabled pupils.

In-service teacher training
Where a particular special educational needs in-service training programme is being considered, a school may wish to consult other schools in the area in order to secure economy of scale with regard to training provision and to draw upon any expertise which may be available.

Grant-maintained status
Where a governing body of a local authority maintained school is considering applying for grant-maintained status under the Education Reform Act 1988, it must ensure that the proposed provision for children with special educational needs will continue to contribute to or enhance the provision of special education in the area, and this may involve revision of the special educational needs policy. Similarly, the governing body of a grant-maintained school wishing to change the character of its school should consult other governing bodies and the local education authority as to the effect of such proposals on the provision of special education in the area.

1.1.6 Duty to report

The annual report for each school shall include a report containing such information as may be prescribed about the implementation of the governing body's policy for pupils with special educational needs (s 161(5)).

The Education (Special Educational Needs) (Information) Regulations 1994,[9] reg 5 and Sch 4 require that the governing body's report should comment on the success of the special educational needs policies in the period since the last report.

---

9 SI 1994/1048, in force as from 1 September 1994.

In doing so, the Code of Practice advises, at para 2:12, that the report should demonstrate the effectiveness of the school's systems for the identification and assessment of pupils with special educational needs; the provision made for those pupils; the school's arrangements for monitoring and record-keeping; and the school's use of outside support services and agencies.

The annual report must describe any significant changes in the policy made or proposed during the year. It should state the reasons for any amendments made and how they will affect the special educational provision, both within the school and in the area served by the school. It must also refer to any consultation carried out by the governing body under s 161(3) and describe the principles under which resources have been allocated to and amongst pupils with special educational needs since the last annual report. This need not take the form of a detailed financial account but might include a description of the deployment of teaching and non-teaching staff and the purchase of any specialist equipment.

The annual report provides governing bodies with a regular opportunity to review the success of the school's policy, and to assess the effectiveness of the policy against its broad principles and objectives and against the criteria laid down in Sch 1, para 11 to the Regulations (Sch 2, para 7 in the case of special schools).[10] Governing bodies may wish to consult other schools, the local education authority and the support services used by the school in drawing up their annual report, and the school may wish to use the annual report to alert parents to the availability of the full special educational needs policy.

1.1.7 Responsibilities in mainstream schools

The Code of Practice provides that the governing body should, in co-operation with the head teacher, determine the school's general policy and approach to provision for children with special educational needs, establish the appropriate staffing and funding arrangements and maintain a general oversight of the school's work. The governing body may choose to appoint a committee to take a particular interest in and closely monitor the school's work on behalf of children with special educational needs. The head teacher has responsibility for the day-to-day management of all aspects of the school's work, including special educational provision and will keep the governing body fully informed. The head teacher will also work closely with the special educational needs co-ordinator or team, who will have responsibility for the day-to-day operation of the school's special educational needs policy. All staff, both teaching and non-teaching, should be involved in the development of the school's special educational needs policy. They should be fully aware of the school's procedures for identifying, assessing and making provision for pupils with special educational needs, and of their individual responsibilities in implementing the policy. However, whatever arrangements are made in a particular school, statutory duties remain with the governing body.[11]

---

10 Maintained special schools, including grant-maintained schools, are devoted to making special educational provision. Therefore, their SEN policies and annual reports will cover the work of the school as a whole. Section 161(1)–(4) of the 1993 Act does not apply to special schools.

11 Code of Practice, para 2:8.

Under the Education (Special Educational Needs) (Information) Regulations 1994, governing bodies of all maintained schools are required to publish prescribed information about the school's policy on special educational needs.

1.2 SCHOOLS' SEN POLICIES

Every school must draw up and publish an SEN policy. This should be made readily available to parents and some schools may wish to provide parents with a copy of the policy. A school's annual report must contain a report on the implementation of the school's SEN policy and a summary of the policy must be included in the school's prospectus.

The issues which schools' SEN policies must address are prescribed in the Education (Special Educational Needs) (Information) Regulations 1994, but the Regulations do not prescribe the contents of those policies nor do they limit the issues which may be addressed. Schools have the freedom to develop their own SEN policies in accordance with their duties and functions and those of the local education authority, in the light of the guidance contained in the Code of Practice, and taking into account the resources available to the school and their most cost-efficient use. In this way, schools are able to reflect their particular specialisms, principles and procedures.

The SEN policies should be kept under regular review and should be an integral part of the school's strategic planning.

1.2.1 Mainstream schools

In formulating their SEN policies, schools must have regard to the Code of Practice. Part 2 of the Code provides practical guidance for schools as to the steps that should be taken to identify and assess pupils with special educational needs, the procedures to be followed in providing for such pupils and the arrangements to be made for reviewing the effectiveness of the provision and further steps to be taken.

The Code of Practice recommends a staged approach intended to match action to the individual child's needs. The head teacher should be kept informed at each stage and the school should work in the closest possible partnership with the parents. Close co-operation and the full exchange of information with outside agencies are also necessary in order to ensure that the needs of the great majority of pupils with special educational needs are met effectively in mainstream schools and without requiring a statutory assessment by the local education authority.

The issues which must be addressed by mainstream schools' SEN policies, set out in Sch 1 to the Education (Special Educational Needs) (Information) Regulations 1994, SI 1994/1048, are as follows.

1.2.2 Basic information about schools' special educational provision

Schools' objectives in making provision for pupils with special educational needs:
Sch 1, para 1
Schools should set out the principles upon which is based their provision for children with special educational needs, both with and without statements, and the objectives which their SEN policies are intended to achieve. Such principles and objectives should be reflected in the arrangements described under the remaining headings in the schools' policies.

The person responsible for co-ordinating the day-to-day provision of education for
pupils with special educational needs (or the SEN co-ordinator): Sch 1, para 2
This may be the head teacher or deputy, the SEN co-ordinator or the head of the special educational needs or learning support team, being a point of reference to whom parents and external agencies may address enquiries.

The arrangements for co-ordinating provision for pupils with special educational needs:
Sch 1, para 3
The Code of Practice advises that, in mainstream schools, a designated teacher should be responsible for:

(1)   the day-to-day operation of the school's SEN policy;
(2)   liaising with and advising fellow teachers;
(3)   co-ordinating provision for children with special educational needs;
(4)   maintaining the school's SEN register and overseeing the records on all pupils with special educational needs;
(5)   liaising with parents of children with special educational needs;
(6)   contributing to the in-service training of staff;
(7)   liaising with external agencies including the educational psychology service and other support agencies, medical and social services and voluntary bodies.

This is the role of the SEN co-ordinator, and in a small school, this role may be taken on by one person, possibly the head or deputy. In larger schools, there may be an SEN co-ordinating or learning support team. Schools may also wish to describe the role of the governing body and the head teacher and the part played by any committee established by the governing body, as well as the consideration given to special educational provision in the strategic management of the school.

Admissions arrangements for pupils with special educational needs but without a
statement: Sch 1, para 4
The Department for Education Circular 6/93, 'Admissions to Mainstream Schools', offers guidance on suitable admissions arrangements. Such arrangements cannot be used either to refuse admission to a child or to give the child lower priority than other applicants simply because the school considers itself unable to cater for his or her special educational needs.

However, admissions arrangements can give priority to children for educational reasons such as the child's special educational needs. The school's SEN policy should state whether admissions arrangements do give priority to children with special needs and, if so, the criteria applied. Where a school's SEN policy states that any specialism is catered for, or where the school is accessible to pupils with disabilities, the SEN policy should also specify whether the school or the local education authority gives priority to pupils who could make use of those facilities, and this will include access arrangements. The percentage of places allocated under special criteria for educational reasons should not exceed 10% of the total intake.

Any SEN specialism and any special units: Sch 1, para 5
The policy must describe any area of specialism which the school may have developed in relation to a particular special educational need and the relevant expertise of teachers. The policy should also describe any special unit within the school, such as a unit for children with speech, visual or hearing impairments, the arrangements for the support of children in such units, and their integration with the work of the school as a whole, in order to fulfil the provisions of s 161(4) of the 1993 Act.

Facilities for pupils with special educational needs: Sch 1, para 6
These may include special units, described above, or may consist of equipment, fixtures and fittings, or characteristics of the school buildings. The desirability of a spectrum of mainstream schools being fully accessible to the disabled is acknowledged, together with the need for their distribution in areas of low population density, where there are fewer schools than in urban areas. It is also acknowledged that good access arrangements will assist in promoting the integration of pupils with special educational needs.

All maintained schools which are accessible to pupils with disabilities should describe their particular arrangements in their SEN policies, including arrangements for wheelchair access, any lighting adaptations or colour codings for visually impaired pupils, and the availability of any special features for hearing impaired pupils. Some of this information will be required by the FAS and local education authority in order to provide information in accordance with regulations made under s 21 of the 1993 Act. In the Department for Education Circular 6/94, 'The Organisation of Special Educational Provision', it is suggested that schools with poor access for disabled pupils may wish to consider the possibility of improvements through minor capital works financed through flexibility in the school's budget.[12]

---

12 Circular 6/94, 'The Organisation of Special Educational Provision', Part I, para 39.

1.2.3 Information about schools' policies for identification, assessment and provision for pupils with special educational needs

How resources are allocated to and among pupils with special educational needs: Sch 1, para 7
All authorities should have schemes which delegate funds to schools for children with special educational needs. In local education authority maintained schools, these funds are received through local management schemes weighted according to the incidence of special educational needs within the authority; in grant-maintained schools the funds are received through their Annual Maintenance Grant, or from the Common Funding Formula.

The allocation of these funds is entirely at the discretion of the governing bodies, but the school's policy should explain how they are applied in fulfilment of the duties contained in s 161(1)(a) of the 1993 Act.

Where the school has delegated funds to meet the needs of pupils with statements, the school's policy should explain how these funds are allocated to ensure that the provision specified in the statements is made, in accordance with the governors' responsibilities.

How the needs of pupils are identified and reviewed: Sch 1, para 8
The policy must include an explanation of the school's identification, assessment, monitoring and review procedures, including the staged procedures adopted, in accordance with the duty to have regard to the Code of Practice.

Arrangements for providing access by pupils to a balanced and broadly based curriculum (including the National Curriculum): Sch 1, para 9
It is suggested in Circular 6/94[13] that schools may wish to consider the following:

(1) the extent to which general curriculum development caters for children with special educational needs;
(2) the range of teaching strategies and approaches used, including differentiation; and
(3) how the school's arrangements for in-class support and/or withdrawal affects access to the curriculum for children with special educational needs.

How pupils with special educational needs engage in the activities of the school together with pupils who do not have special educational needs: Sch 1, para 10
The policy should set out any arrangements for ensuring the integration of pupils with special educational needs in respect of their work in all areas of the curriculum and on school visits and other social activities and during recreation time. It should also state how particular rooms and buildings for pupils with special needs are

---

13 Circular 6/94, Part I, para 44.

utilised so as to avoid physically segregating pupils wherever practicable. This is in pursuance of the governing body's duties under s 161(4) of the 1993 Act.

How the governing body evaluates the success of the education which is provided at the school to pupils: Sch 1, para 11
The school's SEN policy should set out how it is proposed to demonstrate the effective implementation of its policy, measured against the broad principles and objectives set out at the beginning of the policy. The school may wish to identify specific targets against which particular aspects of the policy can be evaluated, and this would then form the basis of the annual report to parents.

Any arrangements made by the governing body relating to the treatment of complaints from parents of pupils with special educational needs concerning the provision made at the school: Sch 1, para 12
The policy should make clear to parents of children with special educational needs how they can make a complaint about the provision made for their child at the school and how the school will subsequently deal with that complaint. The time within which the school will aim to respond should also be indicated.

1.2.4 Information about schools' staffing policies and partnership with bodies beyond the schools

Any arrangements made by the governing body relating to in-service training for staff in relation to special educational needs: Sch 1, para 13
In drawing up policies, schools should be appraised of the local education authority's in-service training policy and consider the training needs of the SEN co-ordinator and how he or she can be equipped to provide training for fellow teachers. The school's policy should set out any arrangements made jointly with other schools.

The use made of teachers and facilities from outside the school including links with support services for special educational needs: Sch 1, para 14
The policy should have regard to the Code of Practice and should explain the sources from which the school seeks external specialist support and any service level agreement with the local education authority.[14]

The role played by parents of children with special educational needs: Sch 1, para 15
The school's policy should clearly state the arrangements for ensuring a close working partnership with parents of children with special educational needs and these should refer to such matters as recording and acting upon parental concern; procedures for involving parents when a concern is first expressed within the school; incorporating parents' views in assessment and subsequent reviews; and

14 Circular 6/94, Part II.

arrangements for ensuring that parents are kept fully informed about procedures and are made welcome at the school.

Any links with other schools, including special schools, and the provision made for the transition of pupils with special educational needs between schools or between the school and the next stage of life or education: Sch 1, para 16
The school's SEN policy should set out any arrangements whereby the school either draws upon the staff and resources of other schools, including special schools, to help the school's provision for pupils with special educational needs, or integrates special school pupils in the mainstream, whether on a full-time or part-time basis. Matters such as standing consultative arrangements with other schools in pursuance of s 161(3) of the 1993 Act,[15] and any arrangements for sharing resources and expertise, may also be covered under this heading.

In drawing up its policy for supporting the transition of pupils between schools or between school and further or higher education or adult life, the school should have regard to the Code of Practice, and, in particular, the advice on the development of agreed pro-formas for recording work with children with special educational needs,[16] and on the transition to adult life or further education of young people without statements but having special educational needs.[17]

Links with child health services, social services and educational welfare services and any voluntary organisations which work on behalf of children with special educational needs: Sch 1, para 17
The policy should set out arrangements for liaison and the exchange of information between the SEN co-ordinator and the designated officers of the district health authority and the department of social services.

1.2.5 Special schools

Special schools (not established in hospitals) should set out in their policies the items listed in Sch 2 to the Education (Special Educational Needs) (Information) Regulations 1994. With appropriate modification to take account of the particular circumstances of special schools, these mirror the items required to be included in the policies of mainstream schools. In formulating their policies, special schools should have considerations similar to those referred to above, as applying to mainstream schools, although it is acknowledged that allowance should be made for the particular circumstances of, and the distinctive issues facing, special schools.[18]

1.2.6 Hospital schools

The SEN policies of special schools established in hospitals will need to take account of the fact that only a small minority of pupils will have learning difficulties

---

15 Circular 6/94, Part III.
16 Code of Practice, para 2:25.
17 Code of Practice, Part 6, especially paras 6:61 and 6:62.
18 Circular 6/94, para 57.

in the sense that the term is normally understood. However, it is likely that there will be some children in hospital schools, who, in their normal school environment, have special educational needs not warranting a statement, and others with statements. In certain specialist hospitals, the latter may account for a substantial proportion. Hospital schools' SEN policies must set out the following:[19]

(1) the name of the person who is responsible for co-ordinating the day-to-day provision of education for pupils with special educational needs at the school (whether or not the person is known as the SEN co-ordinator);

(2) how pupils with special educational needs are identified and their needs determined and reviewed;

(3) how resources are allocated to and among pupils with special educational needs;

(4) how the educational progress of pupils with special educational needs is monitored;

(5) how the contents of a pupil's statement are ascertained and made known to staff;

(6) the arrangements for ensuring continuity of the educational provision set out in a pupil's statement differentiating where necessary between long-stay and short-stay patients;

(7) the arrangements for providing access by pupils with special educational needs to a balanced and broadly based curriculum;

(8) the use made of teachers and facilities from outside the school including links with support services for special educational needs.

---

19 SI 1994/1048, Sch 3.

Chapter 2

SCHOOL-BASED ASSESSMENT

2.1 INTRODUCTION

The Code of Practice on the Identification and Assessment of Special Educational Needs recommends that schools adopt a staged response to give specific help to children who have special educational needs. According to para 2:20 of the Code, this approach is said to recognise that there is a continuum of special educational needs and, where required, to bring increasing specialist expertise to bear on the difficulties that a child may be experiencing.

The model set out in the Code envisages a five-stage approach, where responsibility for pupils within stages 1–3 lies with the school, but with the close involvement of the local education authority at stage 3, and responsibility at stages 4 and 5 is shared by the school and the local education authority.

It is acknowledged in the Code at para 2:22 that it is not essential that there should be five stages, but the Code highlights the importance of differentiation between the stages, which should aim to match the action taken on behalf of a child to his or her needs.

It is envisaged at para 2:23 that the majority of children will not pass through all three school-based stages of assessment and provision since, in many cases, the action taken at one stage will remove the need for the child to move on to the next. Only where a child's progress at any one stage is a continuing cause for concern will the school need to move to the next stage. A relatively large proportion of children may be helped by the stage 1 procedures and a smaller proportion at stages 2 and 3. For the small proportion of children who fail to progress at stage 3, the school should consider referral to the local education authority with a view to statutory assessment. In deciding whether to make a statutory assessment at stage 4, the local education authority will regard the information on the child's learning difficulty and the special educational provision made by the school, assisted by external agencies, up to and including stage 3, as forming an important part of the evidence to be considered. In the case of *R v Secretary of State for Education and Science ex parte Lashford*,[1] it was held that not all children who have special educational needs require a statement.

The Code states at para 2:24 that these stages will not usually be steps on the way to assessment, nor are they hurdles to be crossed before a statutory assessment can be made. Rather, they are intended to assist schools and parents in deciding what special educational provision is necessary and in matching such provision to the child's needs. The Code further states that:

> 'It is for the school, consulting parents, to decide what stage is suitable for a child. If a child's needs require action at stage 2 or 3, even if no action has previously been taken at stage 1, then action should be taken at stage 2 or 3.'[2]

---

1 [1988] 1 FLR 72.
2 Code of Practice, para 2:24.

The Code of Practice also states that:

> 'The school-based stages should be seen as a continuous and systematic cycle of planning, action and review within the school to enable the child with special educational needs to learn and progress. As such, they are a natural extension of the work of schools with children generally.'[3]

At para 1:4, the Code sets out one model of a staged approach to the identification, assessment, monitoring and review of the special educational needs of children without statements in mainstream schools. However, it is not intended to be prescriptive and it is for individual schools to decide the exact procedures they should adopt and the nature and content of special educational provision they should make.

Paragraph 2:6 of the Code requires schools to consult the local education authority when considering the development of a staged approach or any significant changes to such an approach. The model is intended to apply to schools generally but might be adopted differently in a small rural primary school and a large inner-city comprehensive. None the less, according to the Code, the model embodies certain principles which are central to the Code and to which all schools should have regard, namely:

(1)   provision for a child with special educational needs should match the nature of his or her needs;
(2)   there should be careful recording of a child's special educational needs, the action taken and the outcomes;
(3)   consideration should be given to the ascertainable wishes and feelings of the child;
(4)   there should be close consultation and partnership with the child's parents;
(5)   outside specialists should be involved, particularly, but not necessarily only, in the stage preceding any referral to the local education authority for a statutory assessment.[4]

2.2   STAGE 1

At stage 1, the initial identification and registration of a child's special educational needs will take place. This will involve the gathering of basic information about the child and taking early action to meet the child's needs within his or her normal classroom work and monitoring and reviewing his or her progress.

2.2.1   Trigger

Stage 1 will be triggered by the expression of a concern by any teacher at the school, by a parent, or by another professional such as a health or social services worker, that a child is showing signs of having special educational needs, together with evidence for such concern. The concern will, in most cases, be expressed either to or by the

---

3 Code of Practice, para 2:61.
4 Code of Practice, para 2:64.

child's class teacher in a primary school, or, in a secondary school, the form or year tutor.

2.2.2 Roles and responsibilities

Overall responsibility rests with the child's class teacher or form or year tutor. He or she should inform or seek advice from the SEN co-ordinator and consult the child's parents. The head teacher may also be informed.

It is the responsibility of the teacher or tutor to:[5]

(1) gather information about the child and make an initial assessment of the child's special educational needs;
(2) provide special help within the normal curriculum framework, exploring ways in which increased differentiation of classroom work might better meet the needs of the individual child;
(3) monitor and review the child's progress.

It is the responsibility of the SEN co-ordinator to:[6]

(1) ensure that the child is included in the school's SEN register;
(2) help the child's teacher or tutor gather information and assess the child's needs;
(3) advise and support as necessary those who will teach the child.

2.2.3 Information required

The information appropriate to stage 1, which the child's teacher or tutor, with the help of the SEN co-ordinator, should collect and record, includes the following.[7]

(1) From the school:
    – class records, including any from other schools which the child has attended in the previous year;
    – National Curriculum attainments;
    – standardised test results or profiles;
    – Records of Achievement;
    – reports on the child in school settings;
    – observations about the child's behaviour.
(2) From the parent:
    – views on the child's health and development;
    – perceptions of the child's performance, progress and behaviour at school and at home;
    – factors contributing to any difficulty;
    – action the school might take.

---

5 Code of Practice, para 2:73.
6 Code of Practice, para 2:74.
7 Code of Practice, para 2:75.

(3) From the child:
  – personal perception of any difficulties;
  – how they might be addressed.
(4) From other sources:
  – any information already available to the school from health or social services or any other source.

2.2.4 Assessing and meeting the child's special educational needs

The information collected at stage 1 will reveal the different perceptions of those concerned with the child, the immediate educational concerns and the wider context of the child's learning difficulties. On the basis of such information, the child's teacher or tutor will consider how the child's special educational needs may best be addressed.

In particular, the teacher or tutor, in consultation with the SEN co-ordinator, will decide whether:[8]

(1) to continue the child's current educational arrangements, no special help being needed; or
(2) to seek advice and support; or
(3) to give the child special help by differentiation of the curriculum and monitoring and reviewing the child's progress.

Continuing current arrangements
It is possible that the combination of the expression of concern, the gathering of information and the registration and consideration of the child's special educational needs may serve to resolve problems, therefore requiring no further action at this stage. Such a decision should be recorded by the teacher or tutor, and the child's parents and the SEN co-ordinator should be informed. Notwithstanding the decision that no special educational provision is required, the SEN co-ordinator should retain the child's name on the school's SEN register and consult the child's teacher or tutor about the child's progress on a regular basis until it is clear that the child's progress is no longer likely to give any cause for concern.

Seeking advice and support
If it is clear to the child's teacher or tutor and the SEN co-ordinator at the outset that information additional to that available to the school is required or that action at stage 1 would be inadequate, para 2:79 of the Code states that the child should move straight to the appropriate stage.

Giving special help at stage 1
The teacher or tutor, in consultation with the SEN co-ordinator, may decide that the child could benefit from a period of special attention and carefully differentiated teaching within his or her normal classroom work. The nature and aims of such special educational provision should be recorded and a review date set.

---

8 Code of Practice, para 2:77.

2.2.5 Review

The child's parents should always be informed of the action that the school proposes to take and, if it has been decided to give special help at stage 1, of the review date set. The review might be within a term and should focus on the progress made by the child, the effectiveness of the special help and future action.

The following are possible outcomes of the review:

(1) *The child continues at stage 1*
If the child's progress has been at least satisfactory, the teacher or tutor should set targets to be achieved by the next review and, if progress continues to be satisfactory after two reviews, it may be decided to increase gradually the time between reviews.

(2) *The child no longer needs special help*
If a child's progress continues to be satisfactory within this framework of provision and review for at least two review periods, the teacher or tutor may decide that the child no longer needs special help. The SEN co-ordinator should retain the child's name on the SEN register until it is clear that the child's progress is no longer likely to give cause for concern.

(3) *The child moves to stage 2*
If, after two review periods at stage 1, special help has not resulted in the child's making satisfactory progress, according to para 2:83 of the Code, the teacher or tutor and the SEN co-ordinator may decide to move the child to stage 2.

At para 2:69 of the Code, it is observed that all schools recognise the importance of consulting parents whether or not their children have special educational needs and that this is achieved through a variety of means such as parents' evenings and informal discussions when the child is brought to or collected from school. It is further observed that, whilst formal meetings may sometimes be desirable, they are not always necessary or feasible but that parents will have important information to give to the school and, working in partnership with the school, can often help their child at home. The paragraph concludes by stating that parents should always be told about any special help their child receives and about the outcome of that help.

Thus, occasions such as parents' evenings may allow parents to contribute to stage 1 reviews. Parents should always be advised of the outcome and of any steps they can take to help the child at home. It is particularly important that any proposal to move the child to stage 2 is discussed with the parents in person.

2.3 STAGE 2

Paragraph 2:85 of the Code states that at stage 2 the SEN co-ordinator takes the lead in assessing the child's learning difficulty, and in planning, monitoring and reviewing the special educational provision, working with the child's teachers and ensuring consultation with the parents.

2.3.1 Trigger

According to para 2.86 of the Code, the trigger for stage 2 will either be a decision at a stage 1 review, or where, after discussion between teachers and parents of the initial concern expressed, the SEN co-ordinator considers that early intensive action is required.

2.3.2 Roles and responsibilities

The school's SEN co-ordinator takes the lead in co-ordinating the child's special educational provision, in consultation with the child's teachers, who remain responsible for classroom work with the child.

2.3.3 Information required

At stage 2, the SEN co-ordinator and the child's class teacher or form or year tutor should review all the available information, including that gathered at stage 1. The SEN co-ordinator should also always seek information from health and social services and other agencies closely involved with the child.[9]

(1) The school doctor or the child's general practitioner (with the consent of the parents) should be asked to give medical advice.

(2) The social services and/or the education welfare service, as appropriate, should be asked for information on any arrangements under an education supervision order;[10] social services involvement with the child or the family; any concerns about the child's welfare; whether the local authority has the child on the Child Protection Register[11] or has any responsibilities for the child under the Children Act 1989.

Where appropriate, the SEN co-ordinator may also collect information from any other agencies which may be closely connected with the child such as any supplementary school or voluntary organisation that runs leisure activities attended by the child.

---

9 Code of Practice, para 2:88.

10 Education supervision order: an order for which local education authorities can apply under s 36 of the Children Act 1989, to put a child of statutory school age who is not being properly educated under the supervision of the local education authority, with the intention that he or she receives efficient full-time education suited to his or her age, aptitude, ability and any special educational needs, and that sufficient support, advice and guidance are provided to the parents.

11 Child Protection Register: in each area covered by a social services department, a central register must be maintained listing all the children in that area who are considered to be suffering from, or who are likely to suffer, significant harm and for whom there is a child protection plan. This is not a register of children who have been abused but of children for whom there are currently unresolved child protection issues.

2.3.4 Assessing and meeting the child's special educational needs

The SEN co-ordinator, in consultation with the child's class teacher or tutor, should consider all available information, including new information gathered at stage 2 and the reports of any stage 1 reviews.

On the basis of the information available, the SEN co-ordinator should decide whether to seek further advice and/or to draw up an individual education plan.[12]

Seeking further advice
If the information obtained reveals an area of the child's development or performance which requires more detailed investigation or further advice, the SEN co-ordinator should record in the report:

(1) what further advice is being sought;
(2) arrangements for the child pending receipt of advice; and
(3) review arrangements.[13]

Making special educational provision at stage 2: the individual education plan
It is the task of the SEN co-ordinator, working with the child's class teacher or form or year tutor and any relevant curriculum specialists, to ensure that an individual education plan is drawn up setting out the following matters:

(1) the nature of the child's learning difficulties;
(2) action to be taken:
    – the special educational provision;
    – staff involved, including frequency of support;
    – specific programmes/activities/materials/equipment;
(3) help from parents at home;
(4) targets to be achieved in a given time;
(5) any pastoral care or medical requirements;
(6) monitoring and assessment arrangements;
(7) review arrangements and date.[14]

As far as possible, the plan should build on the curriculum being followed by the child alongside fellow pupils and should utilise programmes, activities, materials and assessment techniques readily available to the child's teachers. Implementation of the plan should usually take place either completely or in part in the normal classroom setting and will therefore require the close liaison between all relevant teachers.

The child's parents should always be informed of the action which it is proposed that the school will take and any help they can give their child at home.

---

12 Code of Practice, paras 2:90 and 2:91.
13 Code of Practice, para 2:92.
14 Code of Practice, para 2:93.

The review date set by the SEN co-ordinator should normally be within a term and the co-ordinator should agree with the child's teachers the arrangements for monitoring progress until the review. The parents should be informed of any special arrangements that will apply to their child and for how long.

2.3.5 Review

The review will normally be conducted by the SEN co-ordinator, consulting with the child's teacher or form or year tutor and also with the parents, where this is possible. The review should focus on the following matters:[15]

(1) progress made by the child;
(2) effectiveness of the education plan;
(3) contribution made by the parents at home;
(4) updated information and advice;
(5) future action.

Possible outcomes of the review will be as follows.

(1) *The child continues at stage 2*
If the child's progress has been at least satisfactory, a new individual education plan may be prepared which should set targets based on experience gained in the course of the first plan. If progress continues to be satisfactory after two review periods, the period between reviews may be gradually increased.

(2) *The child reverts to stage 1 or no longer needs special help*
If the child's progress remains at least satisfactory for two review periods, the SEN co-ordinator may decide that the child no longer requires special educational provision at stage 2. The child may then be recorded either as having special educational needs at stage 1, or, if the provision has been completely successful, as no longer needing special help. The child's name should be retained on the SEN register until it is clear that his or her progress is no longer likely to give cause for concern.

(3) *The child moves to stage 3*
If after two review periods at stage 2 the child's progress is unsatisfactory, it will be necessary to seek additional expertise and the child should move to stage 3.

Parents should be given the opportunity to contribute to stage 2 reviews and should always be informed of the outcome. It is of particular importance to discuss with the parents in person any plans to move the child to stage 3.

2.4 STAGE 3

At stage 3, the school will call upon external specialist support to assist the child to progress.

---

15 Code of Practice, para 2:96.

2.4.1 Trigger

Stage 3 will be triggered either by a decision at a stage 2 review or where, after consultation about an initial concern between the SEN co-ordinator, teachers and parents, the SEN co-ordinator, having referred to the head teacher, considers that intensive action with external support is required immediately.

2.4.2 Roles and responsibilities

The SEN co-ordinator continues to play a leading role at stage 3, working in close co-operation with the child's teachers, but responsibilities for the child are now shared with external specialist services relevant to the child's needs. Sources of such support will include teachers in a learning or behaviour support service, peripatetic teachers, for example of the hearing or visually impaired, the educational psychology service, child health or child and adolescent mental health services, social services and advisers or teachers with a knowledge of information technology for children with special educational needs.

The arrangements for securing help from these services will be affected by local policies. The SEN co-ordinator will be appraised of such policies, and local education authorities should provide information to all the schools in their area detailing the range of services available.

The Code of Practice recommends[16] that local education authorities should obtain information from maintained schools concerning pupils in their area who are at stage 3. The head teacher or SEN co-ordinator should advise the relevant local education authority whenever a child moves to stage 3 to ensure that records are kept up to date.

2.4.3 Information required

The SEN co-ordinator and the child's class teacher or form or year tutor will consider all the information gathered by the school over stages 1 and 2 and the reports of stage 2 reviews.

2.4.4 Assessing and meeting the child's needs

The SEN co-ordinator should then enlist the help of an appropriate specialist from a support service. The specialist will be qualified and experienced in the particular field of the child's special educational needs and will be selected from a range of professionals such as those listed at **2.4.2** above. At stage 3, educational psychologists will play a key role in helping the school assess the information collected and the action taken to date, in planning stage 3 special educational provision, and in reviewing such provision.

Based on all the information and advice received including the views of the external specialist, the SEN co-ordinator will decide whether to seek further advice from

16 Code of Practice, para 3:7.

other agencies and/or to draw up a new individual education plan, to include the involvement of the support services.

Whatever course of action is decided upon, the child's parents should be informed, wherever possible in person.[17]

Seeking further advice

If it is considered by the SEN co-ordinator and the external specialist that the information gathered reveals an area of the child's development or performance which requires more detailed investigation or further advice from the outside professionals, the SEN co-ordinator should record:

(1) what further advice is being sought;
(2) arrangements for the child pending receipt of advice;
(3) review arrangements.

Making special educational provision at stage 3: individual education plan and specialist involvement

The new plan should be formulated with the help of outside specialists but should usually be implemented, either wholly or in part, in the normal classroom setting. Therefore, the SEN co-ordinator should ensure close liaison between the relevant teachers. The plan should set out the following matters:

(1) nature of the child's learning difficulty;
(2) action
       – the special educational provision;
       – school staff involved, including frequency and timing of support;
       – external specialists involved, including frequency and timing;
       – specific programmes/activities/materials/equipment;
(3) help from parents at home;
(4) targets to be achieved in a given time;
(5) any pastoral care or medical requirements;
(6) monitoring and assessment arrangements;
(7) review arrangements and date.

The plan should ensure a co-ordinated cross-curricular and inter-disciplinary approach which takes due account of the child's previous difficulties.[18]

The SEN co-ordinator, working in close co-operation with the child's class teacher or form or year tutor and any relevant curriculum specialists and with the assistance of the external specialist, is responsible for ensuring that the plan is drawn up. A range of different teaching approaches, appropriate equipment and teaching materials should be considered, including the use of information technology.

The child may be taught directly by the specialist, or the specialist may act in a supervisory role, supporting the teacher or tutor in implementing the plan. Alternatively, the specialist may recommend additional specialist teaching support

---

17 Code of Practice, para 2:106.
18 Code of Practice, paras 2:107–2:109.

which may be provided by SEN support services. It may be the case that medical treatment or improved management in school based on medical advice will considerably reduce the child's special educational needs. Medical advice may include advice from the school health service and from therapists, in addition to that of the child's general practitioner.

Targets
All aspects of the education plan should carry specified targets and special assessment arrangements made for those targets, including assessment by outside specialists where appropriate.

Parents should always be informed of any action proposed by the school and of any special arrangements that will apply to their child and for how long.

The SEN co-ordinator should set a review date, which should normally be within a term and should agree with the child's teachers and the external specialists involved the arrangements for monitoring the child's progress against the targets established in the plan.

2.4.5 Review

At stage 3, the SEN co-ordinator should convene review meetings, the first of which should focus on:

(1) progress made by the child;
(2) effectiveness of the education plan;
(3) updated information and advice;
(4) future action;
(5) whether the child is likely in future to be referred for statutory assessment.[19]

At the review, the external specialists should offer advice on the appropriateness of the school's analysis of the child and subsequent action. It may be necessary to involve other specialists as a result of such advice.

The following are possible outcomes of the review.

(1) *The child continues at stage 3*
If his or her progress has been at least satisfactory, a new individual education plan may be drawn up setting new targets in the light of the experience of the first plan. If progress continues to be satisfactory after two review periods, the SEN co-ordinator, in consultation with the head teacher and the external specialists, may decide to increase gradually the periods between reviews.

(2) *The child reverts to stage 1 or stage 2*
If a child's progress continues to be satisfactory for at least two review periods, the SEN co-ordinator, in consultation with the head teacher and the external specialists, may decide that the intervention of external specialists and special educational provision at stage 3 is no longer required. The child may then be recorded as having

19 Code of Practice, para 2:113.

special educational needs at stage 1 or 2, and action appropriate to that stage should be taken.

(3) *The head teacher considers referring the child to the local education authority for statutory assessment*
If the child's progress remains unsatisfactory by the second stage 3 review, the head teacher, on the advice of the SEN co-ordinator, should consider informing the local education authority that a statutory assessment may be required. Any such approach should have the endorsement of a responsible person.

Parents should always be invited to attend stage 3 reviews and their attendance actively encouraged. They should always be told of the outcome and consulted in person where there is any likelihood of the child being referred for a statutory assessment.

At the time that the head teacher considers referring the child for statutory assessment, the following information should have been obtained.

(1) Written information on:
  – educational and other assessments, for example from an advisory specialist support teacher or an educational psychologist;
  – views of the parents and of the child;
  – the child's health;
  – social services' or education welfare service's involvement.
(2) Written evidence of:
  – the school's action under the three stages;
  – education plans for the child;
  – regular reviews and their outcomes;
  – involvement of other professionals.[20]

Where a child is referred for a statutory assessment by his or her school, the head teacher is enabled, under regulations made under s 19 of the Education Reform Act 1988, to give a special direction either modifying or disapplying[21] the National Curriculum for the child for a period of up to 6 months although it is the intention that such exceptions should be rare. The Code of Practice warns head teachers against pre-judging the outcome of any statutory assessment and advises that it may be more difficult to carry out an assessment if the child has been excepted from aspects of the National Curriculum. When the local education authority are considering whether to make a statutory assessment or are conducting an assessment, the school, working in partnership with the child's parents and the support services, remains responsible for the child's education, including special educational provision.[22]

The information on the child's learning difficulty and the evidence of the special educational provision made at stages 1–3 will be considered by the local education

---

20 Code of Practice, para 2:116.
21 Disapplication: the removal or lifting of a component of the National Curriculum, including a programme of study, attainment target, assessment, or any combination of these. Also includes entire subjects or the whole of the National Curriculum.
22 Code of Practice, para 2:117.

authority in deciding whether a statutory assessment is necessary. If the support services of the local authority and, in particular, its educational psychologists have been involved in assessment of the child and the review of provision at stage 3, the decision should be reached without delay.

2.5 SUMMARY

To summarise, schools should adopt a staged response to children's special educational needs and should:

(1) employ clear procedures to identify and register children whose academic, physical, social or emotional development is giving cause for concern;
(2) identify children's areas of weakness which require extra attention from their teachers or other academic staff;
(3) develop, monitor, review and record, in consultation with parents and involving the child as far as possible, individual education plans designed to meet each child's identified needs. Such plans should include written information about:
    – individual programmes of work;
    – performance targets;
    – review dates, findings and decisions;
    – parental involvement in and support for the plans;
    – arrangements for the involvement of the child;
    – information on any external advice or support;
(4) assess children's performance, identifying strengths as well as weaknesses, using appropriate measures so that the rate of progress resulting from special educational provision can be assessed;
(5) call upon specialist advice from outside the school to inform the school's strategies to meet the child's special educational needs in particular, but not only, at stage 3.[23]

---

23 Code of Practice, para 2:119.

Chapter 3

STATUTORY ASSESSMENT PROCEDURE

3.1 INTRODUCTION

Section 167 of the Education Act 1993 requires that, where a local education authority is of the opinion that a child for whom it is responsible has special educational needs and that it is necessary for the authority to determine the special educational provision which any learning difficulty the child may have calls for, the authority shall make an assessment of the child's educational needs.

Under s 165 of the 1993 Act, a local education authority has a duty to identify children with special educational needs for whom it is necessary for the authority to determine the special educational provision needed, and the authority has responsibility for a child if that child is in its area and:

(1)   the child is a registered pupil at a maintained, grant-maintained or grant-maintained special school;

(2)   education is provided for the child at a school which is not a maintained, grant-maintained or grant-maintained special school at the expense of the authority or the funding authority;

(3)   the child does not come within (1) or (2) above but is a registered pupil at a school and has been brought to the authority's attention as having (or probably having) special educational needs; or

(4)   the child is not a registered pupil at a school, is not under the age of 2 years or over compulsory school age and has been brought to the authority's attention as having (or probably having) special educational needs.

It is envisaged that the needs of the vast majority of children with special educational needs will be met effectively under the school-based stages, without the statutory involvement of the local education authority. However, in a small minority of cases, estimated at around 2% of children, the local education authority will need to make a statutory assessment of special educational needs.

Statutory assessment is represented at stage 4 of the five-stage model and involves consideration by the local education authority, working in co-operation with the child's school, parents and other agencies, as appropriate, as to whether a statutory assessment of the child's special educational needs is necessary and, if so, conducting such assessment, again working closely with parents, school and other agencies.

Statutory assessment will not lead to a statement in every case, as was highlighted by *Lashford*.[1] The information gathered during an assessment may indicate ways in which the child's needs can be met by his or her school without the need for any special educational provision to be determined by the local education authority through a statement. For example, it may be that the provision of a particular piece

---

1   *R v Secretary of State for Education and Science ex parte Lashford* [1988] 1 FLR 72.

of equipment would allow the school, with appropriate expert guidance and support, to meet the child's needs. This point was recently illustrated in the case of *R v Lambeth London Borough Council ex parte M*[2] where it was held that the provision of a lift at a mainstream primary school to enable a disabled pupil to use the science room and library on the first floor could not be regarded as a provision for an educational need in the context of the local authority's statement of special educational needs.

3.2 ROUTES FOR REFERRAL

A child will be brought to the attention of the local education authority as possibly requiring an assessment by reason of:

(1)   referral by the child's school or other agency;
(2)   a formal request for an assessment from a parent; or
(3)   a formal request from a grant-maintained school directed to admit a pupil under s 13 of the 1993 Act.

3.2.1   Referral by the child's school or other agency

Following action to meet the learning difficulties of a child, a school will conclude in some cases that the child's needs remain such that they cannot be met effectively within the school's normal resources. Therefore, the school may draw the child to the attention of the local education authority with a view to an assessment under the 1993 Act.

In rare cases, a school may consider a statutory assessment to be necessary even though no action has been taken at stages 1–3, where a child demonstrates such significant difficulties that the school considers it impossible or inappropriate to follow its assessment procedure in full. At para 3:24 of the Code, it is cited by way of example that the school's concerns may have resulted in further assessment or examination which indicates that a child has a major sensory or other impairment which will lead to increased learning difficulties without immediate specialist intervention beyond that which the school is equipped to provide.

In such a case, where there is agreement between the school, the child's parents and any relevant consultant or adviser about the child's need for further multi-disciplinary assessment or there is concern that any delay might be deleterious to the child's development, the child may be referred immediately to the local education authority for consideration for statutory assessment.

Children may also be drawn to the attention of the local education authority by the health services and social services departments. This is particularly likely in the case of children under 5 years old who are not yet attending school.

When making a referral for a statutory assessment, the school should state the reasons for referral and provide the following.

2 (1995) *The Times*, 9 May.

(1) Information, including:
   - the recorded views of parents, and, where appropriate, children, on earlier stages of assessment and any action and support to date;
   - evidence of health checks, for example relevant information on medical advice to the school;
   - when appropriate, evidence relating to social services' involvement.
(2) Written individual education plans at stages 2 and 3 indicating the approaches adopted, the monitoring arrangements followed and the educational outcomes.
(3) Reviews of each individual education plan indicating decisions made as a result.
(4) Evidence of the involvement and views of professionals with relevant specialist knowledge and expertise outside the normal competence of the school.[3]

3.2.2 A formal request from a parent

Sections 172 and 173 of the 1993 Act enable parents to request the local education authority to carry out an assessment, under s 172 where the request is for a further assessment in the case of children for whom there are statements, and under s 173 in the case of children in respect of whom the authority does not maintain statements.

The local education authority needs only to comply with the request if such an assessment has not been made within the period of 6 months ending with the date on which the request is made, and it is necessary for the authority to make an assessment.[4]

If, in any case where the above conditions apply, the authority determines not to comply with the request, it must give notice to that effect to the parents and also tell them of their right to appeal to the SEN Tribunal against such determination.[5]

The Tribunal may either dismiss the appeal or order the authority to arrange for an assessment to be made in respect of the child.[6]

Where schools, external specialists, including local education authority support and educational psychology services, and parents have been working in partnership at stage 3, the parental request for a statutory assessment will usually have been discussed between them, and the local education authority will therefore be aware of it.

Alternatively, where a child attends an independent school, a parental request for an assessment may be the first that a local education authority hears about that child. However, the procedure to be followed and the factors to be considered in deciding whether to make an assessment should be the same in each case. The authority will wish to investigate evidence provided by the school and parents as to the child's

---

3 Code of Practice, para 3:8.
4 Education Act 1993, ss 173(1)(b), (c) and 172(3). Note that under the Education Act 1981 the local education authority had to comply with such a request unless it was 'unreasonable' (s 9(1)). Now, following the *Lashford* decision, it is a matter of whether assessment is 'necessary'.
5 See **8.2**.
6 Education Act 1993, s 173(2) and (3).

learning difficulties and evidence about action taken by the school to meet those difficulties.

When a child is referred by a parental request for a statutory assessment, the local education authority should not issue a notice that it proposes to make an assessment under s 167(1) of the 1993 Act but should immediately contact the parents in order to investigate further the nature of their concern, ascertain the degree of their involvement and agreement with the special educational provision which has been made for their child at school and give them full details of the assessment procedure.[7]

The local education authority must advise the child's head teacher that the parents have made a request for a statutory assessment and should also ask the school for written evidence about the child and, in particular, for the school's assessment of the child's learning difficulty and an account of the special educational provision made. The educational psychology service and any other bodies which might later be asked to advise, together with the designated medical officers of the district health authority and the social services department, should also be notified.

3.2.3 A formal request from a grant-maintained school

The governing body of a grant-maintained school which has, under s 13 of the 1993 Act, been directed to admit a child may request the local education authority responsible for the child to conduct a statutory assessment. The power of direction under s 13 will be used very exceptionally and can only be exercised if a child has been refused admission to, or has been permanently excluded from, every school which is a reasonable distance from the child's home and provides suitable education.

The grant-maintained school should consult the parents before requesting the authority to conduct an assessment. On receiving the request, provided that no assessment has been made in the previous 6 months, the local education authority must issue a notice to the child's parents under s 174(2) of the 1993 Act informing the parents that the local education authority proposes to make an assessment of the child's educational needs and of the procedure to be followed in making the assessment.

The notice must give the parents the same information as the notice required under s 167(1) and, as with that notice, a notice issued under s 174(2) must be copied to the district health authority and the social services department and to the child's head teacher.

---

7 Code of Practice, para 3:20.

3.3   PROPOSAL TO MAKE A STATUTORY ASSESSMENT

3.3.1   Notice of a proposal to make a statutory assessment

Having considered the evidence available, the local education authority will consider whether to issue a notice to the parents that it proposes to make an assessment.

Section 167 of the 1993 Act requires that, before making an assessment, the local education authority should write to the child's parents to explain the proposal and also to inform them of the procedure to be followed in making an assessment. In addition, the child's parents should be informed of the name of the officer of the authority from whom further information may be obtained, often referred to as the 'Named LEA Officer', and of their right to make representations and submit written evidence within a given time-limit, which must not be less than 29 days.

The local education authority should encourage parents to make representations and to submit evidence and, where parents make oral representations, a written statement should be agreed with them. The authority may invite parents to indicate formally if they do not wish to make or add to representations in order that it can then immediately consider whether a statutory assessment is necessary.

In explaining to parents the procedures to be followed during statutory assessment and the possible consequent drawing up of a statement, the local education authority should make clear the precise timing of the various stages within the overall 6-month time-limit and how the parents can assist in meeting time-limits, as well as explaining the exceptions to the time-limits.

The Code of Practice recommends that local education authorities should also:

(1)   inform parents about sources of independent advice, such as local or national voluntary organisations and any local support group or parent partnership scheme, which may be able to assist them in considering their feelings about their child's needs and the type of provision they would prefer;[8]

(2)   advise parents about the role of the 'Named Person', as distinct from the Named LEA Officer, who is preferably independent of the authority and can give parents information about their child's special educational needs, and support in their discussions with the authority. If it is subsequently decided to make a statement, the authority must then write to the parents confirming the identity of the Named Person, but it may be of benefit to both the authority and the parents to give consideration to the identity of the Named Person at the start of the assessment process, as that person can then attend meetings and help parents express their views effectively, thereby encouraging parental participation at all stages. The Named Person is likely either to be from, or recommended by, a local parents' group or voluntary organisation;

(3)   invite the parents to nominate someone whom the authority should consult in addition to those whom it is required to approach for educational, medical,

---

8 See Appendix 9, Other useful addresses.

psychological and social services advice, should the authority decide to proceed with the statutory assessment. The authority should make parents aware that they may also present any private advice or opinions which they have obtained and that these will be taken into account;

(4) inform parents about the full range of provision available in maintained mainstream and special schools within the area covered by the authority. This information should be made available as early as possible to enable parents to consider fully their child's future placement and to arrange visits to particular schools so that they may draw upon such information as they have obtained when making representations or expressing a preference for a particular school to the local education authority.[9]

It is recommended at para 3:13 of the Code of Practice that local education authorities should present information to parents in a manner which is not intimidating and which encourages participation. The information should, where possible, be available in the first language of the parents and it is suggested that authorities may wish to consider presenting the information in audio or video-taped form where the parents may find this more readily accessible.

The Code also suggests at para 3:14 that consideration be given to personal delivery of the letter informing the parents of the proposal to assess, thereby giving parents an additional opportunity to ask any questions. At this time, the authority should also seek parental consent to any medical examination and psychological assessment during the making of the statutory assessment as this will save time should the authority decide that a statutory assessment is required.

In most cases where the school and the parents have been working in partnership, the parents will already be aware of the possibility of a statutory assessment. Only in a small minority of cases in which there has been a sudden change in the child's circumstances, for example as a result of an accident, or if the child has very recently moved into the area, will the local education authority's proposal to assess be unexpected. In such cases, the Code recommends that the authority should attempt to forewarn parents of the intention to make an assessment.[10]

3.3.2 Notification to other agencies of a proposal to assess

When informing parents of the proposal to make an assessment, the local education authority must copy the proposal to:

(1) the social services authority;
(2) the district health authority; and
(3) if the child is registered at a school, the head teacher of that school.[11]

The authority is not asking these agencies to provide advice at this stage, but alerting them to the possibility of a request for advice in the near future. There should be an

9 Code of Practice, para 3:11; see Chapter 6.
10 Code of Practice, paras 3:13–3:15.
11 Regulation 5(1) of the Education (Special Educational Needs) Regulations 1994 (SI 1994/1047), which came into force on 1 September 1994.

endorsement on the copy or a notice accompanying the copy informing the recipient of the nature of the help that the authority is likely to request,[12] thus giving an opportunity for collating records and consulting others who might be involved in providing advice. Prompt action within the health service and social services departments at this stage will effectively give them more time to gather advice, and thus help them meet the statutory time-limits.

3.4 TIMETABLE FOR MAKING ASSESSMENT AND STATEMENTS

In response to the Government's review of the Education Act 1981, which revealed that assessments were subject to delays,[13] regulations made under Sch 9 to the 1993 Act set down time-limits in which the various parts of the process of making statutory assessments and statements must normally be conducted.

The cumulative effect of these time-limits[14] is that the period from the receipt of a request for a statutory assessment for the issue of a notice to parents under s 167(1) or s 174(2), to the issue of a final copy of the statement should normally be no longer than 26 weeks.

The timetable may be broken down as follows.

Considering whether statutory assessment is necessary	The period from the issue of a notice under s 167(1) or s 174(2), or the receipt of a request for a statutory assessment from parents to the decision as to whether to make a statutory assessment must normally be no longer than	6 weeks
Making the assessment	The period from the local education authority's decision to make a statutory assessment, to its decision as to whether or not to make a statement must normally be no longer than	10 weeks
Drafting the proposed statement or note in lieu	The period from the local education authority's decision to make a statement, to the issue of a proposed statement or of a notice of its decision not to make a statement, giving full reasons, preferably in the form of a note in lieu, must normally be no longer than	2 weeks

(contd)

---

12 Regulation 5(2) of the Education (Special Educational Needs) Regulations 1994.
13 'Special Educational Needs: Access to the System' (Department for Education, 1992).
14 Regulations 11 and 14 of the Education (Special Educational Needs) Regulations 1994.

Note in lieu	A note issued to the child's parents and the school when the local education authority decides not to make a statement following a statutory assessment. The note should describe the child's special educational needs, explain the decision not to make a statement and make recommendations about appropriate provision for the child. All the advice received during the assessment should be attached to the note sent to the parents and, with the parents' consent, this should also be sent to the child's school.	
Finalising the statement	The period from the issue of the proposed statement to the issue of the final copy of the statement must normally be no longer than	8 weeks
	Total	26 weeks

3.4.1   Considering whether a statutory assessment is necessary

Having notified the parents that a statutory assessment might be necessary or, alternatively, having received a request from the parents for such an assessment, the next task for the local education authority is to decide whether a statutory assessment must be made.

Except in cases where the initiative comes from the parents in requesting a statutory assessment, the parents have 29 days from the date of the notice from the local education authority under s 167(1) or s 174(1), in which to make representations. This period of 29 days forms part of the 6-week period in which the local education authority has to consider whether a statutory assessment is necessary.

3.4.2   Making the assessment and the statement

Once the decision has been reached to make a statutory assessment, the local education authority must seek parental, educational, medical, psychological and social services advice. In addition to this, it must seek any other advice it considers appropriate and consult those named by the parents, where it is reasonable to do so. Such advice should be sought immediately, and all concerned should be asked to respond within 6 weeks.

The health services and social services departments must normally respond within 6 weeks of receiving the request, and, in most cases, the designated medical officer and the designated officer of the social services department will have received prior notice from the local education authority of the possibility of an assessment. At the same time, the local education authority should have sought parental consent to the child being medically examined in the course of any assessment.

However, the health services and social services departments are not obliged to respond within 6 weeks if they have received no relevant information concerning the child prior to receipt of the copy notice to the parents informing them of the local education authority's proposal to make an assessment, or of the local education authority's letter notifying the health services and the social services departments that they have received a request for an assessment. In such circumstances, each department should endeavour to respond promptly. In most cases, the health services will have some knowledge of the child as a result of the child's school having sought medical advice at stages 1–3.

In the normal course of events, the local education authority will be in receipt of all the relevant advice within 6 weeks of the issue of the notice under s 167(4). There then follows a further period of 6 weeks in which documented evidence of the outcome of the assessment must be sent to the parents. A decision to make a statement must be made within 4 weeks and parents should be sent either a proposed statement or written reasons why a statement will not be made, preferably in the form of a note in lieu, within a further 2 weeks, together with notification of their right of appeal to the SEN Tribunal in the latter case. In practice, the decision as to whether to write a statement or a note in lieu will often involve preparing a draft in the alternative, depending on the outcome of the authority's deliberations. The most important point is that parents should normally receive written evidence of the outcome of the assessment within 12 weeks of the start of the statutory assessment.

Upon receiving the proposed statement, parents have the right to state a preference for the maintained school that the child should attend and to make representations to, and attend meetings with, the local education authority.[15]

Within 8 weeks of issuing the proposed statement, the local education authority must normally issue the final statement.

3.5 EXCEPTIONS TO THE TIMETABLE

Inevitably, circumstances will arise where it will not be reasonable to expect the above time-limits to be met by the bodies concerned. The Education (Special Educational Needs) Regulations 1994 address such circumstances by prescribing exceptions to the time-limits in specified situations.

Thus, under reg 11(4), an authority need not comply with the time-limit of 6 weeks (within which parents must normally be told whether the authority will, or will not, make a statutory assessment) if it is impractical to do so because:

(1)   the authority has requested advice from the head teacher of a school during a period beginning one week before any date on which that school was closed for a continuous period of not less than 4 weeks from that date and ending one week before the date on which it re-opens;

---

15 This may result in funds passing out of the area for which the local education authority has responsibility.

(2)   exceptional personal circumstances affect the child or his parent during the 6-week period;[16]

(3)   the child or his parent are absent from the area of the authority for a continuous period of not less than 4 weeks during the 6-week period.

An authority need not comply with the 10-week limit within which an assessment must normally be made if it is impractical to do so because:

(1)   in exceptional cases, after receiving advice sought it is necessary to seek further advice;

(2)   the child's parent has indicated to the authority that he wishes to provide advice to the authority after the expiry of 6 weeks from the date on which a request for such advice was received, and the authority has agreed to consider such advice before completing the assessment;

(3)   the authority has requested advice from the head teacher of a school during a period beginning one week before any date on which that school was closed for a continuous period of not less than 4 weeks from that date and ending one week before the date on which it re-opens;

(4)   the authority has requested advice from a district health authority or a social services authority, and the district health authority or the social services has not complied with that request within 6 weeks from the date on which it was made;

(5)   exceptional personal circumstances affect the child or his parent during the 10-week period;

(6)   the child or his parent are absent from the area of the authority for a continuous period of not less than 4 weeks during the 10-week period;

(7)   the child fails to keep an appointment for an examination or test during the 10-week period.

A district health authority or a social services authority need not comply with the 6-week time-limit within which information must normally be provided if it is impractical to do so because:

(1)   exceptional personal circumstances affect the child or his parent during the 6-week period;

(2)   the child or his parent are absent from the area of the authority for a continuous period of not less than 4 weeks during the 6-week period;

(3)   the child fails to keep an appointment for an examination or a test made by the district health authority or the social services authority respectively during the 6-week period;

(4)   the authority has not, before the date on which a copy of a notice has been served on it, produced or maintained any information or records relevant to the assessment of the child under s 167.

Finally, the authority need not comply with the 8-week time-limit for the making of a statement if it is impractical to do so because:

---

16 An example would be in the case of bereavement.

(1)   exceptional personal circumstances affect the child or his parent during the 8-week period;

(2)   the child or his parent are absent from the area of the authority for a continuous period of not less than 4 weeks during the 8-week period;

(3)   the child's parent indicates that he wishes to make representations to the authority about the content of the statement under para 4(1)(a) of Sch 10 to the 1993 Act after the 15-day period for making such representations provided for in para 4(4) of that Schedule;[17]

(4)   a meeting between the child's parent and an officer of the authority has been held pursuant to para 4(1)(b) of Sch 10 to the 1993 Act, and the child's parent has required that another such meeting be arranged or, under para 4(2) of that Schedule, has required a meeting with the appropriate person to be arranged;

(5)   the authority has sent a written request to the Secretary of State seeking his consent under s 189(5)(b) to the child being educated at an independent school which is not approved by him and such consent has not been received by the authority within 2 weeks of the date on which the request was sent.[18]

The Code states that local education authorities should always strive to ensure that any delay arising from the exceptions should be kept to a minimum and, as soon as the conditions giving rise to an exception no longer apply, they should endeavour to complete the process as quickly as possible. Accordingly, any remaining components of the process should be completed within their prescribed time-limits, irrespective of whether exceptions have caused earlier components to be delayed.

17 See Chapter 6.
18 See **8.4.2** and **10.6.3**.

Chapter 4

STATUTORY ASSESSMENT CRITERIA

4.1 INTRODUCTION

In deciding whether a statutory assessment should be made, a local education authority should pay particular attention to evidence provided by the child's school and the parents as to the extent of and the reason for the child's learning difficulties and also to any special educational provision which has already been made to address and overcome those difficulties. The Code of Practice contains guidance as to the evidence which should be sought, and the questions which should be asked, of schools and parents.

However, the questions set out in the Code should not be regarded as exhaustive, nor should it be assumed that if all the questions were answered in the affirmative, an assessment should always be made. Rather, the local education authority should come to each decision in the light of all the circumstances of the individual case and through close consultation with parents and schools.[1]

The critical question for a local education authority in deciding whether to make an assessment will be whether there is convincing evidence that the child's learning difficulties remain or have not been remedied sufficiently after relevant and purposeful action has been taken by the school with the help of external specialists, and so may require the authority to determine the child's special educational provision.

Thus, in every case, the local education authority will wish to see evidence of the school's assessment of the child's learning difficulties and to establish what action has been taken to address those difficulties. It will require evidence of the child's academic attainment in the school and will seek to understand the reasons for the level of such attainment. Subject to that, the questions to be asked and the evidence to be sought will vary from one case to another and will be determined by the age of the child and the nature of his or her learning difficulty.[2]

4.2 ACADEMIC ATTAINMENT

It has been said that local education authorities will always require evidence of the child's academic attainment and this will be the essential evidential starting point in

---

1 Code of Practice, para 3:47. At para 3:48, the Code suggests that in the interests of establishing an agreed local interpretation of the guidance, local education authorities may consider setting up a moderating group to support the local education authority in the consistent administration of the criteria set out in the Code. Such a group should include head teachers broadly representative of schools in the authority's area, and representation from health and social services, and may include other members such as SEN co-ordinators, teachers, governors and educational psychologists.

2 Code of Practice, para 3:49.

considering whether a statutory assessment is necessary. One of the key indicators of academic attainment will be the results of assessments and tests in the core subjects of the National Curriculum, but this information must always be interpreted in the context of the attainments of the child's peers, the child's progress over time and, where appropriate, expectations of the child's performance.

Local education authorities should be alert to evidence that a child's difficulties may be complex or intractable, such as may be indicated by significant discrepancies between a child's attainment in assessments and tests in core subjects of the National Curriculum and:

(1)   the attainment of the majority of children of his or her age; or

(2)   the performance expected of the child as indicated by a consensus among those who have taught and observed the child, including the parents, and supported by such standardised tests as can be relied upon; or

(3)   the attainment in one core subject or between one core subject and another.

Whilst important evidence will therefore be provided by National Curriculum assessments, the local education authority should not delay its consideration of a child until such up-to-date assessment results are available, but should also have regard to the recorded assessments by teachers of a child's classroom work, the outcome of individual education plans and any portfolio of the child's work compiled to illustrate his or her progress.[3]

When considering the above, local education authorities should simultaneously seek evidence of identifiable non-academic factors which may affect attainment such as:

(1)   problems with the child's health which may have led to recurrent or significant absences from school, or difficulty in concentrating or participating in the full range of curriculum activities while at school;

(2)   sensory impairment, for example hearing loss or visual problems;

(3)   speech and language difficulties;

(4)   poor school attendance;

(5)   problems in the child's home circumstances;

(6)   emotional or behavioural difficulties.[4]

4.3   SPECIAL EDUCATIONAL PROVISION

The information obtained may suggest immediate remedies which would render a statutory assessment unnecessary, or, alternatively, may indicate that a statutory assessment would assist to identify fully the child's learning difficulties. In order to reach a decision, it will be necessary for the local education authority to examine the special educational provision which the school has already made. Thus, except in cases where a child's condition has changed suddenly, the local education authority will normally wish to see clear recorded evidence of the learning difficulties identified and the action taken by the child's teachers at stage 1; the action taken by

---

3 Code of Practice, para 3:51.
4 Code of Practice, para 3:52.

the SEN co-ordinator and teachers, and their evaluation at stage 2; and the action formulated, monitored and evaluated in conjunction with external specialists at stage 3.

However, in exceptional circumstances, for example where it is discovered that the child has a major sensory impairment which will lead to increased learning difficulties without immediate specialist intervention beyond that which the school is equipped to provide, and where there is agreement between the school, the child's parents and any relevant consultant or adviser, the child may be referred immediately to the local education authority for statutory assessment.

Where appropriate, the local education authority should also ask to see evidence that the school has drawn upon information provided by the parents and that, so far as possible, the parents have been involved in the process of addressing the child's learning difficulties. Furthermore, in cases where the concern about the child's progress was first expressed to the school by the parents, the authority should satisfy itself that the school has investigated that concern as thoroughly as it would have done had the child's teacher been first to express a concern.

Finally, local education authorities should seek the medical advice which has been available to the school on the special educational needs of the child as well as information from the parents concerning any medical condition affecting the child's learning.

The considerations set out above will apply to all children referred to local education authorities, either by the parents or the school. However, the precise nature of the evidence which the authority should seek as to the child's learning difficulty, its apparent cause and the provision made by the school, will be determined to some extent by the nature of the learning difficulty or disability, and by the age of the child.

The Code therefore addresses the evidence to be sought and the questions to be asked by the local education authority in certain specified situations, although it states that such guidance does not assume that there are hard and fast categories of special educational need. Rather, it seeks to promote the recognition that each child is unique and thus the practice by the local education authorities of asking questions which reflect the particular circumstances of each child. It also notes that children's learning difficulties may involve more than one area of need.

4.4 LEARNING DIFFICULTIES

It will be possible to identify some children with learning difficulties before they reach school age, and the vast majority should be identified by the early stages of their school careers. Their general academic attainment will be at a level significantly below that of their contemporaries. In the majority of cases, they will experience difficulty in acquiring basic literacy and numeracy skills and many will have significant speech and language difficulties. In some cases, children may have poorly developed social skills and may show evidence of emotional and behavioural difficulties.

In cases of severe or profound and multiple learning difficulties, there will be available to the local education authority a considerable body of existing knowledge resulting from assessments and provision made by child health services or social services which may have been involved with the child and with the family from a very early stage. In many cases, children with severe or profound and multiple difficulties will also have secondary disabilities, the possibility of which should be taken into account in making assessment arrangements.

4.4.1 The child's learning difficulty

Clear recorded evidence of the child's academic attainment should be sought by the local education authority, who should ask whether, for example:

(1) the child is benefiting from working on programmes of study relevant to the Key Stages appropriate to his or her age, or is the subject of any temporary exception from the National Curriculum under s 19 of the Education Reform Act 1988;

(2) the child is working at a level significantly below that of his or her contemporaries in any of the core subjects of the National Curriculum;

(3) there is evidence that the child is falling progressively behind the majority of children of his or her age in academic attainment in any of the National Curriculum core subjects as measured by National Curriculum assessments, other standardised tests and teachers' own recorded assessments of a child's classroom work, including any portfolio of the child's work;

(4) there is any evidence of impaired social interaction or communication or a significantly restricted repertoire of activities, interests and imaginative development;

(5) there is evidence of significant problems in the child's home or family circumstances or in his or her school attendance record;

(6) there is evidence of significant emotional or behavioural difficulties, as indicated by clear recorded examples of withdrawn or disruptive behaviour; a marked and persistent inability to concentrate; difficulties in establishing and maintaining balanced relationships with his or her fellow pupils or with adults; and any other evidence of a significant delay in the development of life and social skills;

(7) there is any evidence of contributory or remediable medical problems or evidence from assessments or interventions by child health services or social services. Information from such assessments and interventions will be particularly important in the case of children with severe or profound and multiple difficulties, whose needs are unlikely to be appropriately assessed without an interdisciplinary perspective.[5]

4.4.2 The child's special educational provision

Having collected evidence indicating the nature of the child's learning difficulty, the local education authority should then consider the action taken by the school and should ask, in particular whether:

5 Code of Practice, para 3:57.

(1)   the school has, in consultation with outside specialists, formulated, monitored and regularly evaluated individual education plans, including structured literacy and/or numeracy support programmes, with clear targets; and the child's progress within such programmes, measured by criterion referenced or standardised tests, is significantly and consistently less than that which may be expected for the majority of children following such programmes;

(2)   the school has sought the views of and involved the child's parents at each stage;

(3)   the school has explored the possible benefits of, and, where practicable, secured access for the child to appropriate information technology, for example word-processing facilities, overlay keyboards and software, providing training in the use of that technology for the child, his or her parents and staff, so that the child is able to use that technology across the curriculum in school and, wherever appropriate, at home;

(4)   the school has implemented its policy on pastoral care and guidance and sought external advice to meet any social, emotional or behavioural difficulties;

(5)   the school has, with the parents' consent, notified and sought the assistance of the school doctor and/or the child's general practitioner, as appropriate.[6]

Where the balance of evidence presented to and assessed by the local education authority suggests that the child's learning difficulties:

(1)   are significant and/or complex;

(2)   have not responded to relevant and purposeful measures taken by the school and external specialists; and

(3)   may call for special educational provision which cannot reasonably be provided within the resources normally available to mainstream schools in the area,

the local education authority should consider very carefully the case for a statutory assessment of the child's special educational needs.[7]

4.5   SPECIFIC LEARNING DIFFICULTIES

In some cases, children will have significant difficulties in gaining literacy or numeracy skills which are not representative of their general level of performance. As with children demonstrating general learning difficulties, these children can become severely frustrated and may also have emotional and behavioural problems.

4.5.1   The child's learning difficulty

The local education authority should seek clear, recorded evidence of the child's academic attainment and, for example, ask whether:

---

6 Code of Practice, para 3:58.
7 Code of Practice, para 3:59.

(1)   there are extreme discrepancies between attainment in different core subjects of the National Curriculum or within one core subject, particularly English or Welsh;

(2)   expectations of the child, as indicated by a consensus among those who have taught and closely observed him or her, appropriately supported by standardised tests of cognitive ability or oral comprehension, are significantly above his or her attainments in National Curriculum assessments and tests and/or the results of appropriately administered standardised reading, spelling or mathematics tests;

(3)   there is clear recorded evidence of clumsiness; significant difficulties of sequencing or visual perception; deficiencies in working memory; or significant delays in language functioning;

(4)   there is evidence of problems sometimes associated with specific learning difficulties, such as severe emotional and behavioural difficulties, as indicated by clear recorded examples of withdrawn or disruptive behaviour, an inability to concentrate, or signs that the child experiences considerable frustration or distress in relation to his or her learning difficulties. Local education authorities should be particularly alert if there is evidence of such difficulties in some classes or tasks such as reading or writing but not in others.[8]

4.5.2   The child's special educational provision

In the light of evidence concerning the child's learning difficulty, the local education authority should consider the action taken by the school and should ask particularly whether:

(1)   the school has taken action to make both the curriculum and the school day accessible to the child by alerting all teachers to the particular needs of the child, helping the child to develop appropriate practices for taking down and recording information, adopting appropriate marking policies and promoting the use of such devices as personal dictionaries;

(2)   the school has formulated, monitored and evaluated, in conjunction with external experts, individual education plans, including structured literacy and numeracy programmes;

(3)   the school, in consultation with external specialists, has monitored the child's progress resulting from the action taken and has clearly demonstrated that the child has not made significant progress and/or that his or her level of attainment is falling further behind that of the majority of children;

(4)   the school has taken account of parental concern, which it has investigated and recorded and has sought to enrol the support of parents by involving them in creating, delivering and evaluating detailed plans to assist the child both inside and outside school;

(5)   the school has, where appropriate and practicable, secured access for the child to information technology, for example word-processing facilities with spell-checkers and other software, and provided the child, his or her parents

---

8 Code of Practice, para 3:61.

and staff with the necessary training to enable the child to use that technology across the curriculum in school, and wherever appropriate, at home;

(6)   the school has closely monitored the emotional and behavioural responses of the child to his or her learning difficulties and, if necessary, has provided help to reduce anxiety and enhance self-esteem;

(7)   the school has, with parental consent, notified and sought the assistance of the school doctor and/or the child's general practitioner, as appropriate.[9]

Where the balance of evidence presented to and assessed by the local education authority suggests that the child's learning difficulties:

(1)   are significant and/or complex;

(2)   have not responded to relevant and purposeful measures taken by the school and external specialists; and

(3)   may call for special educational provision which cannot reasonably be provided within the resources normally available to mainstream schools in the area,

the local education authority should consider very carefully the case for a statutory assessment of the child's special educational needs.[10]

4.6   EMOTIONAL AND BEHAVIOURAL DIFFICULTIES

Children with emotional and/or behavioural difficulties have learning difficulties within the definition contained in s 156 of the 1993 Act.[11] They may not fulfil expectations made of them at school and, in some cases, they may disrupt the education of other pupils.

The possible causes of emotional and behavioural difficulties include abuse or neglect, physical or mental illness, sensory or physical impairment and psychological trauma. In some cases, emotional or behavioural difficulties may arise from or be exacerbated by circumstances within the school environment. They may also be associated with other learning difficulties.[12]

Emotional and behavioural difficulties may manifest themselves in a wide variety of forms including withdrawn, depressive or suicidal attitudes, obsessional preoccupation with eating habits, school phobia, substance misuse, disruptive, anti-social and uncooperative behaviour and frustration, anger and threatened or actual violence. It is recommended in the Code that teachers should carefully record all instances of behavioural disturbance including those with no apparent cause.[13]

---

9   Code of Practice, para 3:62.

10 Code of Practice, para 3:63.

11 See **4.4** (definition of learning difficulties as per s 156).

12 The causes and effects of emotional and behavioural difficulties are discussed in Department for Education Circular 9/94, 'The Education of Children with Emotional and Behavioural Difficulties', where the concept of a continuum of difficulty is developed.

13 Code of Practice, para 3:67.

4.6.1   The child's learning difficulty

The local education authority should seek clear recorded evidence both of the child's academic attainment and of the nature of his or her emotional or behavioural difficulties, discovering whether, for example:

(1)   a significant discrepancy exists between the child's cognitive ability and expectations of the child as assessed by teachers, parents and others directly concerned, appropriately supported by standardised tests and the child's academic attainment as measured by National Curriculum assessments and teachers' own recorded assessments of the child's classroom work, including any portfolio of the child's work compiled to illustrate his or her progress;

(2)   the child is unusually withdrawn, lacking confidence and is unable to form lasting relationships with peers and adults; the local education authority will seek clear, detailed evidence from the school and external specialists based on close observation of the child;

(3)   there is evidence of severely impaired social interaction or communication, or a significantly restricted repertoire of activities, interests and imaginative development;

(4)   irregular attendance at school by the child; the local education authority should seek to establish whether there is any pattern or identifiable cause of the child's non-attendance;

(5)   there is clear recorded evidence of any obsessional eating habits;

(6)   there is clear recorded evidence of any substance or alcohol misuse;

(7)   the child displays any unpredictable, bizarre, obsessive, violent or severely disruptive behaviour. The local education authority should seek to establish whether there is any pattern to such behaviour and obtain examples in the form of specific recorded instances over a period of time, which should not usually be less than a term;

(8)   the child has participated in or has been subject to bullying at school, has been subject to neglect and/or abuse or has faced major difficulties at home. Clear recorded evidence will again be sought;

(9)   there is any suggestion that the child may have a significant mental or physical health problem. The authority should be alert to any sudden unforeseen changes in the child's behaviour which have no obvious cause and which might indicate a developing neurological impairment, epilepsy or other physical cause.[14]

4.6.2   The child's special educational provision

In the light of this evidence, the local education authority should consider the action taken by the school and others to meet the child's needs and will wish particularly to discover whether:

(1)   the appropriate external advice has been sought by the school and that, following thorough discussions with the child, the school has formulated,

14 Code of Practice, para 3:68.

implemented, monitored and evaluated individual education plans, including a behaviour management programme;

(2)   the school has followed the provisions of its policies on behaviour and on pastoral care and guidance;

(3)   the staff have been fully informed of the child's difficulties and have adopted a consistent approach to remedying those difficulties;

(4)   the school has sought a constructive relationship with the child's parents or carers, encouraging them to participate in the child's education and to pay regular visits to the school;

(5)   where appropriate, the school has notified and sought the involvement of the education welfare service and/or the social services department;

(6)   the school has, where appropriate and practicable, secured access for the child to information technology such as word-processing facilities, painting programs and other software which encourages communication and self-expression, as a means of motivating and stimulating the child, together with the necessary training for the child, his or her parents and staff to enable the child to use that technology across the curriculum in school and, where appropriate, at home;

(7)   the school has, with parental consent, notified and sought the assistance of the school doctor and/or the child's general practitioner, as appropriate.[15]

Where the balance of evidence presented to and assessed by the local education authority suggests that the child's learning difficulties:

(1)   are significant and/or complex;

(2)   have not responded to relevant and purposeful measures taken by the school and external specialists; and

(3)   may call for special educational provision which cannot reasonably be provided within the resources normally available to mainstream schools in the area,

the local education authority should consider very carefully the case for a statutory assessment of the child's special educational needs.[16]

4.7   PHYSICAL DISABILITIES

A child's physical disabilities, which may be the result of an illness or injury or may arise from a congenital condition and might have short- or long-term effects, may limit the child's access to the full curriculum unless action is taken by the school or the local education authority. Some children with physical disabilities may also have sensory impairment, neurological problems and learning difficulties.

---

15   Code of Practice, para 3:69.
16   Code of Practice, para 3:70.

4.7.1 The child's learning difficulty or disability

The local education authority should obtain clear recorded evidence both of the child's academic attainment and of the nature of his or her physical disability, and, in particular, discover whether:

(1) a significant discrepancy exists between the child's attainment, as measured by National Curriculum assessments and tests and teachers' own recorded assessments of a child's classroom work, including any portfolio of the child's work, and the attainments of the majority of children of his or her age;

(2) a significant discrepancy exists between expectations of the child as assessed by the child's teachers, parents and external specialists who have closely observed him or her, appropriately supported by the results of standardised tests of cognitive ability, and the child's attainment as measured by National Curriculum assessments and tests;

(3) the child is unable fully to participate in particular aspects of the school's curriculum without close adult supervision and/or substantial adaptation of teaching materials or environment;

(4) the child has significant self-help difficulties in, for example, dressing, toileting or feeding and/or the child's condition gives rise to serious safety issues;

(5) there is clear substantiated evidence based on specific examples that the child's inability fully to participate in school life places the child under significant emotional or physical stress.[17]

4.7.2 The child's special educational provision

In the light of evidence concerning the child's academic attainments and physical disability, the local education authority should consider the action taken by the school and should, in particular, discover whether:

(1) in consultation with the local education authority's support services and, where appropriate, regional organisations expert in information technology for communication difficulties,[18] the school has, where appropriate and practicable, secured access for the child to information technology and provided the necessary training for the child, his or her parents and staff to enable the child to use that technology across the curriculum in school and, wherever appropriate, at home;

(2) the school has formulated, implemented, monitored and evaluated individual education plans to support full access to the curriculum, and has given consideration to such matters as the child's space requirements in the classroom, and the storage and maintenance of equipment;

(3) the school has fully applied the access provisions of its SEN policy in the case of the child concerned and has taken all reasonable steps to improve access to independent learning and the physical environment of the school for the child,

---

17 Code of Practice, para 3:72.
18 Regional Organisations Expert in Information Technology for Communication Difficulties: The Aids to Communication (ACE) Centres in Oxford and Oldham; the Centre for Micro-Assisted Communication at Charlton Park School, London SE7; and Communication Aids Centres funded under the NHS.

obtaining external advice on basic adaptations from the local education authority, the social services department, health and safety experts and voluntary organisations, as appropriate;

(4)   the school has, with parental consent, sought the assistance of the school doctor and/or the child's general practitioner, as appropriate.[19]

Where the balance of evidence presented and assessed by the local education authority suggests that the child's learning difficulties and/or disabilities:

(1)   are significant and/or complex;
(2)   have not been met by relevant and purposeful measures taken by the school and external specialists; and
(3)   may call for special educational provision which cannot reasonably be provided within the resources normally available to mainstream schools in the area,

the local education authority should consider very carefully the case for a statutory assessment of the child's special educational needs.[20]

4.8   SENSORY IMPAIRMENT

Some degree of hearing difficulty, whether temporary or permanent, is experienced by a significant proportion of children. Temporary hearing loss is usually caused by the condition known as 'glue-ear' and occurs most often in the early years Such hearing loss fluctuates and may be mild or moderate in degree. However, it can seriously compound other learning difficulties.

Permanent hearing loss is usually sensory-neural and varies from mild to profound. Children with profound hearing loss may have severe or complex communication difficulties.

In order to ensure that the child's language acquisition, academic achievement and emotional development do not suffer unnecessarily, early recognition, diagnosis and treatment are essential, as is the provision of specialist support for pupils with hearing difficulties.

4.8.1   Visual difficulties

There are many forms of visual difficulty and these have widely differing implications for a child's education. Some children are blind from birth, whereas others lose their sight, either partially or completely, as a result of an accident or illness. In some cases, visual impairment is one aspect of multiple disability.

Whatever the cause of a child's visual impairment, the major issue in identifying and assessing the child's special educational needs will relate to the degree and nature of functional vision, partial sight or blindness, and the child's ability to adapt socially and psychologically, as well as to progress in an educational context.

---

19 Code of Practice, para 3:73.
20 Code of Practice, para 3:74.

4.8.2   The child's learning difficulty/disability

The local education authority should obtain clear, recorded evidence both of the child's academic attainment and the extent and nature of his or her hearing or visual difficulty, discovering, for example, whether:

(1)   a significant discrepancy exists between the child's attainment, as measured by National Curriculum assessments and tests, and teachers' own recorded assessments of a child's classroom work, including any portfolio of the child's work, and the attainment of the majority of children of his or her age;

(2)   a significant discrepancy exists between the expectations of the child as assessed by the child's teachers, parents and external specialists who have closely observed the child, appropriately supported by the results of standardised tests of cognitive ability, and the child's attainment as measured by National Curriculum assessments and tests;

(3)   there is clear recorded evidence of the nature and extent of the child's hearing loss or visual difficulty in the form of the results of appropriate assessments;

(4)   there is clear recorded evidence that the child's hearing or visual difficulty significantly impairs his or her emotional or social development, access to the curriculum, ability to take part in particular classroom activities or participation in aspects of school life;

(5)   there is clear substantiated evidence, based on specific examples, that the child's hearing or visual difficulty places the child under stress, with associated withdrawn or frustrated behaviour.[21]

4.8.3   The child's special educational provision

In the light of evidence about the child's academic attainment and hearing or visual difficulty, the local education authority should consider the action taken by the school and, in particular, should ask whether:

(1)   the school has taken the advice of appropriate external specialists, including, for example, qualified teachers of the deaf or visually impaired, as appropriate, the local education authority's support services and voluntary bodies;

(2)   the school has formulated, implemented, monitored and evaluated individual education plans to support full access to and active involvement in the curriculum and school life, in the case of hearing difficulties, addressing such matters as the child's positioning in class and the use of hearing aids and other relevant equipment, and in the case of visual difficulties, having fully applied the access provisions of its SEN policy, it has followed specialist recommendations regarding physical adaptations to support the child's mobility;

(3)   all teachers and adults in the school have been alerted to the child's hearing or visual difficulty and are aware of the basic measures they should take to overcome or circumvent that difficulty;

(4)   the school has sought the views of, and involved, the child's parents at each stage;

---

21 Code of Practice, paras 3:78 and 3:82.

(5)   the school has explored the possible benefits and, where practicable, secured access for the child to appropriate information technology, providing training in the use of that technology for the child, his or her parents and staff, so that the child is able to use that technology across the curriculum in school and, wherever appropriate, at home;

(6)   the school has, with parental consent, notified and sought the assistance of the school doctor and/or the child's general practitioner, as appropriate.[22]

Where the balance of the evidence presented to and assessed by the local education authority suggests that the child's learning difficulties and/or disabilities:

(1)   are significant and/or complex;

(2)   have not been met by relevant and purposeful measures taken by the school and external specialists; and

(3)   may call for special educational provision which cannot reasonably be provided within the resources normally available to mainstream schools in the area,

the local education authority should consider very carefully the case for a statutory assessment of the child's special educational needs.[23]

4.9   SPEECH AND LANGUAGE DIFFICULTIES

In the majority of cases of speech and language difficulties, these difficulties will have been identified before a child reaches school. However, by the time they start school, some children will still have significant speech and language difficulties which impair their ability to participate in the classroom. This may have a serious effect on the child's academic attainment and lead to emotional and behavioural difficulties. Therefore, the early identification of such difficulties and prompt remedial action are essential.

4.9.1   The child's learning difficulty/disability

The local education authority should obtain clear recorded evidence both of the child's academic attainment and the nature of his or her communication difficulty, discovering, for example, whether:

(1)   a significant discrepancy exists between the child's attainment, as measured by National Curriculum assessments and tests, and teachers' own recorded assessments of the child's classroom work, and the attainment of the majority of children of his or her age;

(2)   a significant discrepancy exists between the expectations of the child as assessed by the child's teachers, parents and external specialists who have closely observed the child, appropriately supported by the results of standardised tests of cognitive ability, and the child's attainment as measured by National Curriculum assessments and tests;

---

22 Code of Practice, paras 3:79 and 3:83.
23 Code of Practice, paras 3:80 and 3:84.

(3)   the child's expressive and/or receptive language development is significantly below that of the majority of children of his or her age as measured by a standardised language assessment test, or a major discrepancy exists between the child's expressive and receptive levels of functioning;

(4)   there is clear substantiated evidence, based on specific examples, that the child's communication difficulties impede the development of purposeful relationships with adults and/or fellow pupils and/or give rise to other emotional and behavioural difficulties;

(5)   there is evidence of a hearing impairment which may exist in addition to, or be the cause of, the speech and language difficulty.[24]

4.9.2   The child's special educational provision

In the light of evidence about the child's academic attainment and communication difficulties, the local education authority should consider the action taken by the school and should particularly ask whether:

(1)   the school has, with parental consent, sought the advice of the school doctor and/or the child's general practitioner, as appropriate, and of a speech and language therapist and other external specialists and has, together with the child's parents and involving all teachers concerned with the child, implemented, monitored and evaluated individual education plans for the child to support full access to, and involvement in, the school and social life;

(2)   the school has closely monitored the child's emotional and behavioural condition and, if necessary, has provided pastoral help to reduce anxiety and enhance self-esteem;

(3)   the school has, in consultation with the local education authority's support services, and, where appropriate, regional organisations expert in information technology for communication difficulties, explored the possible benefits of, and, where practicable, secured access for the child to, appropriate information technology, providing training in the use of that technology for the child, his or her parents and staff, to enable the child to use that technology across the curriculum in school, and wherever appropriate, at home.[25]

Where the balance of the evidence presented to and assessed by the local education authority suggests that the child's learning difficulties and/or disabilities:

(1)   are significant and/or complex;

(2)   have not been met by relevant and purposeful measures taken by the school and external specialists; and

(3)   may call for special educational provision which cannot reasonably be provided within the resources normally available to mainstream schools in the area,

the local education authority should consider very carefully the case for a statutory assessment of the child's special educational needs.[26]

---

24 Code of Practice, para 3:86.
25 Code of Practice, para 3:87.
26 Code of Practice, para 3:88.

4.10   MEDICAL CONDITIONS

If appropriate action is not taken, some medical conditions may have a significant impact on a child's academic attainment or give rise to emotional and behavioural difficulties.

The child's ability to participate fully in the curriculum and the wider range of activities in the school may be impaired by the conditions themselves, while drug therapies, such as those required for the treatment of leukaemia and childhood cancers, may compound the problems of the condition and have implications for the child's education.

Some medical conditions will have an intermittent effect on the child's progress and performance while others will affect progress on a continuous basis throughout the child's school career.

In order to ensure that the child achieves the maximum possible progress and also that he or she is not unnecessarily excluded from any part of the curriculum or school activity because of anxiety about his or her care and treatment, it will be essential for consultation and open discussion to take place between the child's parents, the school, the school doctor or the child's general practitioner, the community paediatrician and any specialist services providing treatment for the child.[27]

4.10.1   The child's learning difficulty

The local education authority should obtain clear recorded evidence both of the child's academic attainment and of the nature of his or her medical condition, discovering, for example, whether:

(1)   a significant discrepancy exists between the child's attainment, as measured by National Curriculum assessments and tests, and teachers' own recorded assessments of a child's classroom work and the attainment of the majority of children of his or her age;

(2)   a significant discrepancy exists between the expectations of the child as assessed by the child's teachers, parents and external specialists who have closely observed the child, appropriately supported by the results of standardised tests of cognitive ability, and the child's attainment as measured by National Curriculum assessments and tests;

(3)   there is clear recorded evidence that the child's medical condition significantly impedes or disrupts his or her access to the curriculum, ability to take part in particular classroom activities or participation in aspects of school life;

(4)   there is clear substantiated evidence, based on specific examples, that the child's medical condition has given rise to emotional or behavioural difficulties;

(5)   there is evidence of significant and recurrent absences from school.[28]

---

27 Department for Education Circular 12/94, 'The Education of Sick Children'.
28 Code of Practice, para 3:92.

4.10.2 The child's special educational provision

In the light of evidence about the child's academic attainment and medical condition, the local education authority should consider the action taken by the school and should ask, in particular, whether:

(1)   the school has, with parental consent, notified and sought the assistance of the school doctor, the child's general practitioner or any specialist child health service, as appropriate;

(2)   all staff have been fully informed of the child's medical condition, and a consistent approach to managing the child's education has been adopted across the school;

(3)   the school has sought the views of, and involved, the child's parents at each stage;

(4)   the school has sought the co-operation of those within the local education authority responsible for the education of children who are at home and, as appropriate, in hospital, as a result of illness.[29]

Where the balance of the evidence presented to and assessed by the local education authority suggests that the child's learning difficulties and/or disabilities:

(1)   are significant and/or complex;

(2)   have not been met by relevant and purposeful measures taken by the school and external specialists; and

(3)   may call for special educational provision which cannot reasonably be provided within the resources normally available to mainstream schools in the area,

the local education authority should consider very carefully the case for a statutory assessment of the child's special educational needs.[30]

---

29 Code of Practice, para 3:93.
30 Code of Practice, para 3:94.

Chapter 5

CONDUCT OF STATUTORY ASSESSMENT

5.1   INTRODUCTION

The Education (Special Educational Needs) Regulations 1994[1] provide that, where a local education authority serves notice on a child's parent under s 167(1) or s 174(2) of the Education Act 1993 that it proposes to make an assessment under s 167, it shall within 6 weeks of serving that notice give notice to the child's parent under s 167(4) or s 174(5) of its decision to make an assessment, or under s 167(6) or s 174(6) of its decision not to make an assessment (reg 11(1) and (2)).

In circumstances where a parent, under s 172(2) or s 173(1), asks the local education authority to arrange for an assessment under s 167, the local education authority shall within 6 weeks of receiving that request give notice to the child's parent under s 167(4) of its decision to make an assessment, or under s 172(3)(a) or s 173(2)(a) of its decision not to make an assessment and of the parent's right to appeal to the SEN Tribunal against that decision (reg 11(3)).

The local education authority must decide whether the evidence obtained from the child's parents and the school suggests that a statutory assessment is required when judged against the criteria as set out in the preceding chapter.

5.2   DECISION NOT TO MAKE A STATUTORY ASSESSMENT

Section 167(6) of the Education Act 1993 provides that, if the local education authority decides not to assess the educational needs of the child concerned, it must give notice in writing to the child's parents of that decision.

Since the decision not to make a statutory assessment may be a serious disappointment to the child's parents and may also be unwelcome to the school, the local education authority should write both to the parents and the school giving full reasons for the decision.

In cases where parents have formally requested a statutory assessment under s 172 or s 173, they may appeal to the SEN Tribunal against the decision not to make an assessment.[2]

The local education authority should try to ensure that the parents fully comprehend the school-based stages and their arrangements for monitoring and review. It should also offer guidelines or suggest action which it considers would help the school to meet the child's needs. Where there is clear disagreement between the parents and the school concerning the child's progress and attainments at

---

1 SI 1994/1047, which came into force on 1 September 1994.
2 See further Chapter 8.

school, the local education authority may consider arranging a meeting between the parents and the school.

5.3 DECISION TO PROCEED WITH A STATUTORY ASSESSMENT

Section 167(4) of the Education Act 1993 provides that where the local education authority decides to proceed with a statutory assessment, it must inform the parents of its decision and the reasons for it.

At this stage, parents should be advised that their child may be called for assessment as part of the process of compiling all the relevant advice. Parental consent to a medical examination and psychological assessment should already have been sought and parents should be informed of their right to attend with the child at any interview, test, medical or other assessment which is carried out for this purpose and should be told of the time and place of appointments. There will, however, be circumstances in which the parent's presence may be counter-productive, such as in an observation of the child in the classroom, and this should be pointed out to parents when advising them of their right to attend.

For the purpose of making a statutory assessment under s 167 of the 1993 Act, the local education authority shall seek the following written advice (reg 6):

(1) parental advice;
(2) educational advice;
(3) medical advice;
(4) psychological advice;
(5) social services advice;
(6) any other advice, such as the views of the child, which the local education authority or any other body from whom advice is sought consider desirable. In particular, advice from the Service Children's Education Authority (SCEA)[3] must be sought where the child's parent is a serving member of the armed forces.

The local education authority must always give to those from whom advice is sought copies of any representations made by or evidence provided by the child's parents under s 167(1)(d). The advice must not be influenced by consideration of the identity of the school at which the child might eventually be placed. The decision as to placement will be made by the local education authority at a later stage and in the light of any preference expressed or representations made by the parents. Discussions between advisers and parents concerning the child's needs and the adviser's written advice may include considerations of the options available, including the scope for mainstream education for the child and the type of school which might best meet the child's needs, for example, mainstream, special or

---

3 The SCEA oversees the education of UK service children abroad. It is funded by the Ministry of Defence and operates in its own schools as well as providing advice to parents on SCEA and UK schools.

residential. However, such discussions and advice should not seek to commit the local education authority, nor pre-empt the parents' statement of a preference.

The local education authority should also ascertain as far as possible the views of the child as to his or her special needs and how these might be addressed.

All requests for advice should be accompanied by notification of the date by which the advice must be submitted.

5.3.1 Parental advice

Parents must be asked to give whatever advice they consider to be relevant. The Code of Practice on the Identification and Assessment of Special Educational Needs sets out guidelines for parents on how to contribute effectively to their child's assessment.[4] The guidelines suggest that the parents' written contribution may be as short or as long as they wish but that the local education authority would find it helpful if the following headings were to be followed, modified as appropriate to the particular circumstances.

A – THE EARLY YEARS

1   What do you remember about the early years that might help?
2   What was he or she like as a young baby?
3   Were you happy about progress at the time?
4   When did you first feel things were not right?
5   What happened?
6   What advice or help did you receive – from whom?

B – WHAT IS YOUR CHILD LIKE NOW?

1   General health – eating and sleeping habits; general fitness, absences from school, minor ailments – coughs and colds. Serious illnesses/accidents – periods in hospital. Any medicine or special diet? General alertness – tiredness, signs of use of drugs – smoking, drinking, glue-sniffing.
2   Physical skills – walking, running, climbing – riding a bike, football or other games, drawing pictures, writing, doing jigsaws; using construction kits, household gadgets, tools, sewing.
3   Self-help – level of personal independence – dressing, etc; making bed, washing clothes, keeping room tidy, coping with day-to-day routine; budgeting pocket money, general independence – getting out and about.
4   Communication – level of speech, explains, describes events, people, conveys information (eg messages to and from school), joins in conversations; uses telephone.
5   Playing and learning at home – how [...] spends time, watching TV, reading for pleasure and information, hobbies, concentration, sharing.
6   Activities outside – belonging to clubs, sporting activities, happy to go alone.

4 Code of Practice, para 3:100.

7   Relationships – with parents, brothers and sisters; with friends; with other
     adults (friends and relations) at home generally; 'outside' generally.

Is […] a loner?

8   Behaviour at home – co-operates, shares, listens to and carries out
     requests, helps in the house, offers help, fits in with family routine and
     'rules'. Moods good and bad, sulking – temper tantrums; demonstrative,
     affectionate.
9   At school – relationships with other children and teachers; progress with
     reading, writing, number, other subjects and activities at school. How the
     school has helped/not helped with your child. Have you been asked to help
     with school work – hearing child read – with what result?

Does […] enjoy school?

What does […] find easy or difficult?

C – YOUR GENERAL VIEWS

1   What do you think your child's special educational needs are?
2   How do you think these can best be provided for?
3   How do you compare your child with others of the same age?
4   What is your child good at or what does he or she enjoy doing?
5   What does […] worry about – is […] aware of difficulties?
6   What are your worries, concerns?
7   Is there any other information you would like to give:
     (a) about the family – major events that might have affected your child?
     (b) reports from other people?
8   With whom would you like more contact?
9   How do you think your child's needs affect the needs of the family as a
     whole?

The Code recommends that parents talk to the Named LEA Officer whom the local education authority named when the proposal to assess the child was first made. The role of the Named LEA Officer will be particularly important if the parents have difficulty in writing, if English or Welsh is not their first language or if they have difficulty in preparing a written report. The Named LEA Officer should prepare a note of the parents' views following discussions with them and this should be agreed with the parents before it is included in advice relating to the assessment.

When a Named Person has been identified at an early stage, the Code states that local education authorities should encourage parents to seek that person's assistance in preparing their advice and should welcome the Named Person at any meetings. Local education authorities should also work closely with local parent or other voluntary organisations in order to develop partnership and support systems and information material on which parents may draw when assessments and statements are being made, in accordance with recommendations contained in the Code.

5.3.2 Educational advice

Advice must be sought from the school currently attended by the child, any other school attended in the preceding 18 months and, if appropriate, from those responsible for providing education otherwise than at school, for example the local education authority's home tuition service. The school must be asked to provide relevant information about the child and evidence of the school's identification and assessment of and provision for the special educational needs of the child. A summary of the records of the school's work with a child at each stage should be appended to the educational advice.

On the basis of the evidence received from the school, the local education authority should consider whether to seek separate advice from a teacher or professional from a learning support service involved with the child during the past year. This should usually be the specialist who has worked with the child and the school at the stage before referral for statutory assessment. If it appears that the child is visually and/or hearing impaired, the local education authority must obtain educational advice from a teacher qualified to teach classes of visually and/or hearing impaired children.

5.3.3 Medical advice

The local education authority must, in all cases, seek advice on all aspects of a child's health and development from the health service. In practice, advice will normally be sought from the designated medical officer for special educational needs who should co-ordinate the advice from all the relevant health specialists. Medical advice may include advice from the child's general practitioner and the school doctor and from therapists, school nurses, health visitors, other community nurses, child and adolescent mental health workers and any other medical specialists who may be involved. If they wish, parents may also submit reports from private professionals and such reports must be considered alongside the professional advice received from the designated medical officer.

The Code recognises that the contribution of the health services to assessment is crucial and observes that medical advice may include information on:

(1) a medical condition which is likely to affect future learning ability;
(2) medical treatment which is likely to affect the child's future learning ability;
(3) general health or developmental problems which may relate to social conditions (for example, social and family disadvantage);
(4) mental health problems which may cause emotional and behavioural difficulties;
(5) shorter-term but acute medical problems (for example treatment for childhood cancer or recovery from serious trauma) which may necessitate special arrangements being made for a child, but with the understanding that the child's special needs are likely to be temporary and that the child will resume full participation in school within a reasonable period of time.[5]

---

5 Code of Practice, para 3:107.

The Code recommends that any medical advice should state the likely consequences for the child's education and may include:

(1) information on any aspects of the child's medical condition which may affect his or her progress in school and advice on how best to manage the condition in the school context (for example, the management of epilepsy or of a tracheotomy);

(2) advice on any special aid or equipment which the child may need;

(3) information on the child's welfare and safety, such as advice on the management of incontinence; feeding; independence and risk taking; and participation and supervision in the playground, while swimming and bathing, and taking part in out-of-school activities;

(4) advice on any non-educational provision which may be needed.[6]

In cases of serious or life-threatening conditions, the Code recommends that medical advice should be sought but that care should be taken to ensure that parents are sensitively informed of the probable outcomes. It recognises that it is not acceptable for parents to receive the first indication of their child's condition (with possible reference to terminal illness) when they see the draft statement.

It is the responsibility of the designated medical officer for special educational needs to co-ordinate the contributions of all health care professionals and to ensure that they have access to information on the current range of services provided by the local education authority in order to inform and reassure parents about the assessment process. Consent should be obtained before medical information is disclosed.[7]

Finally, it is recognised in the Code that for some children with complex needs or specific disabilities or medical conditions, a health perspective will be crucial both in the initial assessment and in any subsequent reviews. It recommends that the health services should:

(1) ensure that there are no additional difficulties or disabilities affecting the child, and monitor the child's general health and development;

(2) help parents and teachers to understand the child's disability or medical condition and provide counselling and support to parents and children if required;

(3) provide access to any specialist advice or services as required; and

(4) advise on any other matters such as access, provision of equipment, and administration of medication.[8]

---

6 Code of Practice, para 3:108.

7 No doctor or other health service worker should disclose medical information without first obtaining the consent of the parents and, where he or she has sufficient understanding, the child. Exceptionally, children under the age of 16, who are judged to be competent by their doctors, may give consent independently of their parents (Code of Practice, para 2:52).

8 Code of Practice, para 3:111.

The Code observes that, in these circumstances, the health services will not only contribute relevant information on the child's special needs, but may also contribute to the setting of objectives and the review process.[9]

5.3.4 Psychological advice

The views of an educational psychologist are essential in fully assessing a child's special educational needs and in planning for any future provision, and advice must be sought from one who is employed or engaged for the purpose by the local education authority. In the report, the educational psychologist should address a wide range of factors which may affect a child's functioning, such as the child's cognitive functioning; communication skills; perceptual skills; adaptive and personal and social skills; the child's approaches and attitudes to learning; his or her educational attainments; and the child's self-image, interests and behaviour. It may be necessary for the educational psychologist to liaise with occupational therapists and physiotherapists when investigating motor skills and their relationship to perceptual skills.

The educational psychologist from whom advice is sought by the local education authority must consult any other psychologist, such as a clinical or occupational psychologist, whom he or she believes has relevant knowledge of or information about the child, and must record any advice received. The local education authority must consider any advice from a fully qualified educational psychologist commissioned independently and submitted by the parents.

5.3.5 Social services advice

Having previously copied the notice of proposal to make a statutory assessment to the social services department, the local education authority must now seek advice as to whether the social services department is aware of any problems affecting the child or can provide advice and information about the child which may be relevant to the assessment. The local education authority should provide the social services department with full information on its statutory assessment arrangements and procedures, and local education authorities and social services departments should agree the procedures to be followed when the local education authority notifies a social services department of its proposal to assess a child's special educational needs.

Having received notification that the local education authority will assess the child, the social services department should provide the local education authority with any relevant information it may have concerning the family or the child.

The Code identifies the particular matters upon which information should be provided, as follows.

(1) If the social services department does not know the child and the family, and if it has no reason to suppose from evidence provided by the school or the local

---

9 Code of Practice, para 3:112.

education authority that it should seek further information, it should say so and need provide no further written advice. But social services departments may combine assessment of children 'in need' under Sch 17 to the Children Act 1989 with statutory assessment under the Education Act 1993. Therefore, given its general responsibilities for children 'in need' and their families and its duty to keep a register of children with disabilities, the social services department may wish to arrange a meeting with the child and his or her family to check whether:
- there are services it should provide for the child or the family;
- the family consider that the child should be registered as disabled (registration being wholly voluntary); and
- there is further information the family should be given.

The results of any such meeting should be passed to the local education authority as part of the social services department's advice for the statutory assessment.

(2)   If the child is receiving social services provision such as day care or is living in a residential or foster home, the social services department should make available to the local education authority any relevant observations, information and reports arising from such placements.

(3)   If the child is 'looked after' by a local authority and therefore has a child care plan, the social services department should give the local education authority full details of that care plan.

(4)   If the child is in the care of a local authority as the result of a court order and the local authority has parental responsibility under the Children Act 1989, the social services department should ensure that any relevant information is provided and that social services staff attend assessments and medical examinations as appropriate.

(5)   If the child is, or may become, subject to child protection procedures, the social services department should give appropriate advice.[10]

Social services departments should give local education authorities information on services generally available for families or children 'in need' (as required under Sch 1 to the Children Act 1989) and should make available to the local education authority any relevant information on planning processes or data collection (such as the register of children with disabilities or the community care plan).[11]

In cases where the child is not currently known to social services, the local education authority should inform the designated officer of the social services department if it seems likely that the child should be educated at a residential school. The social services department will wish to ensure that a parental request for residential education is not made on the basis of lack of support and practical help in their local community and that proper arrangements are made to ensure family contact if the child is placed outside the authority in question.[12]

---

10 Code of Practice, para 3:117.
11 Code of Practice, para 3:118.
12 Code of Practice, para 3:119.

5.3.6   Involvement of the child

It is assumed in the Code that the local education authority will wish to establish the views of children and young people themselves on their special educational needs and the way in which they might be met. The local education authority may consider providing a pupil report for the purpose on which pupils who are able to do so could submit their views. Other pupils will require the assistance of a parent, teacher, educational psychologist, social worker or other person in whom they trust, such as the Named Person. In other cases, the adults closest to the child have a responsibility to establish to the best of their ability the wishes and feelings of the child. However ascertained, the wishes and feelings of the child have a separate identity and, accordingly, it is suggested in the Code that the local education authority may wish to have the child's views set out separately from those of the parents and professionals.[13]

5.3.7   Any other advice

The parents' suggestions of other agencies or individuals who might be called upon for advice should be followed up by the local education authority. In addition, the local education authority should approach any other body whom it considers could helpfully contribute to the accurate and timely assessment of the child. In particular, advice from the Service Children's Education Authority (SCEA) must be sought where the child's parent is a serving member of the armed forces.[14]

---

13 Code of Practice, para 3:120.
14 Code of Practice, para 3:121.

Chapter 6

STATEMENT OF SPECIAL EDUCATIONAL NEEDS

6.1 INTRODUCTION

Section 168(1) of the Education Act 1993 provides that where, in the light of a s 167 assessment, it is necessary for the local education authority to determine the special educational provision which the child's learning difficulty calls for, the local education authority shall make and maintain a statement of his or her special educational needs.

Having conducted the statutory assessment and received advice from relevant agencies and individuals, the authority must decide whether to draw up a statement. A statement will be appropriate where the authority decides that the degree of the child's learning difficulty or disability, and the nature of the provision necessary to meet the child's special educational needs, require the authority to determine the special educational provision for the child through making a statement.

The main ground for making a statement is the conclusion by the local education authority that all the special educational provision necessary to meet the child's needs cannot reasonably be provided within the resources normally available to mainstream schools in the area. In the majority of mainstream schools, the delegated budget will include some funding which reflects the additional needs of pupils with special educational needs, which, in local authority-maintained schools should be received through local management schemes which are weighted for the incidence of special educational needs within the authority. Grant-maintained schools receive this through their Annual Maintenance Grant, which may be determined by replication of the local management scheme or from the Common Funding Formula.

While, in many cases, the issuing of a statement will involve the local authority in making additional resources available to a mainstream school, this will not be appropriate where schools have delegated funds to meet the needs of pupils with statements, except insofar as the authority will be responsible for monitoring the child's progress and reviewing the statement and thereby overseeing the child on a continuing basis. Indeed, this responsibility of the authority to monitor the child's progress through multidisciplinary involvement in the review process and other means may occasionally cause the authority to make a statement even where funding for pupils with statements is not delegated to schools.

Whether or not funding for pupils with statements is delegated to schools, responsibility for arranging the necessary provisions rests with the local education authority. When funding is delegated, local management schemes must include conditions requiring governing bodies to ensure that all the provision specified in the statement is made and should also set out arrangements whereby the local education authority will ensure that these conditions are satisfied.

In the interests of ensuring consistency in the administration of criteria for statutory assessment at a local level, the Code of Practice recommends that moderating groups be set up, such groups being broadly representative of head teachers and including representation from health and social services and optionally, from SEN co-ordinators, teachers, governors and educational psychologists. The Code goes on to suggest that local education authorities may wish to extend the remit of such groups to encourage consistent decisions about whether to make statements by the groups engaging in sampling and retrospective comparison rather than making decisions in individual cases. It is thought that this may help make the practice of the local education authority more robust and clearly understood by schools and parents.

In deciding whether to draw up a statement, the local education authority should consider all the information emerging from the statutory assessment in the light of the evidence put forward by the school at the beginning of the assessment.

In particular, therefore, local education authorities may wish to ask the following questions.

(1) The child's learning difficulties:
  – Is the information on the child's learning difficulties that emerges from the statutory assessment broadly in accord with the evidence presented by the school for consideration by the local education authority?
  – If not, are there aspects of the child's learning difficulties which the school may have overlooked and which, with the benefit of advice, equipment or other provision, the school could effectively address within its own resources?
(2) The child's special educational provision:
  – Do the proposals for the child's special educational provision emerging from the statutory assessment indicate that the special educational provision being made by the school, including teaching strategies or other approaches, is appropriate to the child's learning difficulties?
  – If not, are there approaches which, with the benefit of advice, equipment or other provision, the school could effectively adopt within its own resources?[1]

6.2 CONSIDERATION OF THE PROVISION THAT MAY NEED TO BE MADE AND THE DECISION NOT TO ISSUE A STATEMENT

If it is confirmed by the statutory assessment, that notwithstanding the appropriate assessment and provision made by the school the child is either not progressing or is not progressing sufficiently well, the local education authority should consider what further provision may be necessary and whether such provision can be made within the school's resources.

---

1 Code of Practice, paras 4:8 and 4:9.

The Code of Practice provides the following exemplars to assist in the decision of whether a statement is necessary.[2]

(1) If, as a result of a statutory assessment, the local education authority concludes that, for example, the child's learning difficulties call for:
  – occasional advice to the school from an external specialist;
  – occasional support with personal care from a non-teaching assistant;
  – access to a particular piece of equipment such as a personal word-processing device, an electronic keyboard or a tape-recorder; or
  – minor building alterations such as widening a doorway or improving the acoustic environment,

  the local education authority may conclude that the school could reasonably be expected to make such provision from within its own resources.

(2) But if, as a result of a statutory assessment, the local education authority concludes that, for example, the child requires:
  – regular direct teaching by a specialist teacher;
  – daily individual support from a non-teaching assistant;
  – a significant piece of equipment such as a closed-circuit television or a computer or CD-ROM device with appropriate ancillaries and software;
  – a major building adaptation such as the installation of a lift;[3] or
  – the regular involvement of non-educational agencies,

  the local education authority may conclude that the school could not reasonably be expected to make such provision within its own resources and that the nature of the provision suggests that the local education authority should formally identify in a statement the child's needs, the full range of provision to be made and the review arrangements that will apply. However, the local education authority's conclusions will depend on the precise circumstances of each case, taking into account arrangements for funding schools in the area.

(3) If, as a result of a statutory assessment, the local education authority concludes that a change of placement may be indicated for the child, even if such a change involves moving from a mainstream school to a specialist unit at the same school or from one mainstream school to another, then the local education authority should consider drawing up a statement.

(4) If, as a result of a statutory assessment of a child of parents in the armed forces, the local education authority concludes that the parents' frequent moves might significantly disrupt effective special educational provision for the child, the local education authority should consider drawing up a statement.

(5) If, as a result of a statutory assessment, the local education authority concludes that a day or residential special school placement might be necessary, the local education authority should draw up a statement.

---

2 Code of Practice, para 4:11.

3 See *R v Lambeth London Borough Council ex parte M* (1995) *The Times*, 9 May, where the provision of a lift at a mainstream primary school to enable a disabled pupil to use the science room and library on the first floor was held not to be provision for an educational need in the context of the local authority's statement of special educational needs.

The decision as to whether to make a statement should be determined by the child's identifiable special educational needs in the context of arrangements for funding schools in the area. Local education authorities should arrange for the provision specified in a child's statement to be made in a cost-effective manner, but that provision must be consistent with the child's assessed needs. The efficient use of resources must be taken into account when a local education authority is considering the placement of a child with a statement, once the parents have had an opportunity to express a preference.[4]

Section 169(1) of the Education Act and reg 14(1) of the Education (Special Educational Needs) Regulations 1994 together provide that where a local education authority, having carried out an assessment of a child, decides not to make a statement, it shall within 2 weeks of the date on which the assessment was completed, write to the child's parents with its decision and tell the parents of their right to appeal to the SEN Tribunal against the decision.

The statutory assessment process may lead the local education authority to conclude that the child's special educational needs can be met from within the school's resources, with or without the intervention of a professional service from outside the school. The decision not to issue a statement may be viewed by parents as a denial of additional resources for the child and parents may appeal to the SEN Tribunal over a decision not to issue a statement. The Code of Practice recommends that local education authorities should ensure that parents are aware that resources are available within all maintained schools to meet the majority of special needs of their pupils and that parents fully understand the school-based stages of assessment and the monitoring and review arrangements which will ensure that their child's needs are appropriately met by the school, with external support if necessary.

Since the statutory assessment will have contributed significantly to the school's, the parents' and the local education authority's knowledge of the child, the local education authority should consider issuing a note in lieu of a statement.

A note in lieu of a statement will address similar issues to those contained in a statement and there may therefore be advantage in the format of the note in lieu broadly following the statutory format of the statement. However, it is imperative clearly to distinguish the legal status of the two documents.

The statutory assessment process ends with the decision of the local education authority as to whether to make a statement. That decision must normally be made within 10 weeks of the issue of a notice under s 167(4). The statutory time-limits within which the local education authority must inform parents either that a statement will not be made or issue to parents a proposed statement are then the same; normally, not more than 2 weeks after making the decision and not more than 12 weeks after the issue of a notice under s 167(4) that it will make a statutory assessment, the local education authority must either issue a notice under s 169(1) that it will not make a statement, or issue a proposed statement, together with a written notice under Sch 10, para 2 to the 1993 Act.

---

4 Code of Practice, para 4:12. See also the Education Act 1993, Sch 10, para 3.

6.3   WRITING THE STATEMENT

Regulation 14(1) of the Education (Special Educational Needs) Regulations 1994 requires that, where a local education authority, having made an assessment of a child, decides to make a statement, it shall serve a copy of a proposed statement and a written notice on the child's parent under para 2 of Sch 10 to the 1993 Act within 2 weeks of the date on which the assessment was completed.

The notice must be in the form prescribed in Part A of the Schedule to the Regulations. The statement of special educational needs must follow the format and contain the following information as prescribed by reg 13 and Part B of the Schedule to the Regulations.

PART 1   INTRODUCTION
The child's name and address and date of birth. The child's home language and religion. The names and address(es) of the child's parents.

PART 2   SPECIAL EDUCATIONAL NEEDS (LEARNING DIFFICULTIES)
Details of each and every one of the child's special educational needs as identified by the local education authority during statutory assessment and on the advice received and attached as appendices to the statement.

PART 3   SPECIAL EDUCATIONAL PROVISION
The special educational provision which the local education authority considers necessary to meet the child's special educational needs.

(a)   The objectives which the special educational provision should aim to meet.
(b)   The special educational provision which the local education authority considers appropriate to meet the needs specified in Part 2 and to meet the specified objectives.
(c)   The arrangements to be made for monitoring progress in meeting those objectives, particularly for setting short-term targets for the child's progress and for reviewing his or her progress on a regular basis.

PART 4   PLACEMENT
The type and name of school where the special educational provision specified in Part 3 is to be made or the arrangements for the education to be made otherwise than in school.

PART 5   NON-EDUCATIONAL NEEDS
All relevant non-educational needs of the child as agreed between the health services, social services or other agencies and the local education authority.

PART 6   NON-EDUCATIONAL PROVISION
Specification of relevant non-educational provision required to meet the non-educational needs of the child as agreed between the health services and/or social services and the local education authority, including the agreed arrangements for its provision.

Note: There has been much debate surrounding the question of whether a particular need which has been identified in a statement is one requiring special educational provision or non-educational provision as specified in the statement. The origin of such debate lies in the duty of the local education authority to arrange special educational provision specified in the statement, whereas it may, rather than must, arrange any non-educational provision unless the parent has made alternative arrangements.[5]

SIGNATURE AND DATE
The statement should be signed by a duly authorised officer of the authority and dated.

APPENDICES
All the advice obtained and taken into consideration during the assessment process must be attached as appendices to the statement, and reg 13 provides that the advice appended to the statement must include the following:

(1)   parental representations, evidence and advice;
(2)   educational advice;
(3)   medical advice;
(4)   psychological advice;
(5)   social services advice;
(6)   any other advice, such as the views of the child, which the local education authority or any other body from whom advice is sought consider desirable. In particular, where the child's parent is a member of the armed forces, advice should be obtained from the Service Children's Education Authority (SCEA).

The Code of Practice recommends that local education authorities should draft clear, unambiguous statements and that, where diagnostic or technical terms are necessary or helpful, for example in referring to specific disabilities, their meaning should be amplified in terms which parents and other non-professionals will readily understand.[6]

6.4   CHANGES TO THE STATEMENT

Schedule 10, para 2 to the 1993 Act and regs 12 and 13 together require that, before making a statement, the local education authority should issue to parents a copy of the proposed statement, and a notice setting out the arrangements for the choice of school, the parents' right to make representations about the content of the statement, and their right to appeal to the SEN Tribunal against the contents of the final statement.[7] In that notice, the local education authority must include details of

---

5   For the debate surrounding educational and non-educational provision in relation to speech and
     language therapy, see, inter alia, *R v Secretary of State for Education and Science ex parte E* [1992] 1
     FLR 377; *R v Lancashire County Council ex parte M* [1989] 2 FLR 279; *R v Secretary of State for
     Education and Science ex parte Davis* [1989] 2 FLR 190; *R v Oxfordshire County Council ex parte W*
     [1987] 2 FLR 193.
6   Code of Practice, para 4:26.
7   Code of Practice, para 4:39.

schools approved under s 189 of the 1993 Act and of non-maintained schools; and of maintained schools in the area which cater for children of the appropriate age.

Regulation 14(2) provides that the period from the service of a proposed statement and written notice under Sch 10, para 2 to the service of a copy of a statement under Sch 10, para 6 shall be not more than 8 weeks.

The local education authority must draw up a proposed statement, completing all parts with the exception of Part 4, since the proposed statement must not contain any details relating to where the proposed special educational provision should be made.

The proposed statement together with copies of the advice which has been submitted during the assessment must be sent to the child's parents. At the same time, the local education authority must send the parents a notice in the form prescribed in Part A of the Schedule to the Regulations setting out the procedures to be followed including that for naming the appropriate school.

Schedule 10, para 3 provides that any preference by the parent as to the maintained, or grant-maintained special school at which he wishes education to be provided for his child must be made within 15 days of either the service of the notice or the last of any meetings arranged with an officer of the local education authority to discuss the statement.

Where such a preference is expressed, the name of the school should be specified in the statement unless either:

(1) the school is unsuitable to the child's age, ability or aptitude or to his special needs; or
(2) the attendance of the child at the school would be incompatible with the provision of efficient education for the children with whom the child would be educated or the efficient use of resources.

Before specifying the name of any maintained, grant-maintained or grant-maintained special school, the local education authority must consult the governing body of the school and, if the school is maintained by another local education authority, that authority.

Copies of the proposed statement should also be sent to all those who advised during the making of the statement.

The Code of Practice recommends that the local education authority should consider translating letters sent to parents and the draft statements into the parents' first language if this is not English or Welsh.[8]

In accordance with Sch 10, para 4 to the 1993 Act, at the time of issuing the proposed statement, the local education authority should inform parents that:

(1) they may within 15 days make representations to the local education authority and require that a meeting be arranged with an officer of the local education authority to discuss the contents of the statement;

---

8 See Chapters 8 and 9.

(2)   within 15 days of meeting the officer, the parents may make further representations or, if they disagree with any part of the assessment, require further meetings to be arranged with appropriate people within the local education authority to discuss the advice given;

(3)   within a final 15 days from the last meeting, the parents can make further comments to the local education authority.

It is recommended in the Code of Practice that every effort should be made to ensure that the parents are happy with the proposed statement and that, so far as possible, the child's views are reflected in the proposed statement and that the child understands the reasons for the proposals. At any meetings arising from the proposed statement, local education authority officers should give parents sufficient time and information in order to discuss their anxieties with the Named LEA Officer and seek, as far as possible, to come to a mutual agreement. Parents should also be informed that they may be accompanied by friends, relatives or their Named Person at any meetings. The local education authority may wish to refer parents to professionals in health or other services for clarification of any relevant aspect of the provision proposed which gives rise to concern.[9]

Schedule 10, para 6 to the 1993 Act provides that where a local education authority makes a statement it shall serve a copy on the child's parents and give notice in writing of their right to appeal to the SEN Tribunal against the description in the statement of the child's special educational needs, the special educational provision specified in the statement and the school named, or, if no school is named, the failure to name a school. The local education authority must also give the parents the name of the person to whom they may apply for information and advice about the child's special educational needs.

When amendments are suggested to the proposed statement and agreed by the local education authority and the parents, the final statement should be issued immediately. The local education authority must arrange the special educational provision and may arrange any non-educational provision specified in the statement, from the date on which the statement is made. Where the parents' proposals for amendments to the proposed statement are refused by the local education authority, or the parents are unwilling to accept other amendments to the proposed statement, the local education authority may still proceed to issue the final statement but must inform the parents of their right to appeal to the SEN Tribunal with regard to the provision specified in the statement, including the named school, and the procedures to be followed.[10]

6.4.1   A change of school

The Code of Practice recommends that all concerned with the child should give careful thought to transfer between school phases (eg infant to junior school) and that arrangements for a child's placement should be finalised by the beginning of the child's last term before transfer.

---

9   Code of Practice, paras 4:66 and 4:67.
10   Code of Practice, para 4:68, and see Chapter 8.

Under Sch 10, para 8 to the 1993 Act, parents have the right to request the local education authority to substitute the name of a maintained, grant-maintained or grant-maintained special school for the name of the school in Part 4 of the statement. The local education authority must comply with the request:

(1)   so long as it is made more than 12 months after:
  – a similar request;
  – the issue of the final copy of the statement;
  – the issue of an amendment to the statement;
  – the conclusion of an appeal to the SEN Tribunal over the provision specified in the statement;
  whichever is the latest;

(2)   and so long as:
  – the school is suitable for the child; and
  – the child's attendance at the school would be compatible with the efficient education of other children already there and with the efficient use of resources.[11]

If the above conditions apply, the local education authority must amend the statement to name the school proposed by the parents and must so inform the parents within 8 weeks of receiving the request under reg 14(5). The local education authority must consult the governing body of the school before naming the school and, where appropriate, it must also consult the local education authority by whom the school is maintained. The statement may specify the date on which the child is to start attending the new school, and that date might coincide with the start of a new term or give sufficient time for the school to make the preparations necessary for the child's arrival.

If the local education authority concludes that it cannot name the school proposed by the parents, the parents must be told in writing of their right to appeal to the SEN Tribunal against the decision and should also be given reasons for the refusal of their request. Regulation 14(5) requires that this letter should be sent within 8 weeks of the parents' initial request. If the child is due to transfer between school phases, the local education authority must name a school which will be appropriate for the child. This should be done in the closest consultation with the parents and must follow the procedures for amending statements set out in Sch 10, para 10 to the 1993 Act.

6.4.2   Amending the statement

If, at any time, the local education authority proposes to amend a statement, whether to amend the name of the school in Part 4 or for any other reason, it must write to the child's parents informing them of that proposal and the reasons for it and of their right to make representations within 15 days of the receipt of that proposal. A proposal to amend the statement will most often arise from the annual review.

---

11 Code of Practice, para 6:31.

The authority must then consider any representations made by the parents before deciding whether and how to amend the statement and, if it concludes that an amendment should be made, it must make the amendment within 8 weeks of the original letter setting out the proposal to make an amendment. It must also write to the parents informing them of the decision and the reasons for it, enclosing a copy of the amended statement and any relevant advice, and giving details of the parents' right of appeal to the SEN Tribunal against the description of the child's special educational needs and the special educational provision, including the name of the school. If it is decided not to proceed with the amendment, the authority should write to the parents with an explanation within a similar period of 8 weeks from the letter of proposal.

6.5   DURATION OF THE STATEMENT

6.5.1   Ceasing to maintain a statement

A statement will remain in force until the local education authority ceases to maintain it or ceases to be responsible for the child, for example if the child progresses to further or higher education, or to social services provision, when the statement will lapse. The only grounds for ceasing to maintain a statement for a child is the belief by the authority that it is no longer necessary. Then the authority must write to the child's parents giving notice of the decision to cease to maintain the statement, together with the reasons for that decision and copies of any evidence which prompted it, and explain the parents' right of appeal to the SEN Tribunal.

It should not be assumed that, once made, a statement should be maintained until the local education authority is no longer responsible for a child. Statements should be maintained only when necessary. However, the decision to cease to maintain a statement should be made only after careful consideration of all the circumstances and close consultation with the parents. The authority should consider the results of recent annual reviews, whether the objectives of the statement have been achieved and whether the child's needs could be met in future within the resources of mainstream schools within the area without the need for continuing overseeing by the authority. The local education authority should, therefore, always consider whether, notwithstanding the achievement of some, or even all, of the objectives in the statement, the child's progress would be halted or reversed if the special educational provision specified in the statement or modified provision which justified the maintenance of a statement were not made.[12]

6.5.2   Transfer of statements

When the responsibility for a child with special needs changes from the education authority making the statement to a new authority, the first authority must transfer the statement to the new authority. Upon the transfer of the statement, the new

---

12 Code of Practice, para 6:37.

authority becomes responsible for maintaining the statement and for providing the special educational provision specified in the statement.

The duty to maintain the child at the school named in Part 4 of the statement therefore also transfers to the new authority. However, the new authority may place the child temporarily at a school other than that specified in the statement where it is appropriate and sensible to do so, for example where the distance between the child's new home and the school would be too great, pending the amendment of the statement in accordance with the statutory procedures. Otherwise, the new authority may not decline to pay the fees or otherwise maintain the child at an independent school or non-maintained special school or boarding school named in a statement, unless and until the statement has been formally amended.

Upon the transfer of the statement, the new authority may bring forward the arrangements for the review of the statement and may conduct a new assessment irrespective of the date of the previous assessment. The parents must be told, within 6 weeks of the date of the transfer, when review of the statement will take place and whether it is proposed to make an assessment under s 167. The first authority and the child's school should advise parents of the educational implications of the proposed move, and both authorities should be prepared to discuss these implications with parents.

6.5.3 Maintenance of a statement

When a statement is made, the local education authority should tell the 'responsible person' in the child's school and the responsible person should then ensure that the child's special educational needs are known to all those who will teach him or her. Schools should ensure that teachers monitor and informally review the child's progress during the course of the year. It is imperative that, if a child's special educational needs change for the better or the worse, a review is held as soon as possible to ensure that the provision specified in the statement remains appropriate.[13]

6.6 REASSESSMENT

Section 172 of the 1993 Act permits parents of a child with a statement to request the local education authority to carry out a new assessment of that child under s 167 of the Act. Such a request must be complied with provided:

(1)   no such assessment has been made within the previous 6 months; and
(2)   the local education authority concludes that it is necessary to make a further assessment.

---

13 Code of Practice, para 4:80.

The same procedures as those for assessment should be followed,[14] and, in particular, the authority should consider whether there have been significant changes in the circumstances of the child.

If the authority concludes that a further assessment is not necessary, it must write to the parents giving reasons for the decision and informing them of their right to appeal to the SEN Tribunal. The authority should also write to the child's school and may wish to arrange a meeting between the parents and the school.

If the authority concludes that a further assessment is necessary, the procedures and time-limits for assessment and amendment, set out above, must be followed and the resultant statement will supersede the earlier statement.

6.7   ANNUAL REVIEW

Section 172(5) of the 1993 Act requires a local education authority to review a statement within 12 months of making the statement, or, as the case may be, of the previous review, and on making an assessment under s 167 of a child who already has a statement.

The purpose of an annual review is to integrate a variety of perspectives on a child's progress, to ensure that he or she is achieving the desired outcomes and, if necessary, to amend the statement to reflect newly identified needs and provision. In some cases, the authority will conclude that the objectives set out in the statement have been achieved and that they should cease to maintain the statement. The annual review should focus on achievement by the child as well as on any difficulties remaining to be resolved.

Authorities have the power to review a statement at any time during the year but should aim to secure the agreement of the school and the child's parents before exercising that power. However, authorities must review all statements on an annual basis and the timing of annual reviews should reflect the circumstances of the child and the action which may flow from the review, for example the move to secondary school. Parents should always be notified of an impending review.

The review is initiated by the local education authority's writing to the head teacher of the child's school, with a copy to the child's parents, asking the head teacher to convene a review meeting and prepare a review report.

The authority must give the head teacher at least 2 months' notice of the date by which the review report must be returned to the authority and must also advise the head teacher of those people who should be invited to contribute to the review and to attend the review meeting.

Those invited to the review meeting must include the following:

(1)   a representative from the local education authority;
(2)   the child's parents, or, if the child is looked after by the local authority, his or her carer; and

---

14 See Chapter 3.

(3)   a relevant teacher, who may be the child's teacher or form or year tutor, the school's SEN co-ordinator or some other person responsible for the provision of education for the child, the choice resting with the head teacher.

In preparing for the review meeting, the head teacher must:

(1)   request written advice from the child's parents, all those specified by the authority and anyone else the head teacher considers appropriate; and
(2)   circulate a copy of all advice received to all those invited to the review meeting at least 2 weeks before the date of the meeting, inviting additional comments from those unable to attend the review meeting.[15]

The review meeting will normally take place in the child's school and should be chaired by the head teacher or the teacher to whom responsibility for the school-based elements of the review has been delegated. The review meeting should address the following questions.

(1)   What are the parents' views of the past year's progress and their aspirations for the future?
(2)   What are the child's views of the past year's progress and his or her aspirations for the future?
(3)   What is the school's view of the child's progress over the past year? (What has been the child's progress towards meeting the overall objectives in the statement? What success has the child achieved in meeting the targets set?)
(4)   Have there been significant changes in the child's circumstances which affect his or her development and progress?
(5)   Is current provision, including the National Curriculum, or arrangements substituted for it, appropriate to the child's needs?
(6)   What educational targets should be adopted against which the child's educational progress will be assessed during the coming year and at the next review?
(7)   Is the Transition Plan[16] helping the child's progress to adult life?
(8)   Is any further action required and, if so, by whom?
(9)   Does the statement remain appropriate?
(10)   Are any amendments to the statement required or should the local education authority be recommended to cease to maintain it?

The meeting should then make appropriate recommendations and may recommend amendments to a statement if:

(1)   significant new needs have emerged which are not recorded on the statement;
(2)   significant needs which are recorded on the statement are no longer present;
(3)   the provision should be amended to meet the child's changing needs and the targets specified at the review meeting; or

---

15 Code of Practice, paras 6:10 and 6:13.
16 Transition Plan: a plan which should form part of the first annual review after the child's fourteenth birthday and any subsequent review. The purpose of the plan is to draw together information from a range of individuals within and beyond the school, in order to plan coherently for the young person's transition to adult life.

(4)   the child should change schools, either at the point of transfer between school phases (for example, infant to junior or primary to secondary) or when a child's needs would more appropriately be met in a different school (for example by integration into the mainstream).

The review meeting and the review report may also recommend that the local education authority should cease to maintain the statement.[17]

The process is concluded by the local education authority which considers the review report and recommendations made by the head teacher and then makes any recommendations of its own which are sent to the school, the child's parents and all those invited to the review meeting.

6.8   UNDER 5s

It is a requirement under s 161 of the 1993 Act that those responsible for a school's governance, being the local education authority in the case of a maintained nursery school, shall use their best endeavours to secure that appropriate special educational provision is made for all their registered pupils with learning difficulties.

Thus, the local education authority may expect a nursery class or school to follow broadly the same procedures for identifying and meeting the special educational needs of children under the age of 5 as those recommended in the Code of Practice for children of compulsory school age. However, many young children will be attending child care facilities provided by social services, the health services or the voluntary or independent sectors when concern about a possible special educational need is first raised.

Where a child under the age of 5 is referred to the local education authority by social services or the health services, there should be agreed procedures for acting speedily in order to ascertain whether the child's needs require specific intervention by the authority. In the first instance, the local education authority may wish to invite a pre-school adviser or an educational psychologist to discuss with the service in question how best to take the matter forward, and it may be that at this stage advice will be all that is required. In some cases, referral to a child development centre or team may be the best method of identifying the nature of the child's difficulties; however, in other cases, it may be clear that a child's difficulties are such as to require a statutory assessment.

6.8.1   Criteria for statutory assessment

In considering a statutory assessment, the authority should ask the following questions.

(1)   Where the child is at school, what difficulties have been identified by the school? Has the nursery class or school developed school-based strategies to assist the child?

17 Code of Practice, paras 6:22, 6:28 and 6:29.

(2) Where the child is attending health services, social services, voluntary or private sector establishments, have any concerns been raised about his or her development and has any outside advice been sought regarding the child's:
 – physical health and function;
 – communication skills;
 – perceptual and motor skills;
 – self-help skills;
 – social skills;
 – emotional and behavioural development;
 – responses to learning experiences?

The local education authority will then assess the evidence and decide whether the child's difficulties or developmental delays are likely to be resolved only through a multi-professional approach which will require monitoring and review over a period of time.[18]

6.8.2 Content of the statement

Where children aged between 2 and 5 have needs of such complexity as to require statutory procedures in order to maximise their opportunities, the statement will follow the same format as for any other children, but the contributions of non-educational service providers are likely to be of key significance.

Parents of children under 5 years old may express a preference for a maintained school to be named in the statement and may make representations in favour of a non-maintained or independent school for their child. Authorities must provide parents with lists of independent schools approved under s 189 of the 1993 Act, all non-maintained special schools and of all local education authority maintained and grant-maintained schools in the area which cater for children of the appropriate age. They may also inform parents of such schools in neighbouring areas.

Authorities should informally review a statement for a child under the age of 5 at least every 6 months to ensure that the provision is appropriate to the child's needs. Such reviews would complement the statutory duty to carry out an annual review in accordance with the Regulations but would not require the same range of documentation so long as they reflected the significant changes which can take place in the progress of a child under the age of 5.[19]

6.8.3 Special educational provision

For very young children, access to a home-based learning programme or the services of a peripatetic teacher for the hearing or visually impaired may provide the most appropriate help. In the case of a child with a behavioural difficulty, the advice of the clinical psychologist at a child development centre or of an educational psychologist may enable the child to remain within an existing service. In some cases, it may be decided that a child should attend a nursery class or school (either

---

18 Code of Practice, paras 5:18 and 5:19.
19 Code of Practice, para 5:22.

within a mainstream or special school context), playgroup or opportunity playgroup.

All services working within a local authority with young children, including home-based learning programmes, should have clearly articulated arrangements for access to their services. Such arrangements should be readily understandable by parents of children with special needs, indicate the kind of support which can be provided and state any priority admission arrangements.

The local education authority should have information on nursery school or class places for children with special educational needs, and about places in play or opportunity groups, family centres, day nurseries or other provision for young children in that authority.

6.8.4 Moving to primary school

In some cases, a child under 5 years old may have received considerable support without the necessity for a statement. If it is decided that the child's needs are such that he or she will require a statement prior to entering primary school at the age of 5, careful attention should be paid to the parents' views and to information available from the full range of assessment arrangements within all the relevant agencies making provision for young children with special needs. In particular, attention should be given to the child's general health and development and home environment to ensure that a learning difficulty is not directly related to wider family problems, and in order to provide appropriate support for the parents in making a full contribution to their child's progress at school.

Schools will wish to assess pupils' current levels of attainment on entry in order to ensure that they build on the pattern of learning and experience already established during the child's pre-school years in nursery schools or classes, playgroups and other settings. If the child has an identified or potential special educational need, the head teacher, SEN co-ordinator and the child's class teacher should:

(1) use information arising from the child's early years of experience to provide starting points for the curricular development of the child;

(2) identify and focus attention on the child's skills and highlight areas for early action to support the child within the class;

(3) take appropriate action, for example, developing an individual education plan and monitoring and evaluation strategies to maximise development and alert any relevant support or external professionals at the earliest possible stage;

(4) ensure that ongoing observation and assessment provide regular feedback to teachers and parents about a child's achievements and experiences and that the outcomes of such assessment form the basis for planning the next steps of a child's learning;

(5) use the assessment process to allow children to show what they know, understand and can do, as well as to identify any learning difficulties;

(6) involve parents in developing and implementing learning programmes at home and in school.

Local education authorities should ensure that health services, social services and the voluntary and independent sectors providing services for the under 5s, as well as the parents, fully understand the assessment and referral arrangements and that a child's progress is carefully observed and recorded in order to inform any assessment procedure.[20]

6.9 POST-16 CHILDREN

Some pupils with statements of special educational needs will remain in school after the age of 16. Local education authorities remain responsible for them until they are 19. Others with statements will leave school at 16, moving to college, for example, or social services provision. Whatever the intended future destination of the young person, the annual review has an additional significance as he or she approaches 16.

The first annual review after the young person's fourteenth birthday should involve the agencies which will play an important role during the post-school years. The transfer of relevant information is intended to ensure that the young person receives any specialist support or help during his or her continuing education and vocational or occupational training after leaving school.

The first annual review after the young person's fourteenth birthday will follow the procedure described above with the following exceptions.

(1) The local education authority convenes the review meeting, even when the young person is at school. The authority must invite the young person's parents and relevant member of staff, any people specified by the head teacher and anyone else the authority considers appropriate.

(2) The local authority must also ensure that other providers, such as social services, are aware of the annual review and the procedures to be followed, and must invite the social services department to attend the review so that any parallel assessments under the Disabled Persons Act 1986, the National Health Service and Community Care Act 1990 and the Chronically Sick and Disabled Persons Act 1970 can contribute to and draw information from the review process.

(3) The local authority must invite the careers service to be represented at the review meeting to enable all options for further education, careers and occupational training to be given serious consideration. The careers service will also be able to identify any specific targets which should be set as part of the annual review to ensure that independence training, personal and social skills and other aspects of the wider curriculum are fully addressed during the young person's last years at school.

(4) The local authority prepares the review report and the Transition Plan after the meeting and circulates these to the young person's parents, the head teacher, all those from whom advice was sought, all those attending the review meeting and anyone else the authority considers appropriate. In particular, the local authority should consider passing the review report and Transition Plan

20 Code of Practice, paras 5:29 and 5:30.

to the Further Education Funding Council (FEFC), particularly in cases where a decision might need to be taken about specialist college provision outside the further education sector.[21]

The first annual review after the young person's fourteenth birthday and any subsequent annual reviews until he or she leaves school should include a Transition Plan which will draw together information from a range of individuals within and beyond the school in order to plan coherently for the young person's transition to adult life. Under ss 5 and 6 of the Disabled Persons Act 1986, at the first annual review after a young person's fourteenth birthday, local authorities must seek information from social services departments as to whether a young person with a statement under Part III of the Education Act 1993 is disabled and may require services from the local authority when leaving school. Local authorities should also consult child health services and any other professionals, such as educational psychologists, therapists or occupational psychologists, who may be able to contribute usefully.

Local education authorities should ensure that where a young person has a statement of special educational needs, a copy of the statement, together with a copy of the most recent annual review and any advice appended to it, including the Transition Plan, should be passed to the social services department and the college or other provision that the young person will be attending. Where a decision might need to be taken by the FEFC about the placement of a student in a specialist college outside the further education sector, a copy of the Transition Plan should be sent to the FEFC. Local authorities should seek the agreement of students and parents to the transfer of information, including statements, from school to the further education sector, but should explain the importance of such information and the desirability of the transfer.[22]

The views of young people themselves should be sought and recorded wherever possible in any assessment, reassessment or review during the years of transition. Some young people may wish to express these views through a trusted professional, member of the family, independent advocate or adviser, the Named Person or an officer of the authority. However, effective transition arrangements will involve the young people themselves addressing issues of:

(1) personal development;
(2) self-advocacy;
(3) the development of a positive self-image;
(4) awareness of the implications of any long-term health problem or disability; and
(5) the growth of personal autonomy and the acquisition of independent living skills.[23]

There will be cases of students approaching the age of 16 who may have special educational needs which do not call for a statement but which are likely to require some support if they go on to further education. In such cases, it is important that

---

21 Code of Practice, para 6:44.
22 Code of Practice, para 6:56.
23 Code of Practice, para 6:59.

students receive appropriate help and guidance to ensure that they are able to make decisions and to facilitate their successful transition. This might include the provision of school/college link courses or work placements and should involve the various local agencies concerned. Further education colleges will require a thorough assessment of the young person's needs in order to make well-reasoned decisions about appropriate provision.

6.10   SICK CHILDREN

Section 163 of the 1993 Act empowers the local education authority to arrange for some or all of a child's special educational provision to be made otherwise than at school. Section 164 enables the authority to make arrangements for a child with a statement to attend an institution outside England and Wales. Where such arrangements are made, the local authority may contribute to or pay the fees of the institution and the travelling and other expenses of the child and any person, including a parent, who might accompany the child. Such arrangements may be specified in Part 4 of the statement.

When a child is educated otherwise than at a school, the general timetable and arrangements for the annual review will remain the same as for children in schools. However, in these circumstances the local authority will convene the review meeting, and the range of professionals involved may be wider and in some respects different from those involved in a school-based review. The child's parents must always be invited to the review meeting, which should take place in the most appropriate location, such as the local authority's offices or a hospital and should normally be chaired by the authority.

Where a child is educated otherwise than at school because of major difficulties relating to health or a disability, the views of the child's doctor should be sought. In such circumstances, the attendance of professional advisers from the relevant child health services will be particularly important and the timing of the review meeting should be arranged to ensure that they can participate as far as possible.

PART II

LEGAL REMEDIES

Chapter 7

TRIBUNAL STRUCTURE AND ADMINISTRATION

7.1 GENERAL

The Special Educational Needs Tribunal was established by virtue of Part III of the Education Act 1993.[1] Its jurisdiction is England and Wales. It was created to overcome a perceived problem of delay in the former system under which parents were first required to appeal to a local committee of the local authority and then, if dissatisfied, to appeal to the Secretary of the State.[2] However, the court refused to grant to a parent a remedy for a delay in the former system which was 'unreasonable' but not reprehensible.[3] The intention of the new procedure is not only to make it easier for a parent to appeal but also to ensure that the decisions about a child's future are made as quickly as possible. The Special Educational Needs Tribunal Regulations 1995 ('the Regulations')[4] set a clear timetable for each stage of the appeal process. This will be dealt with more fully in Chapter 9, but it should be noted that it is expected that the timetable will be adhered to. Although there is power to extend the time allowed for doing any act required,[5] an extension will be granted only in exceptional circumstances. The 1995 Regulations replace the 1994 Regulations. The amendments are largely administrative and are intended to tighten up, clarify or simplify the earlier Regulations. They were drafted in consultation with the Special Educational Needs Tribunal and drew upon the experience of the Tribunal's first year of operation. There are some transitional arrangements for appeals determined between January and March 1996. By reg 43 of the 1995 Regulations, the 1994 Regulations will apply to any appeal where the notice of appeal was received by the Tribunal before 1 January 1996, and any appeal received between then and 1 March 1996 may comply with either the 1994 or 1995 Regulations. This chapter refers only to the 1995 Regulations.

The Tribunal was created by s 177 of the 1993 Act and exercises its jurisdiction pursuant to the Regulations.[6] The matters to be dealt with by the regulations are set out in s 180(2). Trevor Aldridge QC was appointed President of the Tribunal in mid-1994. In addition to the President, there are two panels, the chairman's panel and the lay panel.[7] There is a secretariat based in London and Darlington to handle the appeals and service the Tribunal. A list of which members of the secretariat deal

---

1 1993 c 35.

2 Education Act 1981, s 58(6).

3 *R v Gloucestershire County Council ex parte P* [1993] COD 303 (QBD).

4 SI 1995/3113, in force as from 1 January 1996. They replace the 1994 Regulations (SI 1994/1910) which came into force on 1 September 1994.

5 Regulation 41(1). Exceptional circumstances are considered at **9.2**.

6 Section 177(5) and s 180(1).

7 Section 177(2).

with which local education authorities can be found at Appendix 8. The Tribunal has power to regulate its own procedure.[8]

7.2 MEMBERS

The chairman's panel together with the President were appointed by the Lord Chancellor and comprise either solicitors or barristers. The legal members of the Tribunal have a minimum of 7 years' general qualification within the meaning of s 71 of the Courts and Legal Services Act 1990.[9] There are currently 34 chairmen, although more are due to be appointed in mid-1996. The members of the lay panel were appointed by the Secretary of State for Education and Employment (in England) and the Secretary of State for Wales[10] and are individuals who have knowledge and experience of either children with special educational needs or local government.[11] There are approximately 97 lay members. Each member of the chairman's panel and lay panel has been appointed for an initial period of one year and may resign from office by notice in writing (as the case may be) to either the Lord Chancellor or the Secretary of State. Any member is eligible for reappointment for a further period of up to three years if he continues to hold office.[12]

The President determines both the number of Tribunals to be established from time to time and also the times and places that they may sit.[13] The consultation paper on the draft regulations suggested that the Tribunal would sit around the country and, provided suitable accommodation was available, in places which were easily accessible to both parents and the local education authority. Since the members of both panels reside throughout England and Wales, it is anticipated that this expectation will be realised as far as possible. It is clear from the location of sittings which started in January 1995 that this hope has been fulfilled. Subject to one of the lay members being absent at or after the commencement of a hearing,[14] the Tribunal shall consist of a chairman (being either the President or a person selected from the chairman's panel) and two other members selected from the lay panel.[15]

There is power for any act which is required or authorised by the Regulations to be undertaken by the President to be undertaken by a member of the chairman's panel authorised by the President. This has been especially useful, for example, when the President has been on holiday. The 'acting' President may, when carrying out the function of selecting the chairman of a Tribunal, select himself.[17] Any decision made by an 'acting' President is capable of being reviewed as if it were a decision of

---

8 Regulation 35(1).
9 1990 c 41.
10 Section 177(4).
11 Regulation 3.
12 Section 178(4) and (5).
13 Regulation 4.
14 Regulation 28(5): see **10.5** and **10.7**.
15 Regulation 5.
16 Regulation 37(1).
17 Regulation 37(2).

the President, and reg 32 applies except that the reference in that regulation to 'the President' is taken as a reference to the member of the chairman's panel by whom the decision was taken.[18]

In the event of the death or incapacity of the chairman following the decision of the Tribunal in any matter, the functions of the chairman for the completion of the proceedings, including any review of the decision, may be exercised by the President or any member of the chairman's panel[19] except that where a document is required to be signed by the chairman but, as a result of his death or incapacity, he is unable to sign the document, it shall be signed by the other members of the Tribunal who shall certify that the chairman is unable to sign.[20]

7.3 CLERKS AND THE SECRETARY OF THE TRIBUNAL

The Special Educational Needs Tribunal is based at the office of the Tribunal in London,[21] although from early 1996 Tribunals for the north of England have been dealt with from the Department for Education and Employment's office at Darlington.[22] The Secretariat staff 'clerk' all Tribunal hearings although they have no role in deciding the outcome of any appeal. Although the Tribunal initially had 7 staff, the number of appeals received has meant that there are now more than 20 people working for the Tribunal. They are divided into teams and the responsibility for the various local education authorities is divided between the teams. The list of teams is set out in Appendix 8. In addition, the responsibility for arranging hearings and despatching judgments is held by specific individuals. The Tribunal consistently received between 30 and 35 appeals per week in its first year but that increased to an average of 50 per week from November 1995. A clear and helpful guide to the Tribunal has been produced, copies of which are available from the DfEE Publications Centre.[23] Ms Jessica Saraga is the Secretary of the Tribunal and is the senior civil servant in the Tribunal. The Secretary is the person to whom, for example, all documents must be sent, who must be notified of the name and address of a party's representative and who is responsible for notifying the parties of the decision of the Tribunal after a hearing. By reg 38, a function of the Secretary of the Tribunal may be performed by another member of staff of the Tribunal authorised for the purpose of carrying out that function by the President.

For the sake of certainty, the Regulations[24] provide that, unless the contrary is proved, a document purporting to be a document issued by the Secretary of the Tribunal shall be deemed to be a document so issued, and any document purporting to be certified by the Secretary of the Tribunal as being a true copy of a document

---

18 Regulation 37(3).
19 Regulation 37(4).
20 Regulation 39(6).
21 The address and telephone and facsimile number can be found in Appendix 8.
22 The Darlington address can be found in Appendix 8.
23 DfEE Publications Centre, PO Box 6927, London E3 3NZ, tel: 0171 510 0150.
24 Regulation 6(1) and (2).

containing a decision of the Tribunal shall be sufficient evidence of matters contained in it.

7.4   THE TRIBUNAL'S FIRST YEAR: SOME STATISTICS

An analysis of the first year of the Tribunal (to 31 August 1995) gives an indication of both the nature of appeals received and the results obtained by the parents.[25] In the first year, 1,170 appeals were registered, of which 487 were disposed of in one way or another. About 22% of all appeals lodged are withdrawn by the parents – either because an agreement is reached with the local education authority or because there are no grounds upon which to appeal. In the first year, the appeals which were withdrawn totalled 245.

Of the 242 decisions issued by 31 August 1995, 35% were dismissed outright, 46% were upheld outright, 11% were upheld/dismissed in part, 5% were remitted to the local education authority and 3% (seven cases) were struck out.

Of the grounds upon which parents have appealed, it is not surprising that nearly half (49%) of all appeals are against the contents of the statement of special educational needs. Appeals against a refusal of a local education authority to assess a child after parental request account for 21% of appeals, as do appeals against a refusal to make a statement. Only 7% of appeals concern a local education authority's decision to cease to maintain a statement, whereas appeals against a decision not to reassess account for only 2% of cases. The 49% of appeals concerned with the contents of the statement comprise 18% of appeals against the school named, 2% against the refusal of a local education authority to change the name of a school, and 1% against a failure to name a school. The remaining 28% are appeals against the contents, whether in Part 2 or Part 3 of the statement.

It would seem that the expressed wish to ensure that the Tribunal remained informal and relatively free of lawyers has occurred. Only 15% of parents had legally qualified representatives – whereas 23% had non-legal representatives from specialist organisations.

As to the nature of special educational needs of the children whose parents have appealed to the Tribunal, by far the greatest number (40%) have specific learning difficulties. The balance is comprised as follows:

Autism	3%
Emotional and behavioural difficulties (EBD)	6%
Epilepsy	1%
Hearing impairment	4%
Moderate learning difficulty	9%

---

25 I am grateful to the staff of the SEN Tribunal for this information and, in particular, Ms Sue Collins. In addition, the information is contained in the Special Educational Needs Tribunal 1994/95 Annual Report published on 11 December 1995.

Physical handicap	5%
Severe learning difficulty	6%
Speech and language	9%
Visual impairment	1%
'Other'	16%

These statistics are different from those produced at the end of the first 9 months' work. By 31 May 1995, specific learning difficulties accounted for 51% of all appeals, 60% were decided either wholly or partly in the parents' favour (now 57%) and the largest single ground of appeal was refusal to make a statement which accounted for 29% of appeals (now 21%).[26]

To date, 19 cases have gone to the High Court on appeal (see Chapter 12) with only two thus far going to the Court of Appeal. The first case to be heard by the High Court was *S v Special Educational Needs Tribunal and The City of Westminster* which was heard on 25 July 1995.[27] The Court of Appeal gave judgment on the appeal on 13 December 1995.[28] A digest of those cases decided by the Tribunal is published in *Education Law Reports* (Jordans).

7.5 WELSH

The Tribunal has a responsibility to provide its service in Welsh to parents and local education authorities in Wales if they wish. There is a Welsh form of the Notice of Appeal. During the first year of the Tribunal, it was not possible to arrange a hearing exclusively in Welsh for the one parent who requested it because no Welsh-speaking chairman had been appointed. Since 1 September 1995, however, a native Welsh speaker has been appointed as a chairman. There are already a number of lay members of the Tribunal who are Welsh speaking.

7.6 COUNCIL ON TRIBUNALS

By virtue of s 181 of the 1993 Act, the Special Educational Needs Tribunal is supervised by the Council on Tribunals.[29] Its function is both to supervise the procedures and working of the Tribunals and Inquiries and advise government departments. The Council on Tribunals was consulted on the procedural rules of the Tribunal. Members of the Council will visit Tribunal hearings as observers to assess how the procedures are operating. If a member of the Council is present during any appeal hearing, as with everyone except the three members of the Tribunal, they will not be involved in the proceedings or with any decision taken at

---

26 See *Times Educational Supplement*, 9 June 1995, p 14.
27 [1995] 1 WLR 1627, [1996] ELR 102, [1995] TLR 498.
28 [1996] 2 All ER 286, [1996] 1 WLR 382, [1995] TLR 685.
29 Established by the Tribunals and Inquiries Act 1958. It now operates pursuant to the Tribunal and Inquiries Act 1992.

the hearing or in the decision sent to the parties. Further information about the Council's function can be obtained from its Secretary.[30]

---

30 The address can be found in Appendix 8.

Chapter 8

RIGHTS OF APPEAL

8.1 INTRODUCTION

From its creation on 1 September 1994, the Special Educational Needs Tribunal has considered appeals by parents in cases where:

(1)   a local education authority refuses to make an assessment;
(2)   a local education authority refuses to issue a statement[1] after a full assessment has been made;
(3)   parents are unhappy about the way in which their child's needs are described in the statement;
(4)   parents are unhappy about the way in which the provision is described in the statement;
(5)   parents are unhappy about the school named in the statement;
(6)   parents are unhappy that no school is named in the statement;
(7)   a local education authority refuses to reassess a child's special educational needs if it has not made any assessment for at least 6 months;
(8)   a local education authority refuses to change the school named in a statement;
(9)   a local education authority ceases to maintain a statement.

Before each of these is considered in turn, it will be useful to determine who is a party to the appeal and what is meant by a child.

8.1.1   Parent

Although Part III of the Education Act 1993 makes it clear that the right to appeal to the Tribunal rests with the parents of a child, because of the implication for legal aid on appeal to the High Court, the question of whether a child should be a party has already been judicially considered. This matter is more fully discussed in Chapters 11 and 12, but the conclusion of the Court of Appeal is that a child is not a party to the proceedings.

As to who may be described as the parent of the child, Part III of the 1993 Act does not define 'parent' but, by reason of s 305(3), the definition to be found in s 114(1D)–(1F) (as amended by the Education Act 1993) of the Education Act 1944 applies. That section defines a parent so as to include any person who is not a parent of a child or young person but who has 'parental responsibility' for or care of him. In the vast majority of cases, that definition covers the natural parents of a child but does not cover the case of a child who is the subject of a care order in favour of a local authority. By s 33(3)(a) of the Children Act 1989, a care order gives a local authority parental responsibility for a child in its care.

---

1 A 'statement' means a statement of special educational needs as defined by the Code of Practice. See Chapter 6.

Since the parents do not lose their own parental responsibility on the making of a care order, logically it would seem that both the parents and the local authority would be regarded as parents. However, in practice, this will produce a somewhat illogical consequence since, if it is felt by the social services department of a local authority that the education department of the same council has made a wrong decision, in theory the former will have a right to appeal to the Tribunal against the decision of the latter, thus making the authority both parties to the appeal!

A care order does not give a local authority full parental rights. By s 33(6) and (7) of the Children Act 1989, a number of rights are expressly and exclusively retained by the child's parents. Conversely, a care order does give the local authority power to determine the extent to which a child's parent may meet his or her parental responsibility subject to 'any right, duty, power, responsibility or authority' which a parent has in relation to the child by virtue of any Act.[2]

It is possible that this means that an authority has power to direct the parent except in any areas where the parent is specifically mentioned by an Act of Parliament. It is possible, therefore, that, notwithstanding that a local authority is defined as a parent by virtue of having parental responsibility, it may not have the right to appeal to the Tribunal, since that power in the Education Act 1993 is given to a parent rather than expressly given to the person with parental responsibility.

If the authority does have the right to appeal, it does not follow that it can do so, because the Tribunal would then be faced with the prospect of the local authority being both appellant and respondent to the appeal.

There is only one reported case which considers the interrelationship of different departments of the same local authority and, although that case concerning housing legislation, the principle could be just as easily applied in this context. *R v London Borough of Tower Hamlets ex parte B*[3] concerned the housing and social services departments of the same council.

In *Ex parte B* the housing department received a request from the social services department to rehouse a family. The social services department were relying on s 27 of the Children Act 1989. In the Court of Appeal, Lord Justice Russell felt that to construe s 27 to enable one part of the authority to ask another part of the authority for help offended against the plain and natural meaning of the words in that section. Lord Justice Hoffmann said at p 607G–H, 'you cannot ask yourself for help'. It is possible that the courts may feel that it is only a very short step from that view to 'you cannot appeal your own decision'.

Since the decision which the parent appeals against is that of the local authority and not that of the education department, it is fair to conclude that the authority as a whole is bound by the decision and to suggest that it can then appeal itself would seem to stretch common sense to its limits.

---

2 See s 33(9) of the Children Act 1989. It is of interest to note that in Hershman and McFarlane *Children Law and Practice* (Jordans), the authors include at para A[234] the words '(for example, pursuant to the education legislation)' when noting this section.

3 [1993] 2 FLR 605.

It should be noted that the *Ex parte B* appeal failed because the court was being asked to have s 27 of the Children Act construed as enabling one department to ask another for help. This section was also considered when different authorities were involved in *R v Northavon District Council ex parte Smith*[4]. In that case, the House of Lords held that a social services department of one authority did not have power to *require* the housing department of another authority to exercise its powers but that under s 27 the housing authority was required to co-operate with the social services authority to find a solution to the family's housing needs. In other words, the request being made in *Ex parte B* was not wrong. It was the fact that two departments of the same authority were involved that was wrong, not the request.

It is suggested, therefore, that an authority cannot appeal its own decision to the Tribunal, and so children who are in the case of the local authority and who have non-interventionist parents will miss out. It has to be stressed, however, that as there is no reported authority on this point a court may disagree with this interpretation.

If a local education authority is able to appeal against its own decision, the question of who should bring the appeal needs to be considered. As the authority is not a person, it would have to be someone acting on its behalf. The options are the child's foster-parents or social worker. It is difficult to see how the foster-parents would be able to pass the 'parent' test since, as the right to appeal is given to parents, foster-parents are neither 'natural' nor 'statutory' parents. The latter is the authority itself, and foster-parents do not have the legal status of parental responsibility. The appropriate person (if it is indeed possible for an appeal to be brought in these circumstances) would seem to be the child's social worker as a representative of the authority.

8.1.2 Local education authority

By reg 2, the parents' appeal is against the local education authority which made the decision. This is the local education authority for the area in which the child is or was attending school at the time of making the decision appealed against,[5] even if the child now goes to school in a different area or if the family has moved and a new authority has taken over responsibility for the statement (if made). The fact that the former authority cannot implement the Tribunal's decision may mean that the appeal is pointless or, alternatively, could affect the new local education authority without it being able to present any case to the Tribunal. Perhaps, in those circumstances, the 'former' local education authority would be wise to liaise with the 'new' authority and call officers from the new local education authority as witnesses.

A further point which has now become relevant is that from 1 April 1996 a number of local education authorities have been abolished and superseded by unitary authorities. This includes not only all of Wales but also, for example, Humberside. In other areas, such as Brighton and Hove, new unitary authorities have taken over responsibility from the larger county council which will remain in existence for other areas. The Tribunal will continue to hear the appeals in the name of the old

---

4 [1994] 3 WLR 403.
5 Education Act 1993, s 165(3).

authority but will make reference to the new authority (upon whom the decision is binding) in its decision.

8.1.3 Child

Section s 165(3) of the Education Act 1993 defines a child for whom a local education authority is responsible under Part III as being one who is either a registered pupil at a maintained, grant-maintained or grant-maintained special school or for whom education is provided at the expense of the authority at an independent school. In addition, if the child does not come within either of these definitions then, as long as he is a registered pupil at school and has been brought to the local education authority's attention as having (or probably having) special educational needs, the authority will be responsible for him.

A child is also defined as someone who is not a registered pupil at a school, is not under the age of 2 years or over compulsory school age and has been brought to an authority's attention as having (or probably having) special educational needs.[6]

This last subsection is probably the most important since, unless a 'child' is a registered pupil at a school, if he is over the age of 16 years, the local education authority has no statutory responsibility. This would cover a pupil at a college of further education (which is not a school), thereby causing the statement to lapse (see **8.7**). It would also include an individual over compulsory school age who, for example, has not been educated in a school because of a profound disability. Unless the individual becomes a registered pupil, the local education authority will not assist and any appeal to the Tribunal may fail on the basis that there is no legal basis for the parents to appeal.

8.2 REFUSAL TO MAKE AN ASSESSMENT

By virtue of s 173 of the Education Act 1993, a local education authority has to assess the educational needs of a child pursuant to s 167 when asked to do so by the parents of a child, provided that no statement is maintained under s 168 and that an assessment has not been made within the preceding 6 months of the date of the request and it is necessary for the local education authority to make an assessment under s 167.[7] It is important to ensure that, if there is to be an appeal, there was a parental request to assess. Where parents supported a primary school's request for an assessment, the Tribunal accepted that the request had not been made by the parents and so there was no right of appeal. It was struck out.[8]

It is 'necessary' to make an assessment if a child has special educational needs and it is necessary for the authority to determine the special educational provision which any learning difficulty he may have calls for.[9] It is important to note that an assessment is not automatic because a child has a special educational need. The

---

6 Ibid, s 165(3)(d).
7 Section 173(1).
8 Digest of Cases 95/11.
9 Section 167(2).

additional requirement that it is 'necessary' for an authority to determine what special provision that need calls for, excludes such special needs as can be met by the school from its resources. This applies especially to children at stage 2 of the Code of Practice.[10] This decision will depend on the child's needs, so it is possible that a local education authority might conclude, in the light of a parent's request for an assessment, that the special needs of the child can be met without requiring any special educational provision to be made.

Examples of this can be found in the Digest of Cases prepared by the President. In one case, for example, a child was in her final year at junior school and had some difficulty with spelling. The school gave her an individual spelling programme. Without first consulting the school, the mother had asked the local education authority to assess her daughter's needs. The school was starting to implement the Code of Practice and had identified 28 of its 268 pupils as having some form of special educational need. This girl was not among the 28. As the school had a system to identify when a child should be placed on stage 1 of the Code procedure and this girl did not fall into that category, the Tribunal dismissed the parent's appeal.[11]

In another case,[12] a father appealed against the decision of a local education authority not to assess his 12-year-old son who, although of average ability, suffered from an anxiety disorder and received medication for clinical depression. In the preceding year, he had attended school on only 56 of a possible 170 days. The local education authority proposed a case management model to meet the boy's specific needs which combined home tuition with a programme of reintegration into the school. As the resources required for this were available to the school under stage 3 of the Code of Practice, the appeal was dismissed.

If a local education authority has served a notice on the parents indicating that it intends to assess the child, and the period specified in the notice for representation and written evidence has expired, and it remains of the opinion (taking into account the representations and any written evidence) that the child has special educational needs requiring the local education authority to determine the special educational provision which any learning difficulty he may have calls for, it shall make an assessment of his special educational needs[13] pursuant to the provisions of Sch 9 to the Education Act 1993.[14] This is, of course, fully detailed in the Code of Practice.[15] Once a local education authority has decided to make an assessment under s 167, it shall give notice in writing to the child's parents of that decision and the reasons for making it.

If a local education authority, at any time after the service of a notice (that it proposes to make an assessment), decides not to assess the educational needs of a child, it shall give notice in writing to the child's parents[16]. If the assessment is

---

10 See Code of Practice, paras 2:85–2:98.
11 Digest of Cases 95/9. See [1996] ELR 120.
12 Digest of Cases 95/10. See [1996] ELR 121.
13 Section 167(3).
14 Section 168(5).
15 See Chapters 3 to 5.
16 Section 167(6).

instigated by the local education authority after referral by the child's school or other agency (see para 3:5 and following of the Code of Practice) rather than by parental request, there is no right of appeal to the Tribunal. However, it would seem possible, if the local education authority decides under s 167(6) not to assess, for the parent at that time to request an assessment and, if the request is refused, a right of appeal should lie against that decision.[17] The criteria for deciding whether to make a statutory assessment are dealt with in paras 3:46 to 3:95 of the Code of Practice and are considered above.[18] If it is decided to make an assessment after the parental request, a local education authority shall serve a notice on the child's parents informing them that it proposes to make an assessment of the child's educational needs; of the procedure to be followed in making the assessment; the name of an officer of the local education authority from whom further information can be obtained; and the parents' right to make representations (and to submit written evidence) to the local education authority within such period as may be specified in the notice.[19] The length of the period will not, however, be less than 29 days beginning with the day upon which the notice is served.[20] However, the local education authority is only required to arrange the assessment which it considers appropriate. Although the parents can indicate the type of assessment preferred or believed to be in the child's best interest, the parents cannot dictate the assessment to be the statutory assessment.[21]

The local education authority is not required to assess a child if there is already a statement of the special educational needs or there was an assessment within the preceding 6 months.[22] If, however, there is neither a statement in existence nor an assessment, the local education authority may still decide not to comply with the parental request for an assessment. If that happens, the local education authority has to give notice to the child's parents both of the decision and of the parents' right of appeal to the Tribunal.[23]

Examples of where the Tribunal has ordered the local education authority to make an assessment include the case of a 13-year-old boy with admitted dyspraxic special needs. The boy's parents had obtained a number of reports and requested a formal assessment. The local education authority refused to assess, basing their decision exclusively on the reports obtained by the parents. The Tribunal ordered the local education authority to carry out the assessment as it decided that the authority had insufficient evidence to conclude that an assessment was not necessary.[24] In another case, an 8-year-old girl who attended an independent school, had a full verbal IQ score of 128 but her performance in written tests was markedly worse than in verbal tests. She also had gross and fine motor control difficulties. The local education authority took the view that her attainment level was generally age-appropriate and

---

17 Pursuant to s 173(2).
18 See Chapter 4. There is, in addition, a summary chart of the steps leading to a statutory assessment at Appendix 3.
19 Section 167(1).
20 Section 167(1)(d).
21 *R v Surrey County Council ex parte G and Others* [1994] TLR 292.
22 Section 173(1)(b).
23 Section 173(2).
24 Digest of Cases 95/14.

so refused to assess her. Taking into account the fact that the local education authority had not investigated her motor control problems and that the authority's psychologist's report was a 'snapshot' because it had not been possible for it to monitor her progress as she was educated outside the maintained sector, the Tribunal ordered an assessment.[25]

On appeal, the Tribunal may either dismiss the appeal or order the local education authority to arrange for an assessment under s 167.[26]

8.3   REFUSAL TO MAKE A STATEMENT

Once a local education authority has assessed a child's needs pursuant to s 167, it has a duty to make a statement if it is 'necessary' for the local education authority to determine the special educational provision which any learning difficulty he may have calls for.[27] Since the requirement upon the local education authority under the Education Act 1981 was for it to make and maintain a statement where it was 'of the opinion that they should determine the special educational provision that should be made', there has been a clear change of emphasis. The determination of whether a statement is necessary will, inevitably, depend upon each individual child's needs. It may be, for example, that a child has special educational needs but it is not necessary for a statement of those needs to be made by the local education authority.[28] The five-stage process envisaged by the Code of Practice should ensure that there is a greater degree of consistency between local education authorities on this matter as the discretion previously left to authorities highlighted by *Lashford* has been limited. An example of a child who had special needs but did not require a statement can be found in the Digest of Cases.[29] A school had requested the assessment of a bright 15-year-old boy who had difficulties in spelling and presentation. The boy had been given intensive help with spelling and support from the head of the school's special needs department. The boy followed an individual education plan which involved a structured spelling programme. On completion of the assessment the local education authority declined to issue a statement but issued a note in lieu. The Tribunal dismissed the appeal against the refusal to make a statement on the grounds that the school could provide the necessary support from its own resources, that he was making good progress and that his difficulties were being addressed.

By comparison, a local education authority was required to make and maintain a statement for a boy aged 10½ of high average general ability who had specific learning difficulties.[30] The boy attended a small rural primary school with only 72 children on the roll. There were 3.3 teachers in the school, including the head teacher. There were 13 children on the special needs register – 11 at stage 3 and 2 with statements. The school's special needs budget was £5,572 for the year and it

---

25   Digest of Cases 95/15.
26   Section 173(3).
27   Section 168(1). A summary chart of steps and time-limits in making assessments and statements can be found at Appendix 4.
28   *R v Secretary of State for Education and Science ex parte Lashford* [1988] 1 FLR 72.
29   Digest of Cases 95/8. See [1996] ELR 120.
30   Digest of Cases 95/17.

was clear that there were severe limits upon what the school could realistically be expected to provide from its own resources.

The criteria for deciding whether to draw up a statement are considered in paras 4:1 to 4:19 of the Code of Practice[31] and the procedure is set out in Sch 10 to the Education Act 1993.

If, after making an assessment pursuant to s 167, a local education authority decides not to make a statement, it shall give notice in writing of that decision[32] and of the right of appeal to the Tribunal to the child's parents.[33] On appeal, the Tribunal may either dismiss the appeal, order the local education authority to make and maintain a statement or remit the case to the local education authority for it to reconsider whether, having regard to any observations made by the Tribunal, it is necessary for the local education authority to determine the special educational provision which any learning difficulties the child may have calls for.[34] As it is intended that all reasons given by the Tribunal will be in writing,[35] it is also intended that any and all observations made by the Tribunal will be in writing. It will have been seen from the statistics in **7.4** that in the first year of the Tribunal only 5% (12 cases) of appeals were remitted to the local education authority. The only occasion where the Tribunal is empowered to remit a case is where there has been a refusal to make a statement. An example of when it is appropriate to remit a case concerns a 6-year-old boy who suffered from epilepsy, the most serious effects of which were controlled by drugs. He had attention and behavioural problems and was to be referred to a psychiatrist. The local education authority had assessed him but had decided not to issue a statement. The reports obtained on his assessment were substantially out of date at the date of the hearing. The Tribunal considered that they needed to reflect the boy's current functioning and, as there was also evidence that he would benefit from a consistent classroom programme delivered by one person, the case was remitted to the local education authority for reconsideration in the light of the Tribunal's observations.[36]

Since the local education authority is only required to consider the observations of the Tribunal rather than act upon them, it would appear that it will be open for the parents to appeal once again if the local education authority takes no further action. This is on the basis that if the Tribunal remits the case to a local education authority, it is necessary (by virtue of s 169(2)(c)) for the local education authority to reconsider whether to determine the special educational provision. If, after reconsidering the matter, the local education authority still proposes not to make a statement it would seem that it has to give another notice of its decision to that effect to the parents. As there is no power for the Tribunal to review a case after the local education authority has reviewed the case, the only remedy available to the parents would seem to be a fresh appeal against the decision not to make a statement. This

31 See Chapter 4.
32 Section 169(1).
33 Section 169(2).
34 Section 169(3).
35 See Chapter 10.
36 Digest of Cases 96/8.

ability to make a fresh appeal does not seem to exist for other aspects of the Tribunal's work, as discussed in Chapter 13.

8.4 CONTENTS OF THE STATEMENT

The form of the statement is prescribed[37] and must give details of the local education authority's assessment of the child's special educational needs, specify the special educational provision to be made to meet those needs and include details of schools.[38]

This has been the most contentious element of the area of law covering special educational needs, especially the delay in the issuing of a statement. It was also apparent that local education authorities had different policies and practices in the making of a statement and, in some cases, the extent of parental involvement. It was intended and is hoped that the Code of Practice will eradicate some of these differences and difficulties. The Code of Practice considers the contents of a statement between paras 4:23 and 4:73.[39]

There are three occasions when a parent can appeal against the contents of a statement, namely:

(a) when the statement is first made;
(b) where the description in the statement of the authority's assessment of the child's special educational needs, or the special educational provision specified in the statement, is amended; or
(c) where, after conducting an assessment under s 167, the local education authority decides not to amend the statement.[40]

The appeal to the Tribunal is upon the description of the local education authority's assessment of the child's special educational needs. This description should include all learning difficulties identified during the statutory assessment and should also include a description of the child's functioning – that is, what the child can and cannot do.

8.4.1 The exclusion or inclusion of a specific learning difficulty

The first basis of an appeal could, therefore, be against the exclusion or inclusion of any specific learning difficulty (or 'need'). In carrying out an assessment, a local education authority will have obtained advice from several different professional sources which will be attached as appendices to the statement. However, if none of the professional advice in the appendices makes reference to a specific need which the parents contend should have been, but was not, included in the statement, it is difficult to see how it can be said by the parents that that need should have been included as it was not identified as a need in the first place. In those circumstances,

---

37 Section 168(2) and Part B of the Schedule to the Education (Special Educational Needs) Regulations 1994; see also Appendix 5.
38 Section 168(3).
39 See Chapter 6.
40 Section 170(1).

the parents would be best advised to obtain their own report highlighting the need which they contend the child has but which appears to have been omitted and recommending the provision that will be required to meet that need. If a report has not been prepared by the parents before an appeal is made to the Tribunal, it should be obtained in time for the Tribunal hearing. In addition, as parents are usually involved in the process of preparing the statement, any concerns about a specific need should be raised early during the assessment.

Evidence of a need or provision which has been omitted or understated is very important in an appeal under s 170(1). If the parents do obtain reports, it is advisable to bring the author of the report to the Tribunal hearing to give evidence on their behalf. The benefit of up-to-date reports cannot be overemphasised as the President issued a Practice Direction on 15 March 1995 in which he stated that the Tribunal's decision is 'based on what is appropriate at the date of the hearing and should not be a judgement of the correctness of the LEA's decision when it was taken'.[41] The Practice Direction was qualified by a statement from the President dated 9 October 1995,[42] made in contemplation of a challenge of the Practice Direction by an application for judicial review. Although the application has been dropped, the President confirms that, although he may have had no express authority to make a binding Practice Direction in these circumstances, the underlying guidance referred to in the Practice Direction remains.

8.4.2 The specified special educational provision

The second basis of appeal to the Tribunal is against the special educational provision specified in the statement. By virtue of *R v Secretary of State for Education and Science ex parte E*,[43] a local education authority is required to determine and make special educational provision for a child with learning difficulties in respect of each and every educational need identified in the statement. *Ex parte E* concerned a child who was identified as having particular difficulties with numeracy and literacy skills. The local education authority did not include the dyscalcula in the statement as it felt that help with the numeracy problems could have been determined by the school itself. That view was rejected by the Court of Appeal which held that special educational provision had to be included in the statement for each identified special educational need. That decision has been tempered slightly by Lord Justice Leggatt in *Re Leather*[44] when he said 'only if there were a clear failure to make provision for a significant need would the court be likely to conclude that there was such a dereliction of duty by the local education authority as to call for the intervention of the appeal committee or, in default, of the Secretary of State or indeed the High Court'.

In addition, Mr Justice McCullough decided in *R v Hereford and Worcester County Council ex parte P*,[45] that a requirement that a child should receive additional

---

41 [1995] ELR 335; see also the Annual Report.
42 Nature of Appeal: Statement by the President.
43 [1992] 1 FLR 377.
44 (Unreported) 30 September 1992.
45 [1992] 2 FLR 207.

non-educational provision would be met in the statement by setting out 'the general nature of the provision'.

The Code of Practice, on the other hand, states at para 4:28 that the provision 'should normally be specific, detailed and quantified (in terms, for example, of hours of ancillary or specialist teaching support) although there will be cases where some flexibility should be retained in order to meet the changing special educational needs of the child concerned'.

At present, the question of whether various types of therapy should be included in Part 3 is the subject of a number of appeals to the Tribunal. The usual scenario is that a child may require either one or more of speech and language therapy, occupational therapy and physiotherapy. These are normally provided by the local health authority in conjunction with the local education authority either under a formal contract or other arrangement. Parental concern tends to focus around the continuing funding and provision of the therapy should the health authority, for whatever reason, decide it cannot continue to finance the child's needs.

The question of whether speech therapy is or is not an educational need has been considered in two cases. In the first, *R v Oxfordshire County Council ex parte W*,[46] the Divisional Court came to the conclusion that the local education authority was neither irrational nor unreasonable in deciding that a child's speech therapy could be a non-educational provision. That does not, of course, mean that speech therapy cannot be an educational provision, just that it is not wrong to say that it is a non-educational provision. The Court of Appeal in *R v Lancashire County Council ex parte M*,[47] upheld a Divisional Court decision[48] that speech therapy can be special educational provision. It should be noted that 'can' was used and not 'must' or 'will'. Lord Justice Balcombe expressed the position best when he said that '[t]he only question is whether speech therapy for [the] purpose [of enabling a child to communicate so that he may be fully understood by others] is educational or non-educational provision. As we have already said, we do not see how to teach a child to communicate by speech can be any different from teaching him to communicate by writing: both are clearly educational'.[49]

That case was relied upon by a mother who, in her appeal to the Tribunal, invited it to consider whether Part 3 of her son's statement should include the provision of occupational therapy[50] and argued that it was open to the Tribunal to decide whether it was an educational or non-educational need. The boy (aged 15) suffered from a semantic–pragmatic language disorder and dyspraxia, and had Asperger's syndrome tendencies. His gross and fine motor skills were poor. He also had serious difficulties from a lack of mobility and sensory integration/co-ordination and from clumsiness.

As a preliminary issue, the local education authority argued that occupational therapy was a non-educational supportive health service, not specifically mentioned

---

46 [1987] 2 FLR 193.
47 [1989] 2 FLR 279 at p 290.
48 [1989] 2 FLR 279 at p 280.
49 [1989] 2 FLR 279 at p 302B.
50 Digest of Cases 96/12.

in the Code of Practice. The Tribunal concluded that in appropriate circumstances such as where a need, for example relating to motor skills, was identified in Part 2, occupational therapy could constitute a special educational provision which should appear in Part 3.

That decision needs to be treated with caution, however. First, the Tribunal is not bound by its own earlier decisions and so it cannot be relied upon as establishing a precedent to be followed at other Tribunal hearings. Secondly, since the *Lancashire* case deals only with speech therapy, that decision is not binding on the Tribunal insofar as it relates to either occupational therapy or physiotherapy, and so it would appear that the Tribunal's decision was reached by extending Lord Justice Balcombe's view about educational provision mentioned above. Thirdly, the question of physiotherapy was not considered in either of the court cases or the Tribunal hearing so it cannot be assumed that, if the same argument is put forward at a Tribunal hearing, it will necessarily succeed. Until such time as there is a decision from the High Court or the Court of Appeal upon whether occupational and/or physiotherapy should be regarded as educational needs or not, the matter will have to be determined entirely on the facts of each individual appeal.

8.4.3 Placement

The third basis of appeal to the Tribunal concerning the statement refers to the details of the named school. This is, of course, part of the special educational provision being made to meet the identified needs. The starting point is s 160 which requires a local education authority to educate a child in a school which is not a special school provided that to educate a child in a non-special school is compatible with:

(a)   that child receiving the special educational provision which his learning difficulty calls for;

(b)   the provision of efficient education for the children with whom he will be educated; and

(c)   the efficient use of resources.

That requirement is subject to the proviso that a child should not be so educated if a placement at a non-special school is incompatible with the wishes of his parents.

This gives rise to two types of appeal. The first would include a case where the local education authority has determined that it will need to educate a child in a special school but the parents want the child to be educated in a mainstream school. The second is the more familiar argument, namely, that the parents do not want their child educated in the (usually) mainstream school suggested by the local education authority but would prefer either a special or independent special school.

This parental preference can be expressed either at the time of making or amending the statement by virtue of Sch 10, para 3, or at any other time by virtue of Sch 10, para 8 (see **8.6**).

By virtue of s 168(4), the statement shall specify the type of school or other institution which the local education authority considers would be appropriate for the child.[51] One of the most important changes from the old legislation is the right of the parents to express a preference (with reasons) within a 15-day period[52] as to the school to be named in the statement. The school must be named in the statement unless the preferred school is unsuitable or the child's placement there would be incompatible with the efficient education of other pupils there or with an efficient use of resources.[53] The local education authority shall only specify the name of the maintained, grant-maintained or grant-maintained special school for which the parent has specified a preference after it has consulted the governing body of the school or, if the school is in another authority, that local education authority.[54] If, for one of the three reasons mentioned above, the local education authority is not required to name a 'preferred' school, it must name a school or institution which would be suitable for the child.[55]

When the local education authority sends the parents the draft statement to be agreed, the part of the proposed statement which names a school (Part 4) is left blank so that the local education authority does not pre-empt the consideration of any preference for a maintained school which the parents may state or any representations the parents may make in favour of a non-maintained special school or independent school. Clearly there is room for discussion between the parents and the local education authority. If, however, the parents have expressed a preference for a school but, after discussion, a different school is named in Part 4 of the final statement, it may be because the local education authority regards the school it has named as being suitable bearing in mind the criteria set out in the paragraph above. Unless agreement can be reached between the parents and the local education authority to name the school preferred by the parents, rather than spend a considerable time discussing and negotiating upon the matter, it is probably sensible for the parents to agree the contents of the statement and then appeal to the Tribunal on the issue of the name of the school.

Of the first 48 cases published in the Digest of Cases, 19 concern the school named in a statement. It is not proposed to give all those 19 cases as examples, but some may help to highlight the usual issues raised when the Tribunal has to consider this type of appeal.

- A 12-year-old boy had Down's syndrome and had had a statement since he was 5 years old. Although he had attended a small primary school (of only 34 pupils), he had made limited progress with individual support for mornings and afternoons. The revised statement proposed a maintained special school for the boy's secondary placement. The parents favoured a mainstream school. The local education authority argued that, since it would cost about £20,500 to educate the boy in a mainstream school (because of the special education provision he required) and only £8,800 in the special school (as it was already equipped for a child with his needs), to name a mainstream school was not an

---

51 Section 168(4)(a).
52 Schedule 10, para 3(2) to the 1993 Act, and see **6.3** and Code of Practice, paras 4:40–4:67.
53 Schedule 10, para 3(3).
54 Schedule 10, para 3(4).
55 Section 168(4)(b).

efficient use of resources. The Tribunal dismissed the parents' appeal as they accepted that a small special school would be more suitable to the boy's ability, aptitude and needs and also would be a more efficient use of resources.[56]

• A 12-year-old girl had significant specific learning difficulties. These included difficulties with literacy and numeracy skills, weakness in memory coding and her speed of writing and reading. In addition, she lacked self-esteem and confidence. At primary school, she acquired a group of friends who were supportive and encouraging. Her parents wanted their daughter to go to the same grant-maintained school as most of her friends. The local education authority's Senior Medical Officer was satisfied that the girl might develop additional psychological problems if she were not in school with her close, supportive friends. The Tribunal noted that no evidence had been given about the efficient use of resources and named the grant-maintained school.[57]

• A 12-year-old boy who had profound bilateral hearing loss had fallen behind the level expected of a child with his difficulties in both reading and writing. The local education authority had named a 1,077-pupil comprehensive school with a hearing impaired unit in the statement. The parents preferred an independent special school for 148 hearing impaired pupils. Headphones and the right acoustic environment would be available in the hearing impaired unit of the comprehensive school but not in the main school classrooms. At the independent school, the right acoustic environment was available in all curricular subjects. The Tribunal, in considering that the boy needed a suitable aural environment, teaching by specialist teachers of the deaf across the curriculum and an opportunity to participate in class discussions, decided that the statement should name the independent school.[58]

• A 12-year-old girl of average intellectual ability had significant specific learning difficulties and had been educated in the independent sector from the age of 2½. She had been attending a specialist independent school for the last 2 years. The local education authority proposed a placement in the maintained sector. In reaching its decision, the Tribunal did not regard as conclusive the fact that she was attending the independent school (where she was happy) although it was a relevant consideration. The Tribunal accepted that the small classes the girl needed would be the practice at the maintained school and so dismissed the parents' appeal.[59]

• The mother of a 12-year-old boy expressed a preference for a particular Church of England voluntary aided school. The local education authority maintained that any high school in the city where he lived would make suitable provision for him but named a different school from the one proposed by the boy's mother. The governors of the voluntary aided school refused to admit the boy although the evidence showed that the two schools were remarkably similar. The local education authority did not satisfy the Tribunal that the boy's admission to the voluntary aided school would prejudice the efficient education of the other children he would be educated with and therefore held, as a matter of law, that the mother's preference must prevail.[60]

• A 4½-year-old girl had dystonic diplegia cerebral palsy. She had above average cognitive and language skills, but poor motor skills and self-help problems. For 18 months she had been attending a conductive education school for two days a week. Now that the time had come for her to start full-time education, her parents wanted her statement to specify part-time placements at the conductive education school and at her local infant school. The local education authority agreed to her attending the local school but suggested that this be combined with part-time attendance at a maintained special school. The local education authority contended that the alternative would be an inefficient use of resources: the cost of placement at the special school would be notional and would not involve finding further resources, and the cost of transport to the conductive education school would be several times higher than to the special school. The Tribunal ordered that the statement provide for the placement suggested by the authority.[61]

• A 12-year-old boy with very high cognitive ability, but a specific learning difficulty, suffered frustration, lack of self-esteem and unhappiness and developed school phobia and emotional problems on transfer to a middle school and his parents eventually withdrew him. They contended that he needed a small school, with a family ambience and small classes, and they nominated an independent school 21 miles from their home. Given his age and learning delays, the Tribunal considered that the opportunity to go to a new school which would give him educational and emotional stability was necessary to make quick progress. It therefore ordered that the local education authority name the independent school in Part 4 of the statement.[62]

• A 7½-year-old boy with severe visual impairment, delayed mobility skills, communication and severe learning difficulties had attended a maintained special school for pupils with profound and multiple learning difficulties since the age of 2. During the last 3 years, he had made little or no progress in developing new skills. In his statement, the local education authority proposed that he should continue to attend the same school. His parents suggested that he should board at a non-maintained special school for the visually impaired with a range of multiple disabilities. The Tribunal accepted that with his personality and combination of disabilities, the boy was most likely to make progress through consistency, with education and care mutually reinforced on a 24-hour basis and so it ordered that the non-maintained school be named.[63]

A school is not necessarily 'inappropriate' because a better learning environment is available elsewhere. See *R v Surrey County Council Education Committee ex parte H*[64]

---

60 Digest of Cases 95/23.
61 Digest of Cases 96/13; see also Digest of Cases 96/21, discussed at **8.6**.
62 Digest of Cases 96/15.
63 Digest of Cases 96/19.
64 (1984) 83 LGR 219.

and *R v Mid Glamorgan County Council ex parte Grieg.*[65] Independent schools can only be named pursuant to s 189(5) if they have been approved by the Secretary of State for Education and Employment or he consents to the child being educated there. This last point is important. Certain independent schools are approved and the chairmen of the Tribunals have lists of those schools. There are a few, however, which, for whatever reason, are not approved. If parents wish the Tribunal to name a school which has not been approved it is vital that specific consent is obtained by them from the Secretary of State. If the consent is not obtained before the hearing, the Tribunal will be unable to consider it.

8.4.4   Exceptions to the right of appeal

Although there are rights of appeal as set out above, there are exceptions. There is, for example, no appeal to the Tribunal against the amendment of a statement made under an order of the Tribunal either to substitute the name of the school or other institution or to order the local education authority to continue to maintain the statement. There is also no appeal to the Tribunal from the decision of a local education authority not to amend the statement, having previously proposed to do so.

In addition, jurisdiction has not been given to the Tribunal in relation to the contents of all of the statement. If the statement requires arrangements for transport (or other non-educational provision contained in Part 5), the appeal of that issue lies to the Secretary of State as in *R v Hereford and Worcester County Council ex parte P.*[66] Likewise, an appeal from a local education authority's refusal to revoke a school attendance order (pursuant to s 192(4)), it being said by the parents that arrangements have been made for the child to receive a suitable education somewhere other than at school, lies to the Secretary of State.[67] These matters are considered in Chapter 13.

8.4.5   The Tribunal's options

On appeal to the Tribunal on the ground of one of the three matters raised above, the Tribunal may either dismiss the appeal,[68] or order the local education authority to amend the statement so far as it describes that local education authority's assessment of the child's special educational needs or specifies the special educational provision. This will include both the naming of a school and any consequential amendments to the statement.[69] The Tribunal may also order the local education authority to cease to maintain the statement.[70] The Tribunal can only order the local education authority to specify the name of the school in the statement (whether it be in substitution for an existing name or where no school is named) if either the parent has expressed a preference for the school under the

65   *The Independent*, 1 June 1988.
66   [1992] 2 FLR 208.
67   See generally, Chapter 13.
68   Section 170(3)(a).
69   Section 170(3)(b).
70   Section 170(3)(c).

Sch 10 procedure or if, during the Tribunal proceedings, the parent, the local education authority or both have proposed the school.[71] In addition, the Tribunal has powers to correct any deficiency in the statement (before determining any appeal) with the agreement of the parties.[72]

8.5   REFUSAL TO REASSESS EDUCATIONAL NEEDS

Once a child has a statement, a review pursuant to s 167 of that child's needs has to be repeated every year.[73] In addition to a review, Regulations will prescribe the frequency with which assessments are to be repeated in respect of a child.[74] Apart from this reassessment, a parent can also ask for an assessment,[75] and the local education authority must comply with that request, provided that the child has a statement, there has been no assessment in the 6 months preceding the date of the request, and it is necessary for the local education authority to make a further assessment under s 167 of the Act.[76]

Of the cases heard in the first year, none were on the grounds of a refusal to reassess. They accounted for only 2% of the total appeals received in the first year – or 23 cases, none of which features in the Digest of Cases. An example of this type of case would be where the parents of a child are concerned that, notwithstanding the statement of special needs, the description of need or provision contained in the statement is not sufficient. This would normally be because the child's condition has deteriorated or because, as a result of further enquiries, more information has come to light about a child's specific needs. It is likely that this ground will not be used very often as any changes ought to be noticed and acted upon at the annual review.

If, notwithstanding that, the parental request for reassessment was made in excess of 6 months after the last assessment, the local education authority determines not to comply with the request, it must give notice to that effect and of the right of appeal to the Tribunal against that determination to the parents.[77]

On appeal the Tribunal may either dismiss the appeal or order the local education authority to arrange for an assessment.[78]

8.6   CHANGES OF NAMED SCHOOL

It is necessary for every statement[79] to name the school or other institution where the identified special educational provision is to be made. As has already been noted (at

---

71 Section 170(4).
72 Section 170(5).
73 Section 172(5)(b) and see Code of Practice, section 6.
74 Section 172(1).
75 Section 172(2)(a).
76 Section 172(2)(b) and (c).
77 Section 172(3).
78 Section 172(4).
79 See para 4:24 of the Code of Practice.

8.4.3), the parents are able to name a preferred school as part of the process of preparing a statement. In addition, parents are able[80] to ask the local education authority to change the name of the school specified in the statement and substitute the name of a maintained, grant-maintained or grant-maintained special school at a time other than at the making of a new statement or an amended statement. The local education authority must comply with this request[81] unless there are specified objections to the new school or the parents fail to comply with certain time-limits. For example, the parents are unable to make their request within 12 months of either making the previous request, or the date when the statement was served, or the date of giving notice of amendment of a statement, or the date when an appeal to the Tribunal (on the contents of a statement) was concluded, whichever is the later.[82]

The specified objections available to the local education authority are that the proposed new school is either unsuitable for the child's age, ability or aptitude or for his special educational needs or that to name it would be incompatible with the efficient education of other children there or incompatible with the efficient use of resources.[83] These are, of course, identical grounds to those available to a local education authority in refusing to name a certain school in a statement.[84] It is important to note, however, that the school requested has to be a maintained school. The parents cannot request either an independent or non-maintained school. The Tribunal has no jurisdiction to order the local education authority to specify either of the latter two types of school.

If the local education authority determines not to comply with the parents' request, it has to give notice of that fact to the parents and also of the fact that they may appeal to the Tribunal against that decision.[85] On appeal, the Tribunal may either dismiss the appeal or order the local education authority to substitute the name of the school specified by the parents for the name of the school or other institution in the statement.[86] An example of a request for a change of school concerns a 12-year-old girl who had a history of ear problems and undiagnosed hearing loss and, although of average ability, she had difficulty in acquiring literacy and numeracy skills. The question for the Tribunal was whether she should continue to attend the maintained secondary school where she was now placed or transfer to another maintained secondary school for which her parents had expressed a preference. The school which the girl attended had 1,299 pupils, of whom 23 had statements (eight relating to specific learning difficulties). Seven of her contemporaries from primary school had been admitted. The school preferred by her parents had 1,450 pupils, some 35% more than it should accommodate. Twenty-two pupils at that school had statements and 36 of her primary school contemporaries went there. The Tribunal decided that the girl's parents' preference could not prevail because, while her present school was appropriate to her needs, the

---

80 Schedule 10, para 9(1) to the 1993 Act.
81 Schedule 10, para 8(2).
82 Schedule 10, para 8(1)(b).
83 Schedule 10, para 8(2).
84 Schedule 10, para 3(3).
85 Schedule 10, para 8(3).
86 Schedule 10, para 8(3).

other school was over-full, its buildings and physical resources were inadequate, and sending a further child would not be in the interests of the children already being educated there.[87]

8.7 CEASING TO MAINTAIN A STATEMENT

Pursuant to paras 6:36 to 6:37 of the Code of Practice, a local education authority has a duty to maintain the statement as long as it is 'necessary' so to do.[88] If, for whatever reason, the local education authority decides not to continue to maintain the statement, it has to give notice of this to the parents and inform them of their right of appeal to the Tribunal.[89]

A distinction has to be drawn here between those statements which are no longer maintained because the child is no longer the responsibility of the local education authority (because the child has either moved into higher or further education or to social service provision) and cases where, in the light of annual review or other consideration, the local education authority concludes that the objectives of the statement have been achieved and that by ceasing to maintain a statement the additional resources attached to it can be released to help other children.

An example of a case where the local education authority contended that the child's needs could be met by the school rather than by a statement can be found in the Digest of Cases.[90]

Three years before the appeal was heard, the local education authority had made a statement describing the boy as of average overall ability but with weakness in literacy and numeracy. The most recent annual review identified poor spelling, short term memory problems, lack of concentration and an auditory discriminatory problem. His reading age was then 2 years 11 months behind his chronological age, and his spelling age 2 years 6 months behind. He received 40 minutes per week of one-to-one sessions and six sessions of in-class support. Without consulting the parents or school, the local education authority decided to cease to maintain the statement contending that he should be placed at stage 3 under the Code of Practice. There was no evidence before the Tribunal of the level of funding provided under the statement at stage 3, or whether the school would be able to continue to provide his current level of support from its own resources. The Tribunal concluded that the boy's needs did not come within stage 3 and that it was unlikely that the current level of support would be provided by the school from its own resources. The Tribunal, in referring to para 6:37 of the Code of Practice, considered that a change in the boy's support might halt or reverse his progress. As a consequence, it ordered that the local education authority continue to maintain the statement. For an example of a case where the responsibility has been transferred to the further education sector, see *R v Oxfordshire County Council ex parte R* below.

---

87 Digest of Cases 96/21.
88 Schedule 10, para 11(1).
89 Schedule 10, para 11(2).
90 Digest of Cases 95/3. See [1996] ELR 118.

The local education authority can cease to maintain a statement only after it has written to the parents and given them notice of that decision. Although it would appear, however, that an appeal to the Tribunal prevents the local education authority from ceasing to maintain that provision until the appeal is heard,[91] this matter was considered in *R v Oxfordshire County Council ex parte R*.[92] In that case, a 16-year-old girl had severe disabilities and had been at a special school from the age of 3. In March 1995 the local education authority purported to determine that the statement of special educational needs should cease at the end of the summer term – in July 1995. This was because the local education authority has a policy that (with limited exceptions) all the children aged 16 and over with special educational needs should transfer to the further education sector and have their needs met by the Further Education Funding Council. The parents appealed to the Tribunal in May 1995 and failed to obtain an expedited hearing of that appeal.

The parents' solicitors, having failed to persuade the local education authority that the statement should not cease pending the determination of the appeal by the Tribunal, applied for (and were granted) leave to apply for judicial review of that decision.

On the hearing of the full application for judicial review, the court held that a true construction of para 11 of Sch 10 to the 1993 Act allows an authority to cease to maintain a statement pending an appeal to the Tribunal. The conclusion was reached on the basis that, first, the natural and ordinary meaning of the paragraph requires it, and, secondly, a time-limit is imposed by para 11(4) only if parents do not appeal. There is no time-limit imposed if the parents have appealed to the Tribunal since the fate of the statement is determined on the hearing of the appeal. In other words, the existence of the appeal process provides necessary safeguards and, in itself, sets a time-limit in which the statement's status will be resolved. If there is no appeal to the Tribunal, it is wrong to permit an authority to cease to maintain a statement a long time after giving notice of its determination to do so.

On appeal, the Tribunal may dismiss the appeal or order the local education authority to continue to maintain the statement. The order to maintain the statement may require the local education authority either to maintain it in its existing form, or with amendments (as determined by the Tribunal) to the description of the local education authority's assessment of the child's special educational needs or special educational provision specified in the statement and any consequential amendments.[93]

---

91 Schedule 10, para 11(4).
92 Unreported. Hearing took place September 1995, reference no CO/1995/95.
93 Schedule 10, para 11(3).

Chapter 9

PRE-HEARING PROCEDURES

The procedure governing an appeal to the Tribunal is set out in the Special Educational Needs Tribunal Regulations 1995.[1] As one of the reasons the previous appeal system was replaced by the new Tribunal was to achieve greater consistency, the President of the Tribunal has produced some guidance for the Tribunal on the procedures to be followed.

9.1 SENDING, DELIVERING OR SERVING OF NOTICES AND DOCUMENTS

Any notice required to be given under the Regulations shall be in writing and, where a provision is made for a party to notify the Secretary of the Tribunal of any matter, he shall do so in writing.[2] All notices and documents required by the Regulations to be sent or delivered to the Secretary of the Tribunal or the Tribunal may be sent either by post, or by facsimile or delivered to or at the offices of the Tribunal (or other such office as may be notified by the Secretary to the parties).[3] It is important to note that even if the appeal is being processed by the Darlington office, all Notices of Appeal must be sent to London.

Where notices and documents are required to be sent to either party or other person, they may be either sent by first-class post or facsimile or delivered to or at (if the person to receive the documents is a party) his address for service specified in the Notice of Appeal or reply[4] unless the party has given notice to the Secretary of the Tribunal of the change of address for service.[5] If the person is not a party to the appeal, any notice or document directed to that person may either be sent by first-class post or facsimile or delivered to or at his address or place of business or, if such a person is a corporation, the corporation's registered principal office. If any notice or document is sent or given to the authorised representative of a party, it shall be deemed to have been given or sent to that party.[6] If, however, a summons for the attendance of a witness is required, service shall be by the recorded delivery service rather than first-class post.[7]

As to the time for service, if a notice or document is sent by the Secretary of the Tribunal by post in accordance with the Regulations, it is taken to have been delivered to the person to whom it is addressed on the second working day after it

---

1 SI 1995/3113.
2 Regulation 40(1).
3 Regulation 40(2). For the address of the Tribunal, see Appendix 8.
4 Regulation 40(3)(a)(i).
5 Regulation 40(4).
6 Regulation 40(3)(b).
7 Regulation 40(5).

was posted unless it is returned,[8] whilst a notice or document sent by fax is taken to have been delivered when it is received in legible form.[9] However, if for any 'sufficient' reason service of any document or notice cannot be effected in the manner prescribed,[10] the President may dispense with service or make an order for substituted service in such manner as he may deem fit. In those cases, such service shall have the same effect as service in the prescribed manner.[11] Although 'sufficient' is not defined, it would seem to be when the document is returned or not received by fax and ought to include at least two attempts at service.

9.2 TIME-LIMITS

It has already been said[12] that the time-limits must be strictly adhered to and only in very exceptional circumstances will there be an extension of time. The intention is to ensure that an appeal is dealt with as speedily as possible but, even so, the anticipated timetable[13] envisages an appeal taking 6 months to conclude. The time is calculated in working days. This means, therefore, that Saturdays, Sundays and Bank Holidays are not included. Additionally, and most importantly, no day in August is included although hearings can take place during that month.[14]

Any application to extend the time-limit for serving a Notice of Appeal (under reg 7), a reply by the authority (under reg 12), a response by the parents (under reg 8) or any other time-limit, shall be made to the President[15] who may in exceptional circumstances extend the period of time.

Although there is no definition of 'exceptional circumstances' in the Regulations and therefore it is a matter of common sense, an example of what could be considered exceptional circumstances can be found in the Digest of Cases,[16] albeit that it deals with the lodging of an appeal. A statement was issued on 9 September 1994 for a boy. However, his parents were not happy with it and had a meeting with the local education authority on 18 October 1994. Shortly afterwards the boy became seriously ill and was treated in a hospital's intensive care unit. Knowing that the boy's brother had died in tragic circumstances 9 years before, the authority did not press the matter, being aware that the parents were not happy with the outcome of the October meeting. The parents told the local education authority on 15 November 1994 that their son had been discharged from hospital and that they wished to continue with the appeal. The President granted an extension of the 2 months allowed for lodging the appeal, accepting that (under reg 41(1)) there had been exceptional circumstances.

---

8 Regulation 40(6).
9 Regulation 40(7).
10 Under reg 40.
11 Regulation 40(8).
12 See Chapter 7.
13 See Appendix 6.
14 Regulations 2 and 24(7). See **9.14**.
15 Regulation 41(1).
16 Digest of Cases 95/2. See [1996] ELR 118.

There is no prescribed form of application to extend the time but it would be advisable to make the application in writing (as it is in effect a notice) and give the reason for the delay. Excuses such as that it was overlooked will not be treated sympathetically, however. The President may also extend the time-limit of his own motion. Where a period of time has been extended by virtue of reg 41(1), the reference in the Regulations to that period of time shall mean the period of time as so extended.[17] The President has issued a statement about the prompt delivery of replies by local education authorities, which is considered at **9.4**.

9.3 NOTICE OF APPEAL

Any parent wishing to challenge a decision of the local authority may appeal to the Special Educational Needs Tribunal. The local education authority which will be named in the Notice of Appeal is the one which made the decision against which the parent appeals. That appeal shall be made by Notice and must be received by the Secretary of the Tribunal no later than the first working day after the expiry of 2 months from the date on which the local authority gave the parents notice (pursuant to the 1993 Act) that they have a right of appeal,[18] save that if the 2-month period ends in August, the time-limit is extended to 1 September.[19] This time-limit should be calculated carefully and the date that a decision was made should be precisely identified. For example, a local education authority wrote to the parents on 13 May refusing to make a statement but issuing a note in lieu. After parental protest, the authority agreed in a letter dated 1 August to amend the note in lieu but stated that it did not consider a statement justified. The parents then submitted further evidence to the local education authority. The authority replied on 6 October stating that it was still of the view that it should not make a statement. When the parents appealed, the Tribunal decided that the formal assessment procedure ended on 13 May and that the two letters did not represent new decisions. The time-limit expired in July, rather than December.[20]

The Notice of Appeal shall state:

(1) the name and address of the parent making the appeal and, if more than one address is given, the address to which the Tribunal should send replies or notices concerning the appeal;
(2) the name of the child;
(3) that the notice is a Notice of Appeal;
(4) the name of the authority which made the disputed decision and the date on which the parent was notified of it;
(5) the grounds of the appeal;[21]

---

17 Regulation 41(2).
18 Regulation 7(3).
19 See the interpretation of 'working day' in reg 2 (at Appendix 2).
20 Digest of Cases 95/1. See [1996] ELR 118.
21 The draft Notice of Appeal in Appendix 7 contains (at Part 4) 7 grounds from which to choose. Parents are not limited to one ground!

(6)   if a parent seeks an order that a school (other than the one already named in the statement) be named in the statement, the name and address of that school.[22]

It shall be accompanied by a copy of the notice of the disputed decision and, only if the appeal is against the contents of the statement, a copy of the child's statement of special educational needs.[23] The notice may state the name, address and profession of any representative of the parent to whom the Tribunal should send replies or notices concerning the Appeal instead of the parent.[24] The parent must sign the notice of appeal.[25] The Tribunal has produced a booklet entitled 'How to appeal' which includes a *pro forma* Notice of Appeal.[26]

Usually, the parents should send the documents upon which they intend to rely at the hearing at the same time as the Notice of Appeal. If they do not, the documents should be sent with the response (see below). It will be of considerable help for all involved in the hearing if the pages of documents submitted could be consecutively numbered. A suggested list of those documents which it may be helpful to include can be found at Appendix 11.

On receipt of the Notice of Appeal, the Secretary decides whether it is an appeal that the Tribunal could deal with. If the Secretary is of the opinion that, on the basis of the Notice of Appeal, the parent is asking the Tribunal to do something which it cannot, the Secretary will give notice to the parents within 10 working days of receipt of the notice and give reasons for that opinion. The parents will also be told that the Notice of Appeal will not be entered onto the records unless the parents inform the Tribunal that they wish to proceed with it.[27] If parents subsequently inform the Secretary that they wish to continue with the appeal, the appeal is treated as having been received at the time of subsequent notification and not the date of original receipt.[28]

Where, on receipt of the Notice of Appeal, the Secretary of the Tribunal is of the opinion that there is an obvious error in the Notice of Appeal, he may correct that error and notify the parents accordingly. The notification will also state that unless the parents notify the Secretary of the Tribunal within 5 working days that they object to the correction, the Notice of Appeal as corrected shall be treated as the Notice of Appeal.[29]

If the Tribunal is of the opinion that it can deal with the appeal, the Secretary shall enter particulars of it in the records, send to the parents an acknowledgement of receipt and note the case number together with a note of the address to which

---

22 Regulation 7(1)(a).
23 Regulation 7(1)(b).
24 Regulation 7(1)(c).
25 Regulation 7(2).
26 A model Notice of Appeal appears at Appendix 7. Copies of the booklet may be obtained either from the Tribunal or the DfEE Publications Centre, tel 0171 510 0150.
27 Regulation 16(2).
28 Regulation 16(4).
29 Regulation 16(3).

notices and communications to the Tribunal should be sent, as well as notification that advice about the appeal procedure may be obtained from the Tribunal.[30]

If the Notice of Appeal has been lodged later than the 2-month time-limit, no action will be taken by the Tribunal pending a decision by the President as to the extension of that time-limit.[31] The same will apply for a local authority's reply or parents' response if out of time. Appendix 6 contains a summary chart of both the appeal procedure and the appeal timetable.

Assuming that the Tribunal is able to deal with the appeal and either the Notice was lodged within the time-limit or the time-limit has been extended by the President, the Tribunal shall send to the local education authority within 10 working days of receipt of the Notice (or approval by the President) a copy of the Notice of Appeal, any accompanying papers together with a note of the address to which notices and communications to the Special Educational Needs Tribunal should be sent, and a notice stating the time for replying and the consequences of failure to do so.[32]

9.4   THE LOCAL EDUCATION AUTHORITY REPLY

Within 20 working days of receipt of the Notice of Appeal, the local education authority must deliver to the Tribunal a written reply signed by an authorised officer,[33] acknowledging service on it of the Notice of Appeal. The reply must state whether or not the local education authority intends to oppose the appeal and if it does intend to oppose it, the grounds upon which it relies.[34] The reply must quote the name and profession of the representatives of the local education authority and the address for service of the local education authority for the purposes of the appeal.[35] There must be included with the reply, if the local education authority is contesting the appeal, a statement summarising the facts relating to the disputed decision together with the reasons for the disputed decision, if they were not part of that decision,[36] and all written evidence it wishes to submit to the Tribunal.[37]

The President issued a statement in November 1995 about the prompt delivery of replies by local education authorities. It seems that a noticeable number of local education authority replies have been delivered to the Tribunal outside the 20-day time-limit specified in reg 12(3). The President is concerned that this late delivery leads to unjustified extra time being taken to hear the appeal. From December 1995, if the time for delivering the reply has not been extended and, in particular, where no extension of time has been sought, the Tribunal will, as a matter of course and without reference to the local education authority, refer the case to a Tribunal for

---

30 Regulation 16(1)(a) and (b).
31 Regulation 16(6), pursuant to reg 41.
32 Regulation 16(1)(c).
33 Regulation 12(3).
34 Regulation 12(1)(a).
35 Regulation 12(1)(b).
36 Regulation 12(2)(a) and (b).
37 Regulation 12(2)(c).

determination under reg 14. This means that the local education authority will take no further part in the appeal.

Any application to extend time for delivering a reply should be made by letter and sent by post or fax. It must arrive at the Tribunal before the period for delivery of the reply expires and specify the exceptional circumstances upon which the local education authority relies for the extension. By reg 41 the President can only extend time in exceptional circumstances. It is vital, therefore, to apply for the extension in sufficient time to allow action to be taken if the application is refused. If the reply is late, the Tribunal has only two options by virtue of reg 14. It can either decide the case on the basis of the Notice of Appeal alone, or decide that there will be a hearing which only the parents attend.

Two examples will illustrate the point. In the first example, where a local education authority had failed to reply in the period specified in reg 12(3), the Tribunal was satisfied that it had sufficient evidence to determine the appeal and ordered the local education authority to make an assessment. In this case, an 11-year-old girl was of average ability, had specific learning difficulties and satisfied all the criteria for Asperger's syndrome. Her father (who requested the assessment) stated that his daughter had not received help at school under stage 3 and he submitted professional reports to the Tribunal.[38]

In the second example, a 17-year-old boy was attending a non-maintained special school. Details of the precise nature of his needs and of the provision made at the school he attended were not clear from the papers before the Tribunal. However, there was evidence that he continued to have special educational needs and that the current provision was the same as that previously considered appropriate by the local education authority. The Tribunal ordered the local education authority to continue to maintain the statement when it had given notice of its intention to cease to maintain. As the local education authority had failed to reply in the specified time, the Tribunal considered the case on the basis of the Notice of Appeal.[39]

Subject to the President's decision to extend the time-limit for the delivery of a Notice of Appeal, reply or response, the Secretary of the Tribunal shall, upon receipt, send a copy of the reply (under reg 12) and response (under reg 8), together with any amendments or supplementary statements, written representations, written evidence or other documents received from a party, to the other party to the proceedings.[40]

If, on receipt of the Notice of Appeal (or at any stage of the proceedings), the local education authority is of the opinion that an appeal does not lie to, or cannot be entertained by, the Special Educational Needs Tribunal, or that the Notice of Appeal, or the appeal is, or has become, scandalous, frivolous or vexatious or, for want of prosecution, the local authority may apply to the Secretary of the Tribunal for the appeal to be struck out.[41] The Secretary of the Tribunal, upon receipt of the

38 Digest of Cases 95/12.
39 Digest of Cases 95/13.
40 Regulation 16(5).
41 Regulation 36(1) and (2).

application from the local education authority or on direction from the President, shall serve a notice on the parents stating that it appears that the appeal should be struck out on one or both of the grounds put forward by the local education authority or 'for want of prosecution'. The notice served on the parents shall state that the parents may make representations[42] within the period specified in the notice (but, in any event, not less than 5 working days) by either making written representations or requesting an opportunity to make oral representations.[43] The oral representations will not take place within the time specified – all that is required is that the request is made in the specified period.

The Tribunal can determine whether to strike out the appeal without a hearing if there are only written representations. If, however, either party requests the opportunity to make oral representations, this will be done at a hearing which may be held at the beginning of the substantive appeal.[44]

In addition, the President may at any stage of the proceedings order that a reply, response or statement should be struck out or amended on the grounds that it is scandalous, frivolous or vexatious, although before making such an order, he shall give the party against whom he proposes to make the order a notice inviting representations and shall consider any representations duly made.[45]

The 'want of prosecution' ground has, so far as the author is aware, been used only once. In February 1995, a parent appealed against a local education authority's refusal to arrange an assessment for his child. In August 1995, the local education authority offered to arrange an assessment but the Tribunal received no further information. In January 1996, notice of an application to strike out was sent to the parent but there was no response. The appeal was struck out for want of prosecution.[46]

The Regulations are silent upon what is to happen if the local education authority's contention that the appeal should be struck out is dismissed by the Tribunal. Since the local education authority will have applied to have the appeal struck out rather than have set out grounds on which it opposes the appeal, it could be deemed to have failed to reply in the time appointed[47] and so may find that the Tribunal proceeds without any local education authority involvement pursuant to reg 14. The options available to the local education authority would appear to be either: (a) both to apply to have the Notice struck out as well as to serve a reply (pursuant to reg 12) setting out the grounds upon which the appeal is opposed, or (b) to apply under reg 42 for leave to extend time for service of the reply until determination of the preliminary application. The former course of action is the most logical, especially if the point is to be taken at the start of the substantive appeal. It is unclear, however, whether the President will regard the consideration of a preliminary point as giving rise to exceptional circumstances. Of the five cases dealing with

---

42 Regulation 36(3).
43 Regulation 36(8).
44 Regulation 36(4) and (5).
45 Regulation 36(6) and (7).
46 Digest of Cases 96/5.
47 That is 20 working days – see reg 12(3).

applications to strike out an appeal reported in the most recent Digest of Decisions, four of these cases help to illustrate what can happen.

In the first example, on 9 June a parent had received the decision of a local education authority not to arrange an assessment of her son's special educational needs. The Tribunal received a Notice of Appeal on 31 August. The local education authority was required to reply by 9 October. On that day, it applied to the Tribunal by fax to strike out the appeal on the ground that, under reg 7(3), the appeal was out of time. The local education authority also requested that its time for replying begin when the striking out application had been determined as a preliminary issue. The President refused the request for an extension of time. The Tribunal decided at the preliminary hearing that the parent's appeal was not out of time as any day in August is not a 'working day' under reg 2 (see also **9.3**). As the local education authority had not delivered a reply within the time-limit, the Tribunal proceeded to determine the appeal on the basis of the Notice of Appeal.[48]

The second example concerns a parent who expressed a preference for a particular school in response to a draft statement. The local education authority named the school in Part 4 of the final statement but made it clear in a covering letter that the child would be put on a waiting list for the school and that, meanwhile, the child would have to return to the school she had been attending. The parent appealed, but later the local education authority informed the Tribunal that a place had been made available for the child at the school named in the statement. The Tribunal struck out the appeal on the ground that there was no longer any disputed decision to bring it within the Tribunal's jurisdiction.[49] It would have been open to the parent to have withdrawn the appeal rather than have it struck out.

In the third example, the Tribunal struck out a parent's appeal on behalf of a boy aged 16, on the basis that the Tribunal had no jurisdiction. The local education authority argued that since the boy was attending a full-time course at a college of further education, the appeal was outside the Tribunal's jurisdiction. The parent's argument that the boy had not left school voluntarily did not appear to the Tribunal to be relevant since it accepted that, as the local education authority's responsibility under s 165 had ceased, his statement of special needs had lapsed according to para 6:36 of the Code of Practice.[50]

In the fourth example, a parent appealed against the decision of a local education authority not to arrange an assessment for her son. Subsequently, the local education authority informed the Tribunal that it would not oppose the appeal and applied to strike it out. The Tribunal rejected the application since the local authority's decision to agree to the assessment demonstrated that the appeal was well founded. The parent was entitled to the reassurance of an order and the fact that the appeal was not opposed did not, of itself, make the appeal scandalous, frivolous or vexatious.[51] Once again, the parent could have withdrawn the appeal once the local education authority had agreed to the assessment but may have been

---

48 Digest of Cases 96/1.
49 Digest of Cases 96/2.
50 Digest of Cases 96/3.
51 Digest of Cases 96/4.

concerned that, unless she had an order, the local authority might have reneged on the agreement.

9.5 PARENTS' RESPONSE

If the local education authority delivers a reply, the parents may deliver a written response to the Secretary of the Tribunal not later than 15 working days from the date on which they received a copy of the reply from the Tribunal.[52] Unless the parents have already sent to the Tribunal the written evidence upon which they wish to rely, it must be included with the response.[53] It is possible, however, to deliver the written evidence (or further written evidence) after this time. The President may grant permission if it is within 15 working days after the time within which a response should have been delivered. The Tribunal at the hearing may also itself give permission. It should be noted, however, that the permission will be given only in exceptional circumstances.[54] By virtue of reg 29(2), late written evidence cannot be admitted without consent.

9.6 AMENDMENT AND SUPPLEMENTAL GROUNDS

By virtue of reg 8(4), in addition to delivering a response, the parents may in 'exceptional circumstances' amend the Notice of Appeal or response, deliver a supplemental statement of grounds of appeal or amend a supplementary statement of grounds of appeal. This can only be done with the permission of the President (at any time before the hearing) or with permission of the Tribunal at the hearing itself. If permitted by the President, the parents must deliver a copy of the amended document and supplementary statement to the Secretary to the Tribunal before the hearing.[55] Permission from the President will no doubt need to be obtained by applying for directions.

The local education authority has a similar ability to amend[56] either with the permission of the President at any time before the hearing or with the Tribunal's permission at the hearing itself. Whereas amendment by the parents appears to have no costs implications, permission given to the local education authority by the President or the Tribunal may be on such terms as thought fit, including the payment of costs and expenses.[57] As with the parents, the local education authority has to send a copy of every amendment and supplementary statement made before the hearing to the Secretary to the Tribunal.[58]

---

52 Regulation 8(1) and (2).
53 Regulation 8(3). The suggested contents of the evidence to be submitted are found in Appendix 11.
54 Regulation 8(5) for the parents; reg 13(3) for the local education authority.
55 Regulation 8(6).
56 Regulation 13(1).
57 Regulation 13(2).
58 Regulation 13(4).

The Regulations appear to be silent on two points consequential upon amendment. First, if permission is granted to amend any document, it is unclear whether the timetable for the future conduct of the case is affected, and, secondly, if the amended document is served on the day of the hearing, whether the appeal is automatically adjourned. The answer to the first point will need to be resolved by the parties in the directions given by the President on the application to amend, although it would seem illogical not to have a consequential change to the timetable. No doubt the extent of the amendment will have an effect on the timetable – as will the closeness to the hearing and whether there will be sufficient time for the party on whom the amended document is served to deal with it satisfactorily.

The second point would seem to be partially dealt with in reg 13(2) where a local education authority can be required to pay costs or expenses. Since parents can claim expenses for attending the hearing,[59] it is no doubt envisaged that a local education authority which serves an amendment on the day of the hearing will be required to pay the parents' expenses if the appeal is not dealt with on that day. The decision as to whether to adjourn will no doubt be dependent upon the nature of the amendment and whether the parents are able to respond to it quickly. The decision in that instance will be made by the Tribunal either on the application of either party or of its own motion if the members of the Tribunal feel that they are unable to deal properly with the appeal.[60]

9.7   REQUEST FOR DIRECTIONS

Reference has already been made in this chapter to applications to the President for directions. Any application for directions made before the hearing shall be made in writing to the Secretary of the Tribunal and, unless it is accompanied by the written consent of the other party, shall be served by the Secretary of the Tribunal on the other party.[61] The Regulations state that if the other party objects to directions sought, the President shall consider the objection. However, the Regulations do not set out the mode of objection or a time-limit in which to object. Common sense would suggest that it would be appropriate for any party seeking a direction to write to the other side setting out the proposed direction. This would appear to be the only way it would be possible for the applying party to send the written consent of the other party to the Tribunal. As to the time in which to object, since time-limits are both relatively short and strictly applied, it would be advisable to deal with the matter promptly – within 5 working days of receipt of the request from the other side or within such time as may be set by the Tribunal in the letter informing the other party of the request for directions would be sensible.

The President will consider both the request for directions and the objections.[61] He does not have to hear the parties to determine the application and will only give them the opportunity of appearing before him if he considers it necessary. There is no guidance as to which directions may require attendance.

---

59 See Chapter 11.
60 Pursuant to Regulation 24(5).
61 Regulation 18(4).

9.8 DIRECTIONS

There are a number of matters upon which directions may need to be sought or required. Directions are given by the President to enable the parties to prepare for the hearing or to assist the Tribunal to determine issues.[62] For example, the President may give directions requiring any party to provide such particulars or supplementary statements as may reasonably be required for the determination of the appeal.[63] This direction (as with the direction for the disclosure of documents and other materials pursuant to reg 21[64]) may be given either on the application of a party or of the President's own motion.[65] A witness summons, however, may only be issued on the application of a party.[66]

The President may, by summons, require any person in England and Wales to attend as a witness at a hearing of an appeal at such time and place as may be specified in the summons and, at the hearing, to answer any questions or produce any documents or other material in his custody or under his control which relates to any matter in question in the appeal.[67] However, the person summoned can only be required to give such evidence and produce such documents or material as he would be compelled to give or produce in a court of law[68].

A person needs only to attend the hearing and give evidence or produce documents in obedience to the summons if the necessary expenses of his attendance are paid or tendered to him.[69] There is no definition of the 'necessary expenses' contained in the Regulations. However, as the power given by reg 22 is similar to the procedure in the county court,[70] the same financial requirements ought to apply. In the county court, a witness, if a police officer, is to be paid or have tendered to him the sum of £6; £8.50 is to be paid or tendered to any other person in addition to a sum reasonably sufficient to cover his expenses in travelling to and from court[71]. The money is to be paid or tendered at the time of service of the summons. As the provisions in reg 22 are not identical to Ord 20, r 12 of the County Court Rules 1981, it should not be assumed that this is the correct approach but it cannot be regarded as wholly wrong.

The President, in exercising his powers under reg 22, has to take into account the need to protect any matter that relates to intimate or financial circumstances or consists of information communicated or obtained in confidence.[72]

Parties to an appeal wanting the President to issue a witness summons should be aware that no one shall be required to attend in obedience to a witness summons

---

62 Regulation 18(1).
63 Regulation 20.
64 See **9.9**.
65 Regulation 19(2).
66 Regulation 19(3).
67 Regulation 22.
68 Regulation 22(a).
69 Regulation 22(d).
70 Under Ord 20, r 12 of the County Court Rules 1981.
71 Order 20, r 12 of the County Court Rules 1981.
72 Regulation 22(b).

unless he has been given at least 5 working days' notice of the hearing. If the witness has been given less than 5 working days' notice, he may still be required to attend if he has informed the President that he accepts such notice as he has been given.[73]

9.9 DISCOVERY

There are four aspects to discovery, namely: discovery, disclosure, inspection and production. One of the directions to be given by the President concerns the disclosure of documents and other material. A party may be required[74] to deliver to the Tribunal any documents or other material which the Tribunal may require and which it is in the power of that party to deliver. The other party will be supplied with a copy of the documents or other material by the Tribunal but it is a condition of supplying the documents that the party to whom they are supplied shall use such documents only for the purposes of the appeal.[75] A useful power of discovery is contained in reg 21(2). This enables the President to grant to a party such discovery and inspection of documents (including taking copies) as might be granted by a county court. Discovery and inspection in the county court is governed by ss 52 and 53 of the County Courts Act 1984 and Ord 14 of the County Court Rules 1981. This book is clearly not the place to set out a full and detailed study of the county court rules for discovery and inspection. The matter is fully dealt with in *The County Court Practice*.[76] However, the general rule is that a party is entitled to discovery and production of all documents that relate to the matters in issue and this right does not depend upon the admissibility of the documents in evidence.[77] Pursuant to Ord 14, r 1 of the County Court Rules 1981, a party seeking discovery may apply on notice to the President for 'order for discovery' which directs the other party to make a list of the documents 'which are or have been in his possession, custody or power relating to any matter in question in the proceedings and may at the same time or subsequently also order him to make an affidavit verifying such a list'.[78] This apparently wide power is limited by Ord 14, r 8 of the County Court Rules 1981 inasmuch as the President, on the hearing of an application, will only order discovery if he feels that it is necessary. Consequently, the President may either dismiss or adjourn the application for discovery if he is of the opinion that the discovery, disclosure, production or supply is not necessary either for the disposing fairly of the appeal or for saving costs.

To enable a document that is in the possession of one party to be disclosed by an order of the President, therefore, it will be necessary for the applicant not only to show that it is necessary but also that it is relevant. The test of relevance is not the probative value of the document but whether it might reasonably be expected to

---

73 Regulation 22(c).
74 Regulation 21(1).
75 Regulation 21(1).
76 Order 14 starts at p 246 of the 1996 edition. In addition, there is a useful procedure table (No 8) on p 530 of the 1996 edition.
77 See *O'Rourke v Darbishire* [1920] AC 581 and *Rush and Tomkins Ltd v Greater London Council* [1989] AC 1280.
78 Ord 14, r 1(1) of the County Court Rules 1981.

provoke a line of enquiry which would be of assistance to a party.[79] Assuming that an order for discovery has been made by the President and has not been refused by him, the party against whom the order is made must disclose every document he has in his possession whether he is bound to produce it or not.[80]

There are two important additional points to make. First, discovery can be ordered against a party in respect of documents in the possession of an employee as long as that document was created or obtained in the course of his employment.[81] This would seem to cover documents prepared by a teacher who is employed by a local education authority and would enable the President to order discovery of documents which may be held by the school but not disclosed by a local education authority when replying to the appeal. Secondly, a party will not be required to produce documents which are privileged. However, it is not sufficient simply to say that the document is privileged.[82] The list to be made as a result of an order for discovery must state the facts upon which the objection to discovery by reason of privilege is based. Likewise, if an affidavit[83] is required, that too must set out the grounds of the objection and verify the facts upon which the objection is grounded.

By virtue of Ord 14, r 2 of the County Court Rules 1981, the President may on the application on notice of any party make an order directing the other party to make an affidavit 'stating whether any document or any class of document, specified or described in the application is or has at any time been in his possession, custody or power and, if not still in his possession, custody or power, when he parted with it and what has become of it'.[84] This order can be made notwithstanding that the party has already made or been required to make a list or affidavit under Ord 14, r 1.

Once the list has been made in compliance with a request or order, the party making the list shall allow the applicant to inspect the documents referred to in the list (other than those which he objects to having to produce) and to take copies of them. Consequently, at the same time as the list of documents is served, a notice shall also be served stating a time within 7 days after service at which the document may be inspected at a place specified in the notice.[85]

If, however, the party who is required to permit inspection either fails to serve a notice, or objects to the production of a certain document or offers inspection at a time or place which is in the opinion of the President unreasonable, on the application of the party entitled to the inspection the President may, subject to Ord 14, r 8 of the County Court Rules 1981 referred to above, make an order for the production of documents for inspection at such time and place and in such manner as the President thinks fit.[86] The application for the order has to be supported by an affidavit specifying or describing the documents of which inspection is sought and

---

79 See *The Captain Gregos* (1990) *The Times*, 21 December.
80 See generally the note to Ord 14, r 1 of the County Court Rules 1951.
81 *Macmillan Inc v Bishopsgate Investment Management (No 1)* [1993] 1 WLR 1372.
82 *Gardner v Irvin* (1879) 4 Ex D 49.
83 Pursuant to Ord 14, r 1(1) of the County Court Rules 1981.
84 Ord 14, r 2(1) of the County Court Rules 1981.
85 Ord 14, r 3 of the County Court Rules 1981.
86 Ord 14, r 5 of the County Court Rules 1981.

stating the belief of the person making the affidavit that they are in the possession, custody or power of the other party and that they relate to a matter in question in the proceedings.

Those documents which are usually not produced are often protected on the grounds of privilege. This privilege extends to copies as well as to the original document.[87] The most usual claim of privilege is that of professional privilege and is created when there is either a communication which is confidential or in the ordinary professional dealings between one party and his solicitor or his counsel in the course of, or with a view to, litigation.[88] Consequently, such privilege does not apply to communications with advisers who are not legally qualified.[89] The test is to see whether the communication was made confidentially for the purpose of legal advice, construing such purposes broadly.[90]

The taking of copies of documents is dealt with by virtue of Ord 14, r 4A of the County Court Rules 1981. A party who is entitled to inspect a document may, at or before the time when inspection takes place, serve on the party who is required to produce such documents for inspection, a notice requiring that party to produce a true photocopy. The notice must contain an undertaking to pay the proper charges. Once received, the party upon whom the notice is served must within 7 days after the receipt supply the copy requested together with an account of the proper charges.[91] If a party fails to supply the other party with a copy of any document, the President may make such orders as to supply of that document as he thinks fit.[92] This could mean either the dismissal of the appeal or reply,[93] but this must be read in the light of reg 23 which deals specifically with a failure to comply with directions.

9.10 VARIATION OR SETTING ASIDE OF DIRECTIONS

Where a person to whom a direction (including any summons) given by the President pursuant to the Regulations is addressed has no opportunity to object to the giving of such direction, he may apply to the President by notice to the Secretary of the Tribunal to vary or set it aside. The President shall not set aside or vary the direction without first notifying the person who applied for the direction and considering any representations made by that person.[94]

---

87 *Re Fuld (No 2), Hartly v Fuld* [1965] P 405.
88 *Wheeler v Le Marchant* (1881) 17 Ch D 675 and see the notes to Ord 14, r 5 of the County Court Rules 1981.
89 *New Victoria Hospital v Ryan* [1993] ICR 201.
90 *Balabel v Air India* [1988] Ch 317.
91 Ord 14, r 5A(2). The proper charges shall not exceed the sums shown in Appendix A, item 4 of Ord 38, r 3(1) of the County Court Rules 1981. See p 1653 of *The County Court Practice* (1996 edition). The cost allowed in 1996 is 25p for each A5 or A4 page and 50p for each A3 page.
92 Ord 14, r 5A(3).
93 Ord 14, r 10(1).
94 Regulation 19.

This provision enables a party or witness to make representations as to why the direction should not be made. A witness may object to the production of documents for whatever reason and, although the President has to consider certain matters pursuant to reg 22,[95] there may be other reasons to prevent the production which need to be put before the President.

There is no apparent time-limit within which to apply to vary or set aside the directions contained in the Regulations but it would be advisable to apply as soon as the direction has been received and, in any event, before the time within which the direction is to be complied with, otherwise it could be possible that the party objecting to the direction will be deemed to have failed to comply with it and may find the appeal determined either without a hearing or in the absence of a party in default of that direction.[96]

9.11 FAILURE TO COMPLY WITH DIRECTIONS

Any direction issued by the President pursuant to the Regulations containing a requirement upon one or other party shall, as appropriate, include a statement of the possible consequences for the appeal (as provided by reg 23) where the party or parties fail to comply with the requirement in the time allowed by the President.[97]

The direction shall also contain a reference to the fact that, under s 180(5) of the 1993 Act, any person who without reasonable excuse fails to comply with directions regarding discovery or inspection of documents or regarding attendance to give evidence and produce documents, shall be liable on summary conviction to a fine not exceeding level 3 on the standard scale.[98] If the person to whom the direction is addressed did not have an opportunity of objecting to the direction at the time of it being made, the direction shall contain a statement to the effect that the person may apply to the President under reg 19 to vary or set aside the direction.[99]

If a party has not complied with a direction to it within the time specified in the direction (the 'party in default' – as directed by reg 23(2)), the Tribunal may, where the party in default is the parent, dismiss the appeal without a hearing.[100] If the defaulting party is the local education authority, the Tribunal may determine the appeal without a hearing.[101] The third available option is that the Tribunal may hold a hearing without notifying the party in default at which the party in default is not represented. Alternatively, where the parties have been notified of the hearing under reg 24, the Tribunal may direct that neither the party in default nor any person whom he intends should represent him be entitled to attend that hearing.[102] As can

---

95 See **9.8**.
96 Pursuant to reg 23.
97 Regulation 18(5)(a).
98 The current level, imposed by the Criminal Justice Act 1982, s 37, is a maximum of £400.
99 Regulation 18(5)(b).
100 Regulation 23(1)(a).
101 Regulation 23(1)(b).
102 Regulation 23(1)(c).

be seen, therefore, the consequences of not strictly adhering to the time-limits can be severe and fatal to either party's case.

9.12 WITHDRAWAL OF APPEAL

A parent (as opposed to the parent's representative) may either at any time before the hearing of the appeal withdraw his appeal by sending to the Secretary of the Tribunal a notice signed by him stating that he withdraws his appeal or withdraw the appeal at the hearing.[103] It should be noted, however, that although the Tribunal shall not normally make an order in respect of costs,[104] it may make an order against a parent who has withdrawn his appeal if the Tribunal is of the opinion that the parent acted frivolously or vexatiously or that his conduct in making or pursuing an appeal was wholly unreasonable.[105] However, no order for costs shall be made against a parent without first giving that parent an opportunity of making representations against the making of such an order.[106] If the parent has lawyers acting for him in the appeal, it is important to note that the lawyers cannot withdraw the appeal on the parent's behalf. It must be withdrawn by the parent. It is also possible that if it is clear to the Tribunal that the appeal cannot continue for whatever reason, the Secretary of the Tribunal may write to a parent asking whether he wishes to withdraw his appeal. If, however, the parent does not withdraw the appeal, it is possible for a local education authority to apply to strike it out (see **9.4**).

9.13 ENQUIRIES BY THE SECRETARY OF THE TRIBUNAL

At any time after the Secretary of the Tribunal has received the Notice of Appeal, he shall enquire of each party whether or not the party intends to attend the hearing, whether the party intends to be represented at the hearing and, if so, the name of the representative.[107] The Secretary shall also enquire whether either party wishes the hearing to be in public, whether the party intends to call witnesses and, if so, the names of the proposed witnesses[108] and whether the party or witness will require the assistance of an interpreter.[109] The parties are required to supply the Secretary of the Tribunal with this information by virtue of reg 10(1) for parents and reg 15(2) for the local education authority.

The Secretary shall also enquire of the parents whether they wish any persons (other than the parents' respresentative or any witness they propose to call) to attend the hearing if the hearing is to be in private and, if so, the names of such persons.[110] It

---

103 Regulation 9.
104 See **11.2**.
105 Regulation 33(1)(a).
106 Regulation 33(3). For the amount and scale, see **11.20**.
107 Regulation 17(a)(i) and (ii). See also **10.3**.
108 Subject to the limit of two witnesses and a request for directions if more are required.
109 Regulation 17(a)(iii), (iv) and (v).
110 Regulation 17(b).

should be noted, however, that by virtue of reg 26(8), where the parents have named more than two persons in response to this enquiry, only two persons shall be entitled to attend the hearing unless the President has given permission before the hearing or the Tribunal gives permission at the hearing for a greater number to attend.

9.14 NOTICE OF HEARING

Unless the appeal is determined without a hearing,[111] the Secretary of the Tribunal shall fix the time and place of the hearing after consultation with the parties and, not less than 10 working days before the date so fixed (or such shorter time as the parties agree), send to each party a notice that the hearing is to be at such time and place.[112]

If, however, the hearing is to take place under reg 14 (failure to reply and absence of opposition), reg 31 (review of the tribunal's decision) or reg 36 (power to strike out), the period of notice required is shortened to 5 working days.[113]

The Secretary of the Tribunal shall include with the notice of hearing information and guidance (in a form approved by the President) as to the attendance of parties and witnesses, the bringing of documents and the right of representation or assistance.[114] The notice will also explain the possible consequences of non-attendance, and the right of a parent and local education authority (if it has presented a reply) who do not attend and are not represented to make representations in writing.[115] The parent should send the additional written representations in support of his appeal to the Secretary of the Tribunal not less than 5 working days before the hearing.[116] The same provision applies to the local education authority.[117] If a parent or local education authority is represented but does not attend, it would seem that no written representations can be made by that party.

If it is necessary to alter the time and place of the hearing, the Secretary of the Tribunal shall give the parties not less than 5 working days' (or such shorter time as the parties agree) notice of the altered hearing date. Unless the parties agree, the altered hearing date shall not be before the date notified for the hearing under reg 25(1).[118] It should be noted that the Secretary of the Tribunal is not obliged to consult or to send a notice to any party who by virtue of any provision of these Regulations is not entitled to be represented at the hearing.[119]

The Tribunal has the power from time to time to adjourn the hearing and, if the time and place of the adjourned hearing are announced before the adjournment, no

---

111 See **10.1**.
112 Regulation 24(1) and (2)(b).
113 Regulation 24(2)(a).
114 Regulation 24(3)(a). See also **10.2**.
115 Regulation 24(6)(b).
116 Regulation 10(2).
117 Regulation 15(3).
118 Regulation 24(4).
119 Regulation 24(6).

further notice shall be required.[120] If, therefore, the parties are present but not represented they should ensure that they are fully aware of the date of any adjourned hearing before they leave as they will not be sent a notice of the new date.

A 'working day' for the purposes of this section is defined[121] as being any day other than a Saturday, a Sunday, Christmas Day, Good Friday or a day which is a Bank Holiday within the meaning of the Banking and Financial Dealings Act 1971.[122] The relevance of this is that in reg 2, a 'working day' is defined as also excluding a 'day in August'. This means that although August does not count for the delivery of the Notice of Appeal it does count and will be used for hearings.

9.15   TRANSFER OF PROCEEDINGS

Where it appears to the President that an appeal pending before a Tribunal could be determined more conveniently in another Tribunal, he may at any time, upon the application of any party or of his own motion, direct that the proceedings be transferred so as to be determined in that other Tribunal. However, no such direction shall be given unless notice has been given to all parties concerned giving them an opportunity to show cause why such a direction should not be given.[123]

9.16   IRREGULARITIES

An irregularity resulting from a failure to comply with any provision of the Regulations or of any direction of the Tribunal before the Tribunal has reached its decision shall not of itself render the proceedings void.[124] Where any such irregularity comes to the attention of the Tribunal, the Tribunal may, and shall, if it considers that any person may have been prejudiced by the irregularity, give such directions as it thinks fit before reaching its decision to cure or waive the irregularity.[125]

Clerical mistakes in any document recording a decision of the Tribunal or a direction or decision of the President produced by or on behalf of the Tribunal, or errors arising in such documents from accidental slips or omissions may at any time be corrected by the chairman or the President (as the case may be) by a certificate under his hand.[126] The Secretary of the Tribunal shall send a copy of any corrected document containing reasons for the Tribunal's decision to each party[127] and, if the parents have stated the name of a representative, send him a copy of the document as well.[128]

---

120 Regulation 25(5).
121 Regulation 24(7).
122 1971 c 80.
123 Regulation 34.
124 Regulation 39(1).
125 Regulation 39(2).
126 Regulation 39(3).
127 Regulation 39(4).
128 Regulation 39(5).

Chapter 10

HEARING PROCEDURE

10.1 DETERMINATION WITHOUT A HEARING

The Tribunal has power to determine an appeal on any particular issue without a hearing. The power can be exercised either if the parties agree in writing[1] or if the local education authority either:

(1) does not send a reply within the time-limit or states that it does not resist the appeal or withdraws its opposition to the appeal;[2] or

(2) fails to comply with a time-limit set out in any direction given.[3]

For those reasons set out in (1), in addition to determining the appeal without a hearing, the Tribunal can hold a hearing without notifying the authority and at which it is not represented.[4] It should be noted that the failure of parents to comply with a time-limit does not mean that the appeal is determined. It is dismissed.[5] In determining the appeal without a hearing, the Tribunal shall consider any representations in writing submitted by that party in response to the notice of hearing, and any reply by the authority and response by the parents are treated as representations in writing.[6] Even if the appeal is determined without a hearing, the decision will still be notified in writing.[7]

In addition, if both parties agree in writing upon the terms of a decision to be made by the Tribunal, the Tribunal may, if it thinks fit, give a decision in accordance with the agreement.[8]

10.2 NON-ATTENDANCE OF A PARTY

If a party fails to attend or be represented at a hearing of which he has been duly notified, the Tribunal may, unless it is satisfied that there is sufficient reason for such absence, hear and determine the appeal in the party's absence[9] or may adjourn the hearing[10] and may make such orders as to costs and expenses as it thinks fit.[11] Before disposing of an appeal in the absence of a party, the Tribunal shall consider any representations in writing submitted by that party in response to the notice of hearing and the Notice of Appeal, and any reply or amended reply submitted by the

---

1 Regulation 25(1)(a).
2 Pursuant to reg 14(a).
3 Pursuant to reg 23(1)(b).
4 Pursuant to reg 14(b).
5 Regulation 23(1)(a).
6 Regulations 25(2) and 27(2).
7 See **10.6**.
8 Regulation 35(2).
9 Regulation 27(1)(a).
10 Regulation 27(1)(b).
11 Regulation 33(1)(b).

local education authority and any response, amended Notice of Appeal or amended response.[12] As before, the decision would have to be notified to the parties in writing.

10.3 REPRESENTATION

The consultation paper on the draft Tribunal regulations published by the Department for Education in February 1994 expressed the wish that the use of lawyers should be kept to a minimum[13] with the legally qualified chairman resolving points of law when they occurred. The consultation document expressed the hope that a 'concordat' would be established between local education authorities and voluntary bodies whereby the local education authority would not bring a lawyer to the Tribunal if the parents were not legally represented. That concordat was not implemented. It is too early to be certain whether parents will be legally represented in increasing numbers of cases but they were for the very first appeal to be heard.[14] It would appear that about 15% of cases have legal representation at the moment, with 23% having non-legal representatives.[15]

If parents have not stated the name, address and profession of a representative in the Notice of Appeal[16] they may at any time before the hearing notify the Secretary of the Tribunal in writing of the name, address and profession of a representative to whom the Tribunal should send any subsequent document or notices concerning the appeal instead of to the parents.[17] Further, the parents are able, whether they have named a representative either in the Notice of Appeal or subsequently, to notify the Secretary of the Tribunal in writing either of the name, address and profession of a replacement representative or that the representative is no longer acting and that from thereon it is the parents to whom documents should be sent.[18]

Where the parents have named a representative,[19] all references to documents and notices which the Regulations require should be sent or given to the parties or a party shall, in the context of the parents, be treated as references to sending documents to or giving notice to the representative.[20] That provision will not apply, however, if the parents have notified the Secretary of the Tribunal either that they do not wish it to apply,[21] or that no person is acting as their representative or the representative named has notified the Secretary of the Tribunal in writing that he is not prepared or no longer prepared to act in that capacity.[22] If the person named does so notify the Secretary of the Tribunal, he shall notify the parents of that decision and send any subsequent notices or documents to the parents themselves.[23]

---

12 Regulation 27(2).
13 Paragraph 36.
14 *Times Educational Supplement*, February 1995.
15 Details supplied by the Tribunal and correct as at 31 August 1995.
16 Regulation 7(1)(c).
17 Regulation 11(1).
18 Regulation 11(2).
19 Pursuant to either reg 7(1)(c) or reg 11(1) or (2).
20 Regulation 42(1).
21 Regulation 42(2)(a) and (b).
22 Regulation 42(2)(c).
23 Regulation 11(3)(a) and (b).

At the hearing or any part of a hearing of the appeal, the parents may either conduct the case (and have assistance from one person if they wish) or may appear and be represented by one person whether or not that person is legally qualified provided that, if the President gives permission before the hearing, or the Tribunal gives permission at the hearing, the parents may obtain assistance or be represented by more than one person.[24]

Although it is clear from the Regulations that parents who have legal representation need to obtain permission to be represented by two people if, for example, they have both a solicitor and barrister at the hearing, until the end of 1995 that permission was automatically given by the President.[25] However, the President issued a statement on 1 December 1995 stating that with effect from 1 January 1996 permission would not automatically be given for a solicitor to attend the hearing as well as a barrister. It is still possible, however, to apply under the Regulations in advance of the hearing for permission in an individual case. However, as the permission will not be given as a matter of routine, the application must show why, in the interests of justice, it should be allowed in that case. The President has determined that it will not normally be sufficient to say that it would be convenient to have a note-taker or that the barrister is unknown to the parent. Any application for the attendance of two lawyers should be made in sufficient time before the hearing to enable appropriate arrangements to be made depending on the outcome of the application.

The President decided to reconsider the matter because too many people attending a hearing does not help to create an informal atmosphere and also because unrepresented parties had made representations that they felt a second representative made the experience of facing a party represented by a lawyer even more intimidating. The decision was made after consultation with the Bar Council, The Law Society, The Law Society's Local Government Group and the Education Law Association.

The parents may feel that for reasons of cost, they should have only one lawyer present. It would appear possible to name a representative and have that person attend if a hearing has already started and has then been (for whatever reason) adjourned to another date, since reg 11(4) expressly includes the phrase '. . . or any part of a hearing . . .'. There may be problems of the representative knowing what has happened at the previous hearing, however.

A local education authority will, of course, have to be represented by a person, whether or not that person is legally qualified, and the same proviso as to the number of legal or other representatives also applies.[26] The decision about representation will normally be made some time before the hearing takes place since the Secretary of the Tribunal has to enquire (at any time after receipt of the Notice of Appeal) of each party whether or not that party intends to attend the hearing, whether or not the party wishes to be represented at that hearing and, if so, the name of the representative together with the names of any proposed witnesses and whether an

---

24 Regulation 11(4).
25 Presidential Guidance.
26 Regulation 15(1).

interpreter will be required.[27] The Secretary of the Tribunal will also at the same time enquire whether the party wishes the hearing to be in public,[28] whether the parents wish any persons (other than a representative, or any witnesses they propose to call) to attend the hearing and the names of such persons.[29]

It should be noted, however, by virtue of reg 26(8), that where the parents have named more than two persons in response to this enquiry by the Secretary of the Tribunal, only two persons shall be entitled to attend the hearing unless the President has given permission before the hearing or the Tribunal gives permission at the hearing for a greater number to attend.

A hearing by the Tribunal shall be in private unless the parents and the authority request that the hearing shall be in public[30] or the President at any time before the hearing, or the Tribunal at the hearing, orders that the hearing shall be in public.[31]

In addition to the parties, their representative and witnesses, a number of other people are entitled to attend the hearing of an appeal, even though it is in private.[32] Those entitled include the parent of the child who is not a party to the appeal,[33] as well as any two persons named by the parents in response to the enquiry by the Secretary of the Tribunal,[34] unless the President has determined that any such person shall not be entitled to attend the hearing and notified the parents accordingly.[35] The clerk to the Tribunal and the Secretary of the Tribunal as well as the President, any member of the chairman's or lay panel (when not sitting as a member of the Tribunal) and a member of the Council of Tribunals are also entitled to attend, as are any persons undergoing training as either a member of the chairman's or lay panel or the clerk of the Tribunal, any person acting on behalf of the President in the training or supervision of clerks to the Tribunal, and an interpreter.[36]

A party to the proceedings should be aware, however, that, with the exception of a parent of the child who is not a party to the appeal,[37] no one entitled to attend the hearing by virtue of reg 26(2) shall take any part in the hearing or (even when entitled or permitted to remain) in the deliberations of the Tribunal.[38] This does not include, however, the clerk of the Tribunal or an interpreter taking part in the hearing as their respective duties require. They do not, however, take any part in the deliberations of the Tribunal. It does include in the list of those who cannot take part those other people whom the parents may wish to attend in addition to their representative and witnesses.

27 Regulation 17(a)(i), (ii), (iv) and (v).
28 Regulation 17(a)(iii).
29 Regulation 17(b).
30 Regulation 26(1)(a).
31 Regulation 26(1)(b).
32 Regulation 26(2).
33 Regulation 26(2)(b).
34 Under reg 17(b).
35 Pursuant to reg 26(2)(a) and (8).
36 Regulation 26(2)(c)–(h).
37 Regulation 26(7).
38 Regulation 26(6).

Power is also given to the Tribunal (albeit with the consent of the parties or their representatives actually present), if the appeal is in private, to permit any other person to attend the hearing[39] and it may exclude from the hearing or part of it any person whose conduct has disrupted or is likely, in the opinion of the Tribunal, to disrupt the hearing.[40]

10.4 WITNESSES

Neither party is entitled to call more than two witnesses to give evidence orally unless permission is given by the President before the hearing or by the Tribunal at the hearing.[41] These are two witnesses in addition to the parents themselves and any witness who has made a written statement whose personal attendance is required by the Tribunal.[42] There should be considerable thought given to the question of who should give evidence. This is more fully explored at **10.5**.

The Regulations are silent as to what happens if one party does not accept a written statement supplied by the other party. Presumably, the solution would be to apply for a witness summons pursuant to reg 22 after the parties have reviewed the evidence. Most witnesses (such as educational psychologists, other experts or head teachers) will have produced a report as part of the evidence originally submitted. Regulation 7 requires certain documents to accompany the Notice of Appeal and by reg 8(3), the parents shall include all written evidence they wish to submit to the Tribunal. Likewise, the local education authority has to submit its written evidence with its reply by virtue of reg 12(1)(c) or, at the latest (with permission of the President) within 15 working days from the date on which the parents could have delivered a response.[43] If, on receipt of the written evidence, a party feels it requires the attendance of an author of a certain statement or report, the matter is best resolved by applying for directions. However, parties should be aware that the Tribunal only pays the expenses of two witnesses called by the parent. Nothing will be paid for further witnesses, even though consent has been given to calling them.

10.5 CONDUCT OF THE APPEAL

10.5.1 Procedure

The Tribunal shall conduct the hearing in such manner as it considers most suitable to the clarification of the issues and generally to the just handling of the proceedings and it shall, so far as appears to be appropriate, seek to avoid formality in its proceedings.[44] At the beginning of the hearing, the chairman shall explain the order of proceedings which the Tribunal proposes to adopt[45] and shall determine the

---

39 Regulation 26(3).
40 Regulation 26(4).
41 Proviso to reg 29(1).
42 Regulation 29(2).
43 Regulation 13(3).
44 Regulation 28(2).
45 Regulation 28(1).

order in which the parties are heard and the issues to be determined.[46] Experience thus far has shown that dealing with different aspects of the case in turn rather than the whole case at one time has prevented muddle.[47] The discussion at the hearing need not be limited to points raised by the chairman.

The Tribunal may, if it is just and reasonable to do so, permit a party to rely on grounds not stated in its Notice of Appeal or, as the case may be, that party's reply or response and to adduce any evidence not presented to the local education authority before or at the time it took the disputed decision.[48] It should be noted that if, either at or after the commencement of any hearing, a member of the Tribunal other than the chairman is absent, the hearing may, with the consent of the parties, be conducted by the other two members and, in that event, the Tribunal shall be deemed to be properly constituted and the decision of the Tribunal shall be taken by those two members.[49]

10.5.2 Evidence

In the course of the hearing, the parties shall be entitled to give evidence, to call witnesses, to question any witness and to address the Tribunal on the evidence and generally on the subject matter of the appeal.[50] Subject to the limit (unless permission is given) of two witnesses the evidence may be given orally or by written statement.[51] It should be remembered that written evidence has to be submitted by certain time-limits.[52] The Tribunal may receive evidence of any fact which appears to the Tribunal to be relevant.[53] It would seem, therefore, that the normal rules of evidence – such as hearsay and corroboration – do not apply. However, simply because all evidence is admissible, it does not mean that it must be admitted. There will be no benefit to either party in the admission of irrelevant or time-wasting evidence. The relevant evidence will, of course, be the documents prepared for the assessment or statement or whatever. The relevant documents to be submitted by the parents are set out at **9.3** and a suggested list of documents can be found at Appendix 11.

Both parties should bear in mind that the Tribunal has the papers in advance and does not expect the witnesses at the hearing to go through their evidence or reports in detail. The parties, in preparing for the hearing, therefore, should try to ensure that each point they want to make is in the Notice of Appeal, reply or response and that wherever possible there is documentary evidence to support each point being made.

Although it will not be normal for evidence to be given on oath, the Tribunal has power to require any witness to give evidence on oath or affirmation or require

---

46 Regulation 28(3).
47 Author's own experience.
48 Regulation 28(4).
49 Regulation 28(5).
50 Regulation 29(1).
51 Regulation 29(2), but note the possibility of the author of a written statement being required to attend by the Tribunal. See **9.4**.
52 See **10.4**.
53 Regulation 29(3).

evidence given by written statement to be given by affidavit.[54] If it is required for evidence to be given on oath or affirmation, the oath or affirmation will be administered in due form. Although it is the usual practice for the local education authority to present their evidence (see **10.5.3**), as the hearing ought to be issue-based, each party will take it in turns to deal with various aspects of the case. Questions will be asked by the Tribunal members as the case proceeds rather than at any set times, and questions by either party should also be asked at the appropriate time. These questions should not, however, turn into a statement of case. The purpose of a hearing is so that the parties can participate in what amounts to an 'informed discussion'.

By virtue of the President's Practice Direction of 15 March 1995[55] (as qualified by the President's statement dated 9 October 1995 and considered at **8.4.1**) that the Tribunal decision is to be based on what is appropriate at the date of the hearing, the Tribunal will find it very useful to have up-to-date reports to hand. It should be noted, however, that reports circulated to members of the Tribunal before the hearing are able (simply because of the constraints of time) to be considered more freely than those handed to the clerk less than half-an-hour before the hearing. Reports which were prepared up to 4 years previously in the preparation of a statement of special educational needs will be the target of easy and persuasive criticism if it becomes clear that they do not adequately reflect the current needs and provision required for the child. It should be noted, however, that that direction was the subject of a judicial review, both as to the President's jurisdiction to make directions and as to what should be the nature of an appeal to the Tribunal. That judicial review was dropped, however, and so the underlying guidance as to the nature of appeals stands. The President is satisfied[56] that, although the legislation gives him no express authority to make a binding Practice Direction on a question of law, the guidance which the March 1995 Direction gave is right. This view is supported by the decision of the Divisional Court in *R v Secretary of State for Education ex parte Davis*.[57] Although that case concerned the Education Act 1981, local appeal committees of local education authorities and appeals to the Secretary of State, as this was the structure which the Tribunal replaced it is suggested the same principles should apply to the Tribunal.

In his judgment, Mr Justice Auld made it clear that it is the present and future, not the past, that needs to be considered and that, unless an appeal is approached with the most up-to-date information, it is not possible to determine that the most suitable provision is made for the child. Until the case is determined, the Direction of 15 March 1995 is, and must be, the best way to approach a hearing.

In addition to having up-to-date evidence, it is important for both the parents and the local education authority fully to consider long before the hearing what they are trying to achieve. For example, from the local education authority's point of view, there will be little help given to the Tribunal from an educational psychologist who has neither seen the child nor knows the school. A far better witness would be the

---

54 Regulation 29(4).
55 [1995] ELR 335.
56 'Nature of Appeal: Statement by the President', 9 October 1995.
57 [1989] 2 FLR 190.

teacher (or special needs co-ordinator) who has or will have daily responsibility for implementing a statement (or whatever). A witness will need to know what is offered by the school and why it is felt appropriate either not to assess, not to statement or not to change the name of the school to the one named by the parents.

From the parents' point of view, it is much more helpful to have the authors of reports present to provide background information, rather than friends. An educational psychologist who can explain why his or her report and conclusion are more perceptive than those of the local education authority's expert is invaluable. Likewise, a teacher from the proposed school or even the teacher from the child's current school will assist. If the current school teacher refuses (or is not permitted) to attend, the parents should apply for a witness summons.

10.5.3   Order of proceedings

Although the parents have brought the appeal, it will be normal for the local authority to present its case first. This was the order of presentation most often used in the local appeal committees which preceded the Tribunal and will have the benefit that most if not all of the relevant facts are brought out. The parties should be aware that it is anticipated that the Tribunal will direct the parties' attention to the main issues and suggest that they be examined first. However, it may not always be appropriate, especially if parents are unrepresented, for this course of action to be adopted.

10.5.4   Notes of evidence

In addition to the tape-recording of the proceedings the chairman will take detailed notes of the oral evidence, which will be retained by the Tribunal in case the decision is challenged. These notes will be available for the members of the Tribunal to refer to when reaching their decision.

10.5.5   Children at the hearing

It is not advisable for the parents to bring the child who is the subject of the appeal to the hearing. If it is intended to bring a child, prior warning should be given to the secretariat and provision made (if necessary) for appropriate child-minding. The clerks will not be able to do this for the parents. The only reason for the child to be present at the hearing is if he or she is giving evidence. Normally, however, a letter or other document is just as good. A child should not attend (and will not be allowed to stay) if either his or her presence will disrupt the hearing or where what needs to be said could be hurtful or harmful to the child or where the child's presence could inhibit witnesses. It is much better to assume that the child will not attend.

10.6 CONSIDERATIONS

10.6.1 Interests of the child

Save for the need to have regard to the Code of Practice[58] and as to the naming of a school,[59] the Regulations and the 1993 Education Act give the Tribunal no guidance about the criteria to be used to determine appeals. Consequently, the President has decided that the guiding principle in deciding all appeals must be 'the interests of the child' or, more accurately, 'must never be against the interests of the child'. Since the child is not a party to the proceedings, the hearing must not be seen as a question of which party succeeds but of seeing which course of action is in the interests of the child.[60]

Although according to the standard imposed by the Children Act 1989, 'the child's welfare shall be the court's paramount consideration', this cannot be appropriate in some decisions to be made by the Tribunal as it lies in conflict with the statutory requirement[61] that there has to be an efficient use of resources.

10.6.2 The Code of Practice

The Tribunal has a statutory duty to have regard to any provision of the Code of Practice which appears to be relevant to any question arising on the appeal.[62] Parties should, therefore, be familiar with the appropriate paragraphs of the Code of Practice. The local education authority is under a duty to have regard to the Code[63] but, if the local education authority has not taken it into account, that will not of itself be grounds for the Tribunal to reject the authority's contentions.

The fact that the Code of Practice envisages a five-stage process of assessment with the statutory assessment beginning only at stage 4[64] ought to make it clear to all that it is neither necessary nor appropriate to have a statement of special educational needs for every child. In the great majority of cases, the special needs provision required should be met effectively by the school from its own resources.[65] A statement is not the necessary consequence of providing special educational needs.[66] Indeed, even if a proposed statement is served on the parents, it does not mean that a statement has to be made.[67]

---

58 Section 157(3) of the Education Act 1993.

59 Section 160 of the Education Act 1993.

60 That a child is not a party to the appeal was decided in *S v Special Educational Needs Tribunal and the City of Westminster* [1996] ELR 102, [1995] 1 WLR 1627, [1995] TLR 498. That decision was appealed and the Court of Appeal unanimously agreed that a child was not a party to an appeal. See [1996] 1 WLR 382, [1995] TLR 685.

61 See s 160(2)(c), for example.

62 Section 157(3).

63 Section 157(2).

64 See generally section 3 of the Code of Practice, and Chapter 4 (above).

65 Paragraph 3:1 of the Code of Practice.

66 *R v Secretary of State for Education and Science ex parte Lashford* [1988] 1 FLR 72.

67 *R v Isle of Wight County Council ex parte RS and Another* [1993] 1 FLR 634, and see **8.3**.

10.6.3   Naming a school

The general statutory policy[68] that parental preference has priority is tempered by the provisions of the Education Act 1993. Although a local education authority is required to educate a child in a mainstream school instead of a special school, it is not obliged to do so if three conditions are satisfied.[69] These conditions are:

(1)   the child is receiving the special educational provision which his learning difficulty calls for;

(2)   the child being educated in a mainstream school does not affect the efficient education of the children with whom he is educated; and

(3)   (and possibly the most crucial) by doing so the local education authority is ensuring an efficient use of resources.

Since the parents have the opportunity to express a preference as to the local education authority school to which their child should go, the school must be named[70] unless the local education authority establishes one of the criteria set out in paras 3 or 8 of Sch 10 to the 1993 Act, namely that the school is unsuitable to the child's age, ability or aptitude or to his special educational needs or that the attendance of the child at the school would be incompatible with the provision of efficient education for the children with whom he would be educated or the efficient use of resources. Consequently, on appeal, the Tribunal can order the local education authority only to specify the name of a school when either the parents have expressed a preference for the school or, in the proceedings, the parents, the local education authority or both have proposed the school.[71]

It would be possible, therefore, that in some cases the Tribunal could be faced with a choice of schools, one being named by each of the parties. First, the Tribunal will see whether the local education authority has successfully established in respect of the school proposed by the parents any of the grounds of opposition specified in Sch 10, paras 3(3) and 8(2) of the 1993 Act (as set out in the preceding paragraph). If the ground of opposition is established that school is eliminated. If, however, more than one school is available for the Tribunal to order the local education authority to name, the choice by the Tribunal should be made in the interests of the child.

But does a named school have to admit the child? By virtue of s 168(5)(b), a maintained, grant-maintained or grant-maintained special school is obliged to admit a child if the school is named in the statement. The problem will arise if an independent school is suggested by the parents but contested by the local education authority. If this occurs, it would be of obvious assistance for the Tribunal to know at the hearing whether there is a place available for the child if the school is named as it cannot order an independent school to admit a child. Before an independent school can be named, it is necessary to be sure that it is approved by the Secretary of State for Education and Employment as being suitable for the admission of children for whom statements are maintained.[72] The chairman of the Tribunal will have a list of independent schools currently approved by the Secretary of State at any hearing

---

68 Introduced by the Education Reform Act 1988.
69 Section 160(2) of the Education Act 1993.
70 By virtue of para 3 of Sch 10 to the Education Act 1993.
71 Section 170(4).
72 Section 189(5)(a).

at which the school is in issue. In some cases, however, the parents may wish the Tribunal to name a school which is not approved by the Secretary of State. The course of action the parents should take in those circumstances is to seek the consent of the Secretary of State to the child being educated there[73]. If parents do wish to have their child educated at such a school, they will no doubt have been in contact with that school (and may even ask the head teacher to give evidence) and so should be aware whether consent is required. It is imperative that consent is obtained before the hearing. If no consent has been received, the Tribunal will not be able to name the school.

The grounds of opposition cannot automatically be met, however, by either the local education authority proving that the parents' favoured choice is more expensive than the local education authority's favoured alternative or by the authority stating that it has no available funds. The Tribunal is not empowered or required to consider the purposes to which the funds of a local education authority are put. However, it is not necessarily a conclusive answer to the local education authority's opposition to show that either the school favoured by the parents makes better provision than the adequate provision offered by the local education authority alternative (if the local education authority provision is inadequate, however, it would be a conclusive answer) or that the child is already attending the school favoured by the parents. This latter point is only relevant if the local education authority is not yet paying for the child at that school.

It will be of help in assisting the Tribunal to reach a conclusion on the suitability of the alternative schools if information about them (such as prospectuses) can be made available. School size, class sizes, teaching ratios, specialist facilities and resources may all be relevant. If there is to be an argument about the efficient use of resources, comparative financial information may be necessary.

10.7 DECISIONS

The decision of the Tribunal will usually occur at least 5 months after the appeal was lodged. It is not intended that the appeal will be a review of what happened at the time of the hearing. The President issued a Practice Direction[74] stating that decisions are to be based on what is appropriate at the date of the hearing and not a judgment of the correctness of the local authority's decision when it was taken. In the light of the fact that that Direction was being challenged by an application for judicial review,[75] the President issued a statement on 9 October 1995, in which he confirmed that the guidance given in the Direction of March 1995 was correct whilst at the same time accepting that the legislation gave him no express authority

---

73 Section 189(5)(b).
74 15 March 1995. See [1995] ELR 335 at p 336.
75 See **10.5.2**.

to make a binding Practice Direction. That application for judicial review has now been withdrawn and so the guidance stands (see **8.4.1**).

A decision of the Tribunal may be taken by a majority[76] and, where the Tribunal is constituted by two members only,[77] the chairman shall have a second or casting vote. However, no decision of the Tribunal shall contain any reference to the decision being by a majority (if that is the case) or to any opinion of a minority.[78] Although the Regulations enable the Tribunal to give the decision orally (either at the end of the hearing or on a reserved date)[79] the President has stated that a standard procedure will be adopted.[80] The parties will be told by the chairman at the start of the proceedings and he will announce at the end of the hearing that the parties will be notified of the decision in writing. The notification will be sent by the Secretary of the Tribunal to the parties or notified representative and normally will not be delayed longer than 2 weeks (10 working days) from the date of the hearing, although with the number of appeals now being heard that cannot be assured.

The decision shall be recorded in a document which, save when the decision was made with the consent of both parties, shall contain (or have annexed to it) a statement of the reasons (in summary form) for the Tribunal's decision and each document shall be signed and dated by the chairman.[81] The decision will also (in an accompanying letter) give guidance about a party's right to appeal.[82] Every decision of the Tribunal shall be entered into the records[83] and shall be treated as having been made on the date on which a copy of the document recording the decision is sent to the parents.[84] Where parents have stated a name of a representative, the Secretary of the Tribunal shall send a copy of both the decision and guidance as to the circumstances in which there is a right to appeal to both the parents and the representative.[85]

It will be recalled that pursuant to reg 26(2) a number of people are entitled to attend the hearing of an appeal. The decision of the Tribunal is the decision of only the three members of the Tribunal but in reaching that decision or determining any question of procedure the Tribunal may permit certain individuals to remain in the room,[86] although they will have no part to play in reaching the decision.

The question of whether a statement of the reasons (in summary form) was adequate was considered in *S v Special Educational Needs Tribunal and the City of*

---

76 Regulation 30(1).
77 Under reg 28(5).
78 Regulation 30(3).
79 Regulation 30(2).
80 Presidential guidance.
81 Regulation 30(2).
82 Regulation 30(5).
83 Regulation 30(4).
84 Regulation 30(7).
85 Regulation 30(6).
86 Those people specified in reg 26(2)(c)–(f).

Westminster.[87] Mr Justice Latham after considering two cases[88] considered that the balance was to be properly struck by requiring that the statement of the reasons should deal, but in short form, with the substantial issues raised in order that the parties can understand why the decision has been reached. It is necessary for the Tribunal to deal with all the issues of substance raised, albeit in a summary way. This will not mean that every point raised in argument in support of a party's case needs to be dealt with but rather that the Tribunal needs to make its conclusion intelligible in relation to the issue itself.[89] Decisions of the Tribunal should have a short form conclusion as to what evidence has been accepted and what evidence has been rejected, with a short form reason for that conclusion. Where it is not always possible to identify the precise reason for accepting the evidence of one witness as opposed to another, there may have to be a simple assertion of the Tribunal's preference.[90]

A decision will be given if there has been a hearing and in certain other limited circumstances. However, if the case was not completed for whatever reason and had to be adjourned, since no conclusion could have been reached, no formal decision will be produced. The same applies if the parent chooses to withdraw the appeal either before the hearing date or at the hearing. Since the withdrawal brings the proceedings to an end, the Tribunal will not need to act and so will not make a decision.

If the Tribunal is required to determine a particular point, such as a point of law or application to strike out at a preliminary hearing, or if the appeal is determined without a hearing, a formal decision will be produced.

If the parties reach an agreement, either before or at the hearing, since the appeal is being determined, a formal decision will be required, even if that decision simply recites the contents of the agreement.

10.8   REVIEW OF DECISION

Any party may apply to the Secretary of the Tribunal for the decision of the Tribunal to be reviewed on the grounds that either its decision was wrongly made as a result of an error on the part of the Tribunal staff,[91] or a party who was entitled to be heard at a hearing but failed to appear or to be represented has good and sufficient reason for failing to appear,[92] or there was an obvious error in the decision of the Tribunal which decided the case,[93] or the interests of justice so require.[94] Any application shall be made not later than 10 working days after the date upon which

---

87   [1996] ELR 102, [1995] 1 WLR 1627, [1995] TLR 498. The Court of Appeal decision is reported at [1996] 1 WLR 382 and [1995] TLR 685.
88   *Poyser and Mills Arbitration* [1964] 2 QB 467 and *William Hill Organisation Ltd v Gavas* [1990] IRLR 488.
89   At p 112C, and [1995] 1 WLR 1627 at p 1636D.
90   At p 112D, and [1995] 1 WLR 1627 at p 1636F.
91   Regulation 31(1)(a).
92   Regulation 31(1)(b).
93   Regulation 31(1)(c).
94   Regulation 31(1)(d).

the decision was sent to the parties.[95] The application shall be in writing and state the grounds in full.

An application made by a party may be refused by the President or by the chairman of the Tribunal which decided the case if, in his opinion, it has no reasonable prospect of success.[96] If, however, the application for a review is not refused, the parties shall have an opportunity to be heard on any application for review and the review shall be determined by the Tribunal which decided the case or, if it is not practicable for it to be heard by that Tribunal, it will be heard by a Tribunal appointed by the President.[97]

In addition to a party applying to the Secretary of the Tribunal for a decision to be reviewed, the Tribunal may of its own motion review its decision on any of the four grounds referred to above.[98]

If the Tribunal proposes to review its decision, it shall serve a notice on the parties within 10 working days of the decision being sent to the parties. The parties shall have an opportunity of being heard on the proposal for review.[99]

Whether on an application by a party or of its own motion the Tribunal is satisfied as to any one of the four grounds set out above, it may review and, by certificate under the chairman's hand, set aside or vary the relevant decision.[100] If the decision is set aside (as opposed to varied) the Tribunal shall substitute such decision as it thinks fit or order a rehearing before either the same or a differently constituted Tribunal.[101] If any decision is set aside or varied by virtue of reg 31 or altered by an order of a superior court, the Secretary of the Tribunal shall alter the entry in the records to conform with the chairman's certificate or order of a superior court and shall notify the parties accordingly.[102]

10.9   REVIEW OF THE PRESIDENT'S DECISION

If on the application of a party to the Secretary of the Tribunal or of his own motion the President is satisfied that either a decision by him was wrongly made as a result of an error on the part of the Tribunal staff, or there was an obvious error in his decision, or the interests of justice so require, the President may review and set aside or vary the relevant decision of his.[103] As with an application to review a decision of the Tribunal, an application to review the decision of the President shall be made not later than 10 working days after the date on which the party making the application was notified of the decision and shall be in writing stating the grounds in full. Where the President proposes to review his decision of his own motion he will

---

95 Regulation 31(2).
96 Regulation 31(3).
97 Regulation 31(3)(a) and (b).
98 Regulation 31(4).
99 Regulation 31(4)(a) and (b).
100 Regulation 31(5).
101 Regulation 31(6).
102 Regulation 31(7).
103 Regulation 32(1).

serve notice of that proposal on the parties within the same period.[104] The parties shall have an opportunity to be heard on any application or proposal for review of the President's decision and the review shall be determined by the President.[105] If the President does decide to set aside or vary one of his decisions, the Secretary of the Tribunal shall alter the entry in the records and notify the parties accordingly.[106]

104 Regulation 32(2).
105 Regulation 32(3).
106 Regulation 32(4).

Chapter 11

FINANCIAL MATTERS

11.1 LEGAL AID

Legal aid is not available for representation before the Tribunal. However, to ensure that parents are properly advised at the early stages of the appeal process, they are able to apply for legal aid under the Green Form scheme to obtain initial advice and assistance. This legal advice and assistance covers a number of matters such as general advice, writing letters, negotiating, obtaining an opinion from a barrister and preparing a written case to go before the Tribunal. The Green Form legal aid enables people who are financially eligible to get help from a solicitor free of charge until the solicitor's charges reach a total of 2 hours' worth of work. Solicitors cannot claim more without the authority of the area office of the Legal Aid Board. Legal advice and assistance is available in both England and Wales.

To apply for legal advice and assistance, parents must make an appointment to see a solicitor at his office. At the appointment, the solicitor will need information about their income and savings in order to complete a legal aid application form. Based on this information, the solicitor will be able to tell them whether they qualify for legal aid on financial grounds. Only once they have signed the application form can the solicitor start to give them advice and assistance. Although children are eligible for legal advice and assistance, because the appeal to the Tribunal is brought by the parents it is not sensible, necessary or appropriate for the application to be in the name of the child.[1]

The financial qualifications for Green Form legal aid are the limits for disposable income and disposable capital set from time to time. If either disposable income or disposable capital is above the limit, parents will not be eligible for legal advice and assistance but if both are within the limits then, even if there is disposable capital, no contribution will be called for from it. It is fair to say that, if a person is receiving income support, family credit or disability working allowance or has an income below £75 per week, he will be eligible for legal advice and assistance. Once the solicitor has decided (by assessing the parents' means) whether the parents are financially eligible, he must then decide whether advice and assistance is available. There are certain conditions which need to be met to ensure that this is possible. As long as the solicitor does not take any steps in the proceedings (such as submitting the application for appeal or other documents), the information given to assist the

---

1 The question of whether a child should be the appellant in a case appealed from the Tribunal was considered in *S v Special Educational Needs Tribunal and the City of Westmister* [1996] ELR 102, [1995] 1 WLR 1627, [1995] TLR 498. See Chapter 12. The Court of Appeal decision is reported at [1996] 1 WLR 382, [1996] 1 FLR 663 and [1995] TLR 685. It confirms that a child is not a party to the appeal to the Tribunal.

parents would be covered by Green Form legal aid as the conditions are met by an appeal to the Tribunal.

It should be noted, however, that it will not be possible without authority from the Legal Aid Board for a solicitor to give advice and assistance on the same matter as another solicitor's advice has been sought within a short period of time (such as 6 months) merely because the advice given by that solicitor does not accord with the views of the parents (as opposed to the parents being dissatisfied with the service provided) and the parents are seeking a second opinion.[2]

Although there is an initial limit on the amount of advice given (2 hours' work), it is possible for an extension of time to be given by the Legal Aid Board. This depends upon the Legal Aid area office being satisfied that it is reasonable for the advice and assistance to be given and that the estimate of costs to be incurred in giving it is reasonable. Any solicitor making application for an extension must provide sufficient information to the Legal Aid area office to enable the office to make a decision about what the problem is, what work has to be done, what needs to be done (and why) and the estimated costs of the work to be done. If it is thought appropriate to take an opinion from a barrister, an estimated cost of that opinion (whether in writing or in conference) should be sought from the barrister and included in the request. The extension will be granted if the problem is one of English law and legal aid is not available. It will also be necessary to decide whether the prospects of success justify the expenditure, and whether it is reasonable for the client to deal with some of the steps involved himself having regard to the circumstances of the case.

There is a blank Notice of Appeal at Appendix 7, a draft letter setting out what steps ought to be taken by the parents at Appendix 10, and a suggested bundle of documents for submission to the Tribunal at Appendix 11.

11.2 COSTS

The Tribunal will not normally make an order for costs against a party.[3] However, it may make a costs order against a party (including any party who has withdrawn his appeal or reply) if it is of the opinion that the party has acted frivolously or vexatiously or that his conduct in making, pursuing or resisting an appeal was wholly unreasonable.[4] If a party fails to attend or be represented at a hearing of which he was duly notified, a costs order may be made.[5] An order may also be made against a local education authority which has neither delivered a written reply nor acknowledged receipt of the Notice of Appeal[6] and where the Tribunal considers the disputed decision was wholly unreasonable.[7] The order in respect of costs and

---

2 There are certain exceptions, for example where a solicitor has moved firms or the parents have moved some distance away.
3 Regulation 33(1).
4 Regulation 33(1)(a).
5 Regulation 33(1)(b).
6 Regulation 33(1)(c).
7 Regulation 33(1)(d).

expenses made against a party may be made in respect of any costs or expenses incurred or any allowances paid or the whole or part of any allowance paid by the Secretary of State to any person for the purpose of or in connection with his attendance at the Tribunal.[8]

No order for the payment of costs or expenses shall be made against a party without first giving that party an opportunity of making representations against the making of the order.[9] Any order made for the payment of costs and expenses may require the party against whom it is made to pay the other party an unspecified sum in respect of the costs and expenses incurred by that other party in connection with the proceedings, or the whole or part of such costs as taxed (if not agreed).[10] Any costs that are to be taxed by an order of a Tribunal may be taxed in the county court according to such of the scales as shall be directed in the Tribunal's order prescribed by the County Court Rules 1981 for proceedings in the county court.[11] No provision has been made in the Regulations to specify in which county court the taxation is to take place. Unless a particular court is mentioned in the order, the most sensible choice would seem to be the county court for the district in which the person by whom the sum is payable resides or carries on a business.

The procedure to have the costs taxed is to apply for a taxation by way of an originating application[12] to which should be annexed the bill of costs. Taxation will take place on the hearing of the originating application.[13]

There are three county court scales of costs. The lower scale covers claims exceeding £25 but not exceeding £100; scale 1 is for claims exceeding £100 and not exceeding £3,000; and scale 2 is for claims exceeding £3,000.

Notwithstanding an order for taxation of the costs and expenses, it may be possible that the party ordered to pay the costs refuses to pay them. As the order made by the Tribunal for payment was not made under the County Court Rules 1981, it cannot be enforced until it is so made. This is done by applying to the court ex parte by filing a certificate verifying the amount remaining due to the applicant and by producing the order or agreement under which the sum is payable (or a duplicate) and filing a copy.[14] There is a special form to use.[15] As the proceedings to enforce an award arise from a failure to honour the award, a cause of action distinct from the issue before the Tribunal occurs and any time-limits run from the failure to honour the award and not from the date of the original decision appealed against.[16]

---

8 Regulation 33(2)(a) and (b).
9 Regulation 33(3).
10 Regulation 33(4).
11 Regulation 33(5).
12 The procedure of issuing an originating application is set out in Ord 3, r 4 of the County Court Rules 1981.
13 Per Ord 38 of the County Court Rules 1981 in general, and Ord 38, r 22 in particular.
14 Order 25, r 12 of the County Court Rules 1981 and the notes thereto at p 357 of *The County Court Practice* (1995 edition).
15 Form N 322A.
16 *Agromet Motoimport Ltd v Maulden Engineering Co (Beds) Ltd* [1985] 1 WLR 762.

11.3 EXPENSES

The Tribunal is empowered to pay such allowances for the purposes of or in connection with the attendance of persons at the Tribunal.[17] This is limited to two witnesses, although a party may wish (and be permitted) to call more than two witnesses. Any witnesses in addition to the two allowed will not be paid their allowances. A form is provided by the Tribunal for completion and submission.

17 Education Act 1993, s 180(3).

Chapter 12

APPEALS FROM DECISIONS OF THE TRIBUNAL

12.1 WHO CAN APPEAL?

The Tribunal is able to hear appeals in three broad areas. The first is as a result of a local authority's refusal to make a statement after an assessment,[1] the second is as to the contents of a statement[2] and the third is against a local authority's refusal to assess.[3] In each of the three sections, the right of appeal to the Tribunal is given to the parents, not the child.

The ability to appeal the decision of the Tribunal to the High Court is given by s 181 of the Education Act 1993. This somewhat technical section adds the Special Educational Needs Tribunal to those Tribunals from which an appeal lies to the High Court.[4] The relevant part of s 11 of the Tribunals and Inquiries Act 1992[5] permits 'any party to proceedings before' the Tribunal to appeal. There is, however, no definition in the 1993 Act as to who are to be parties to an appeal before the Tribunal.

However, Mr Justice Latham sitting in the High Court in *S v Special Educational Needs Tribunal and the City of Westminster*[6] in reviewing the overall structure of appeals to the Tribunal concluded[7] that the only parties to an appeal to the Tribunal are the parents and the local education authority. It follows, therefore, that only the parents or the local education authority can appeal to the High Court. The appellant in *S v Special Educational Needs Tribunal and the City of Westminster* was a child and so the court was unable to hear the appeal. The obvious reason that the appeal was brought in the name of child rather than by the parents was because of the question of legal aid. Legal aid is more easily granted to a child than his or her parents. That this is so has been confirmed by the solicitor who acted for the child in that case.[8]

On 13 December 1995, the Court of Appeal unanimously dismissed the child's appeal against this decision. Lord Justice Leggatt delivering the judgment of the court said that a 'child' was defined in reg 2 of the Tribunal's regulations as meaning 'the child in respect of whom the appeal is brought'. He also said that the term 'party' in s 11(1) of the Tribunals and Inquiries Act 1992 was to be treated as a litigant and not a beneficiary to litigation. He concluded that the court had no

---

1 Education Act 1993, s 169, but see more specifically Chapter 8.
2 Section 170.
3 Section 172.
4 Tribunals and Inquiries Act 1992, s 11.
5 Section 11(1).
6 [1996] ELR 102, [1995] TLR 498, [1995] 1 WLR 1627.
7 [1996] ELR 102 at p 106F; [1995] 1 WLR 1627 at p 1631B.
8 See *Times Educational Supplement*, 4 August 1995, p 3.

jurisdiction to entertain the appeal and that Mr Justice Latham, although he had reached the right conclusions on all the issues before him, should not have entertained the appeal. In passing, Lord Justice Leggatt noted that the opportunity given to the mother to be substituted as a party was deliberately declined.[9] It will be noted when *S v Special Educational Needs Tribunal and the City of Westminster* is considered more fully below that, in fact, Mr Justice Latham did conclude that he could not entertain the application.

In two other cases heard together,[10] Mr Justice Latham was again dealing with appeals brought by children. He determined, once again, that appeals should be brought in the name of the parents and not the child. He gave leave to withdraw the appeals and launch amended proceedings. In addition, bearing in mind the definition of a 'party' in s 151 of the Supreme Court Act 1981, he held that the correct respondent was the chairman of the Tribunal, rather than the Tribunal. Although it is unclear from the judgment, the chairman of the Tribunal would seem to be the legally qualified person who chaired the hearing, rather than the President – unless of course the President is chairing the hearing. This is somewhat surprising as the chairman does not have an automatic right to appear and be heard.

It should be noted that one of the two appeals was made seriously out of time. The time to appeal was extended 'reluctantly and exceptionally'. Mr Justice Latham commented that delay by 'an agency which holds itself out as competent to advise and act for a person in this field' was not of itself good reason to extend time for entering an appeal. He was applying similar reasoning relating to delay by solicitors in the unreported case of *Regalbourne v East Lindsey District Council*.

12.2 PROCEDURE TO BE FOLLOWED

As has already been said, by virtue of the Tribunals and Inquiries Act 1992, s 11(1) the right of appeal lies against the decision of the Tribunal to the Divisional Court or the Queen's Bench Division of the High Court by way of case stated[11] or the High Court on a point of law.[12] The first step to conduct such an appeal is to write to the Tribunal defining the legal point which it is considered arises. As the cost of litigation can be considerable, any parents wishing to appeal are recommended to consult a solicitor to be advised upon their rights and how to exercise them or to consult a local Citizens Advice Bureau. The time within which to appeal is to be calculated from the day upon which the decision is sent to the parents as that is the date on which the decision is treated as having been made.[13] Any decision of the Tribunal which is altered in any way by a superior court is altered in the records by the Secretary of the Tribunal and shall be notified to the parties accordingly.[14]

---

9 [1996] 1 FLR 663, [1995] TLR 685, [1996] 1 WLR 382.
10 *S and C v Special Educational Needs Tribunal* (unreported: Crown Office list).
11 Pursuant to Ord 56 of the Rules of the Supreme Court 1965.
12 Pursuant to Ord 55 of the Rules of the Supreme Court 1965.
13 Regulation 30(7).
14 Regulation 31(7).

In addition to being governed by the Tribunals and Inquiries Act 1992, the appeal from the Tribunal is also governed by Ord 94 of the Rules of the Supreme Court 1965 and, in particular, rr 8 and 9. Rule 8 is concerned with an appeal under Ord 55 and deals with appeals on a point of law if a party is dissatisfied with the decision of the Tribunal, and r 9 is concerned with case stated under Ord 56. If the parents' request to the Tribunal to state a case for the decision of the Divisional Court on any question of law arising in the proceedings is not complied with by the Tribunal, the party to the proceedings may apply to the High Court for an order directing that the Tribunal does so state a case.[15]

It would appear, therefore, that there are two routes to appeal the decision of the Tribunal. The appellant in *S v Special Educational Needs Tribunal and the City of Westminster*[16] questioned whether the appropriate procedure would be to use Ord 55 or Ord 56 of the Rules of the Supreme Court 1965. Although Mr Justice Latham found that he could not entertain the application as it was brought by a child rather than his or her parents (and so any other matter in his judgment is strictly obiter), he decided that s 11 of the Tribunals and Inquiries Act 1992 made it clear that for the purposes of the Education Act 1993 an appeal could be made in either form.[17] However, an appeal under Ord 55 is appropriate if a decision of the Tribunal is being challenged without reference to it. In addition, the Tribunal may of its own motion (or at the request of either party) state a case on a question of law arising during proceedings. Consequently, a case stated may not necessarily be directly challenging the decision of the Tribunal but may be seeking to resolve a question of law that has arisen.

It must be stressed that an appeal has to be on a point of law and not on the facts in the case. That point was made very strongly by Mr Justice Latham in *Joyce v Dorset County Council*[18] when he said 'In this case, the appellant has sought ... to pursue an argument on the merits ... But I can only interfere if a Tribunal has made an error of law or failed to give adequate reasons for its decision ... The appellant has sought to ... elevate decisions of fact to issues of law'.

12.2.1 Appeal under Order 55

An appeal is on a point of law and is brought by originating motion. The notice must state the grounds of the appeal and whether the whole or only part of the order is appealed against.[19] The bringing of an appeal does not act as a stay of the decision appealed against and so if it is necessary to seek to stay the original order an application has to be made to the Tribunal.[20]

The notice of motion must be served on the Tribunal and any other party to the proceedings within 28 days after the date of the order appealed against.[21] In this

---

15 Order 94, r 9(2).
16 [1995] 1 WLR 1627, [1996] ELR 102, [1995] TLR 498.
17 [1996] ELR 102 at p 107A; [1993] 1 WLR 1627 at p 1631E.
18 (Unreported), Crown Office, 25 January 1996.
19 Order 55, r 3(1) and (2).
20 Order 55, r 3(3).
21 Order 55, r 4(2).

regard, the date is not the date of the hearing but the date on which the decision was received by the parents.[22]

There are powers to amend the grounds of appeal[23] and make interlocutory applications.[24] The Court has power to receive further evidence of fact.[25] The person appealing has to apply to the Tribunal for a signed copy of any note made by the chairman of the proceedings and provide a copy of that note of evidence for the court.[26]

On hearing the appeal, the court can make an order which ought to have been made by the Tribunal, make any further or other order as the case may require, or remit the matter to the Tribunal (with the court's opinion) for rehearing and determination.[27] It is important to note, however, that the court shall not be bound to allow the appeal merely on the ground of misdirection or of the improper admission or rejection of evidence. This will only occur if the court is of the opinion that a substantial wrong or miscarriage has thereby been occasioned.[28]

12.2.2 Case stated under Order 56

The power of the High Court to hear a case stated is conferred by Ord 56, r 7 of the Rules of the Supreme Court 1965. A request to state a case has to be made within 21 days of the Tribunal's decision. If the request (under Ord 94, r 9 of the Rules of the Supreme Court 1965) to the Tribunal to state a case has met with a refusal, the procedure of asking the High Court to direct the Tribunal to state a case is commenced by originating motion and notice is to be served on the Secretary of the Tribunal and every party to the proceedings to which the application relates. The notice of motion has to state the grounds of the application and the question of law upon which it is sought to have the case stated and any reasons given by the Tribunal for its refusal to state a case.[29] If the Tribunal refuses to state a case when asked, the notice of motion must be entered and served within 14 days after receipt of the notice of refusal of the request to state a case.[30]

A case stated by the Tribunal must be signed by the chairman or President of the Tribunal.

Once a case stated has been prepared by the Tribunal, either as the result of a request or order of the court or of its own motion, the Tribunal has to serve it on the party at whose request or application to the court the case was stated and any other party.[31] It is also necessary to give notice to all parties that the other parties have been served. Once the party who requested or applied to the court for an order that there

---

22 Regulation 30(7).
23 Order 55, r 6.
24 Order 55, r 6A.
25 Order 55, r 7(2), and see **12.4**.
26 Order 55, r 7(4).
27 Order 55, r 7(5).
28 Order 55, r 7(7).
29 Order 56, r 9(1) and (2).
30 Order 56, r 8(3).
31 Order 56, r 9.

be a case stated has been served by the Tribunal with the case stated, that person must begin the proceedings for the determination by the High Court of a case stated. This is done by originating motion. If, however, the case was stated by the Tribunal without a request or order, it shall begin the proceedings by originating motion.[32] The notice of motion must set out the applicant's contentions on the question of law to which the case stated refers.[33] The notice of motion must be entered for hearing and served within 14 days of the service on the applicant of the case stated.[34] If the applicant fails to enter the motion within 2 weeks of service of the case stated, any other party may, within 2 weeks of the expiry of the 14-day time-limit imposed on the applicant, begin proceedings for the determination of the case.[35] If that happens, that party has to undertake the issuing and serving of the notice of motion.

There is power for the court to amend the case or order it to be returned to the Tribunal for amendment.[36] The person by whom the case was stated may appear and be heard at the hearing.[37]

12.3 SHOULD THE TRIBUNAL BE A PARTY TO THE APPEAL?

Pursuant to Ord 55, r 4 of the Rules of the Supreme Court 1965, the notice of motion has to be served on the chairman of the Tribunal and every party to the proceedings in which the decision appealed against was given. In principle, therefore, one would expect that the Tribunal was enabled to appear and be heard, but by Ord 55, r 8 only certain persons are entitled to appear. Mr Justice Latham in *S v Special Educational Needs Tribunal and the City of Westminster*[38] concluded that the Tribunal had no right to appear under an appeal brought pursuant to Ord 55.

Comparing Ord 55, r 8 with Ord 56, r 12, he noted that the latter had been amended (in 1990) to extend the categories of persons entitled to appear and be heard to chairmen or Presidents of Tribunals by whom the case was stated. Mr Justice Latham concluded that the Tribunal could not appear before the court as of right in any appeal under Ord 55 but that the court had power to permit the Tribunal to appear and be heard in appropriate matters – such as where issues of general principle as to jurisdiction and procedure were raised. It follows from the comparison by Mr Justice Latham that the Tribunal can appear as of right in a case stated pursuant to Ord 56.

However, in *S and C v Special Educational Needs Tribunal*,[39] Mr Justice Latham held that the correct respondent to an appeal (bearing in mind the definition of a 'party' in s 151 of the Supreme Court Act 1981 – which was not referred to in *S v Special*

---

32 Order 56, r 10(1).
33 Order 56, r 10(2) and (3).
34 Order 56, r 10(4).
35 Order 56, r 10(5).
36 Order 56, r 11.
37 Order 56, r 12.
38 [1996] ELR 102 at p 107; [1995] 1 WLR 1627 at p 1632A.
39 (Unreported), 7 November 1995.

Educational Needs Tribunal and the City of Westminster) was the chairman of the Tribunal rather than the Tribunal, notwithstanding that he does not have an automatic right to appear and be heard.

12.4   CAN ADDITIONAL EVIDENCE BE FILED ON APPEAL TO THE HIGH COURT?

The court has power to receive further evidence (which will be in affidavit form) pursuant to Ord 55, r 7 of the Rules of the Supreme Court 1965. The question is whether it should. The answer lies in the contents of the affidavits. Order 55, r 7 makes it plain that the court can only receive affidavits as to fact. In *S v Special Educational Needs Tribunal and the City of Westminster*, Mr Justice Latham[40] held that an affidavit which stated what was or was not taken into account by the Tribunal and the conclusions are matters of fact in relation to the decision-making process and are therefore able to be received by the court. The judge was alert to the fact that the affidavit should be genuinely directed to telling the court what happened at the time the decision was taken by the Tribunal and not be used to give the court an ex post facto rationalisation.[41]

It is important to note that the procedures under Ords 55 and 56 are alternatives and not cumulative, so either an appeal on a point of law or a case stated by the Tribunal should be pursued. An appeal to the Court of Appeal is possible from the decision of the Divisional Court, although such an appeal lies only with the leave of the Divisional Court or the Court of Appeal.

It is not appropriate to go into full details about what steps are required in appealing under Ord 55 or asking for a case to be stated under Ord 56. Likewise, it is not possible to set out the requirements to be met in an appeal to the Court of Appeal, save that it should be noted that there is usually a 28-day time-limit in lodging an appeal to the Court of Appeal. Any party seeking to take either step should seek legal advice from a solicitor or the Citizens Advice Bureau at the earliest opportunity.

---

40   [1996] ELR 102 at p 112H; [1995] 1 WLR 1627 at 1637A–B.
41   [1996] ELR 102 at p 113A; [1995] 1 WLR 1627 at p 1637C.

Chapter 13

MATTERS OUTSIDE THE SCOPE OF THE TRIBUNAL

13.1 EDUCATION ACT 1944

The Tribunal is empowered to hear appeals arising from certain acts or omissions of a local education authority.[1] However, as already mentioned, if a complaint is made against certain other aspects of an authority's action, action lies in a different direction, namely towards either the Secretary of State for Education and Employment or the Secretary of State for Wales, or possibly to the Local Government Ombudsman.

If, for example, a parent wishes to complain about the way in which a local education authority carried out an assessment or the length of time it took, the Tribunal has no power to act. The Code of Practice sets out the time-limits for the making of assessments and statements.[2]

If a local education authority makes a statement of special educational needs, that statement will identify both the needs of the child and the help necessary to meet those needs.[3] However, the local education authority may arrange to provide the help in a way which is not to the liking of the parents. The arrangements are distinct and different from the description contained in the statement and whereas the description is capable of being appealed, the arrangements are not.

The Tribunal is concerned with appeals from decisions (or lack of them) of the local education authority. This relates almost exclusively to the statutory assessment procedure (or stages 4 or 5 of the Code of Practice). Many children will have special needs identified and met within the schools they attend. If a parent is unhappy about the way a school is meeting that child's needs, the Tribunal cannot act. If, however, the parents are concerned that the school should be seeking the statutory assessment and it is not, the parent can make a formal request to the local education authority for an assessment.[4] In addition to containing details of a child's special educational provision, a statement of special educational needs will contain details of all the relevant non-educational needs as agreed between, for example the health service, social services or any other agency and the local education authority, and specify which non-educational provision is required to meet those identified non-educational needs. An example is the provision of transport to and from special schools.[5] Any matters concerning either the description of the non-educational need

---

1 See Chapter 8.
2 See paras 3:27 to 3:45 of the Code of Practice, regs 11 and 14 of the Education (Special Educational Needs) Regulations 1994, and Chapter 3 (above).
3 See para 4:24 of the Code of Practice, and Chapter 6 (above).
4 Education Act 1993, s 173(1).
5 See *R v Hereford and Worcester County Council ex parte P* [1992] 2 FLR 207.

and both the help required and arrangements to provide that help are outside the scope of the Tribunal. There is a difference, however, if the parents contend that something which is in Part 5 of the statement as a non-educational need should be in Part 3.[6]

If a statement is amended under order of the Tribunal either by substituting a name of a school or other institution or by ordering the local education authority to maintain the statement, no appeal lies to the Tribunal if the local education authority fails to comply. If an authority proposes to amend the statement but fails to do so there is, likewise, no right of appeal to the Tribunal.

An appeal against the refusal to revoke a school attendance order does not lie to the Tribunal nor does failure to keep to time-limits for assessment and making the statement or for failing to make provision set out in the statement.

In all the above cases, parents might first wish to discuss the matters with the school or local education authority. If, however, the parents are still unhappy about what is being done, a complaint may be made to the Secretary of State for Education and Employment or the Secretary of State for Wales that the school or local education authority is either acting unreasonably or failing to carry out its duty. The power is established by ss 68 and s 99 of the Education Act 1944. An alternative may be to complain to the Local Government Ombudsman.

If the Secretary of State agrees with the complaint, he may direct the school or local education authority to put matters right. If the parents are still not satisfied, they can apply to the High Court for judicial review of the decision of the local education authority.

13.2   JUDICIAL REVIEW

As with matters covered in Chapter 12, this is not the appropriate place to set out a detailed exposition on the law relating to judicial review. It is, however, a very important part of administrative law and there are several good books written on the subject.[7] All that is intended to be given in this section is a thumbnail sketch of what steps need to be taken. Anyone wishing to apply for judicial review of a decision of a local authority should take advice from a solicitor or the Citizens Advice Bureau.

An application for judicial review is governed by Ord 53[8] and can only be brought if the leave of the court has been obtained. It is necessary, therefore, to apply for leave.[9]

---

6 See **8.4**.
7 For example, Aldous and Alder *Applications for Judicial Review: Law and Practice of the Crown Office*, 2nd edn (Butterworths, 1993).
8 Rules of the Supreme Court 1965.
9 See Ord 53, r 3.

This is achieved by filing at the Crown Office a notice in form 86A which will contain the name and description of the applicant, the relief sought and the grounds upon which it was sought, the name and address of the applicant's solicitors (if any) and the applicant's address for service.[10] In addition, an affidavit verifying the facts relied on must be filed at the same time.[11]

The judge may determine the application without a hearing and if the application is refused by the judge without a hearing or granted on terms, the applicant can renew it by applying to a judge in open court.[12] The application to renew it has to be made within 10 days of being served with the notice of the judge's refusal and such notice of intention to renew has to be lodged on form 86B.[13]

The court will not grant leave unless it considers that the applicant has a sufficient interest in the matter to which the application relates and, if leave is granted, the court may impose such terms (as to costs and security) as it thinks fit.[14] An application for leave to apply for judicial review has to be made promptly but in any event within 3 months from the date when grounds for the application arose. The court does have power to extend the time-limit if there is good reason but an extension will not normally be granted.[15]

Although judicial review is outside the scope of the Tribunal's normal appeal procedure, it has not stopped two attempts to challenge the decision of the Special Educational Needs Tribunal. The first case, *R v Special Educational Needs Tribunal ex parte F*,[16] concerned a severely handicapped 7-year-old child. Leave was given ex parte to challenge a Tribunal decision. It is not clear whether the leave was given with or without a hearing. The Tribunal applied to set aside the leave[17] on the grounds that first, any appeal should have been brought using the statutory procedure under Ord 55[18] and, secondly, that the Tribunal was not the proper respondent to a statutory appeal, although it was to a judicial review. There has to be a query about the accuracy of the first part of this second ground in light of the decision in *S and C v Special Educational Needs Tribunal*.

Mr Justice Popplewell held that any appeal should have been brought under the Ord 55 (statutory) procedure and so set aside the leave previously granted to bring an application for judicial review. The judge stated that, save in exceptional circumstances (which he did not apply in this case), judicial review would not be granted where a statutory right of appeal existed and had not been exercised.

---

10 Order 53, r 3(2)(a).

11 Order 53, r 3(2)(b).

12 Order 53, r 3(3) and (4).

13 Order 53, r 3(5).

14 Order 53, r 3(7) and (9).

15 Order 53, r 4.

16 (Unreported), Crown Office, 11 October 1995.

17 Applying the procedure in the notes to Ord 53 at 53/1–14/34 of the Rules of the Supreme Court 1965.

18 See Chapter 12.

The second case to consider the use of judicial review proceedings was *R v Special Educational Needs Tribunal, ex parte South Glamorgan County Council.*[19] Mr Justice Turner granted leave to apply for judicial review to South Glamorgan County Council at a hearing at which it was decided by the Treasury solicitors that there was no need for the Tribunal to be represented. Instead, they wrote to the court drawing attention to the decision of *S v Special Educational Needs Tribunal and the City of Westminster* and *ex parte F* (discussed above), suggesting that the correct route for challenging the Tribunal's decision was by way of appeal under Ord 55. The Tribunal applied to set aside the leave but this was refused. The Tribunal then appealed the refusal of Mr Justice Turner to set aside the leave to the Court of Appeal. The Court of Appeal unanimously allowed the appeal and set aside the leave. It was referred to *R v Inland Revenue Commissioners, ex parte Preston*[20] in which Lord Templeman said that the 'judicial review process should not be allowed to supplant the normal statutory appeal procedure' and *R v Secretary of State for the Home Department ex parte Swati*[21] in which it was said that '... where Parliament provides an appeal procedure, judicial review will have no place, unless the applicant can distinguish his case from the type of case for which the appeal procedure was provided' and 'the process of judicial review is not appropriate for a purely factual challenge'.

The Court of Appeal was also made aware by the Tribunal that the provisions of Ord 55 were wider than those of Ord 53. Particular reference was made to r 3(1), which provided that the appeal should be by way of re-hearing, to the court's power under r 7(2) to receive further evidence and make directions for oral evidence and affidavits, and to the court's ability under r 7(5) to make any order which ought to have been made by the Tribunal.

Once leave has been granted, an application for judicial review has to be made by originating motion. This has to be served on all persons directly affected within 14 days of the grant of leave to apply. In addition to the notice of motion, an affidavit giving details of the names and addresses of (and the places and dates of service on) all persons served.[22] Also, the statement in support of the application for leave must be served although the court can allow it to be amended. If the applicant either intends to amend his statement or use further affidavits, he must give notice of that intention and any proposed amendments to the other party.[23]

The court at the hearing of the application for judicial review may quash the decision of the local education authority (by an order of certiorari) where the authority acted without jurisdiction or exceeded its authority, or failed to comply with the rules of natural justice (where those rules are applicable), or where there is an error of law on the face of the record or the decision is unreasonable.[24] The latter point may be the best one to rely upon.

---

19 First instance decision is unreported, but the Court of Appeal decision is reported at [1995] TLR 669.
20 [1985] AC 835 at p 862.
21 [1986] 1 WLR 477.
22 Order 53, r 5.
23 Order 53, r 6(3).
24 Notes to Ord 53 at 53/1–14/6.

The test was established in *Associated Provincial Picture Houses Ltd v Wednesbury Corporation*[25] and is known as the *Wednesbury* principle. This is that a decision of the local education authority will be quashed or otherwise dealt with in judicial review proceedings where the court concludes that the decision taken by the authority is such that no body properly directing itself on the relevant law and acting reasonably could have reached that decision. It is possible to appeal to the Court of Appeal from a decision of the court on an application for judicial review, although leave is required.[26]

Anyone considering applying for judicial review is strongly urged to look at the notes to Ord 53 as they not only clearly set out the stages to go through and a table of points but also give details of what to include in any bundles to be submitted to the court. They also contain a commentary on the scope of judicial review, when it is available and the types of relief available.

13.3 EDUCATION APPEAL COMMITTEES

These committees hear appeals against the decisions of local education authorities (and the governors of voluntary aided schools) relating to school admissions[27] and appeals over the permanent exclusion of a child from a school.[28] It has been noted that the Council on Tribunals favours the transfer of appeals relating to the exclusion of a child to the Special Educational Needs Tribunal.[29] However, that has not yet occurred and so those appeals are still outside the Tribunal's jurisdiction.

Admission appeals are not easy to categorise as one has to balance the ability of a parent to express a preference for a particular school[30] with criteria used by local education authorities (or voluntary aided school governors) to restrict that choice. In addition, grant-maintained schools have to establish their own admission appeal system as they are responsible for their own admission policy.

The exclusion appeals deal solely with permanent exclusions. Since most exclusions at schools are for a fixed period (a certain number of days) this ought not to be a frequent occurrence. However, since indefinite period exclusions have been abolished,[31] the number of these appeals may grow as schools begin to feel that they have no alternative but to exclude permanently children who cannot be dealt with in any other way.

---

25 [1948] KB 223.

26 See notes to Ord 53 at 53/1–14/9.

27 Education Act 1990, s 7.

28 Education (No 2) Act 1986, s 26 and Sch 3.

29 By Dr Neville Harris, Reader in Law at Liverpool University, in an article entitled 'Access to justice for parents and children over schooling decisions – the role and reform of education tribunals' (1995) *Child and Family Law Quarterly* vol 7, no 3, p 81.

30 Education Act 1980, s 6(1).

31 Education Act 1993, s 261.

13.4   LOCAL GOVERNMENT OMBUDSMAN

The Commissioner for Local Administration, more familiarly called the Local Government Ombudsman, investigates complaints against a number of different types of authorities (including local educational authorities) when a complainant believes that he has been unfairly treated to the extent that he has suffered injustice through maladministration.[32]

Maladministration can occur when a local authority does something the wrong way, does something it should not have done or fails to do something it should have done. A leaflet is produced by the Local Government Ombudsman[33] and gives examples of maladministration as being such things as unreasonable delay, muddle, bias, failure to follow proper procedures and a decision badly made. The Ombudsman cannot question what a council should have done simply because someone does not agree with the local authority. Before a complaint is made, however, the local authority must be given a chance to deal with it. A letter to the education department or the authority's chief executive to discover the authority's complaints procedure is the first step. If the complainant is not satisfied by the action taken by the authority (or if the authority takes no action) a councillor should be asked to look into the matter but, likewise, if no action is taken or the matter is not dealt with satisfactorily, a complaint can be made to the Ombudsman. The complaint must be in writing and is usually made on a form which can be found at the end of the leaflet produced by the Local Government Ombudsman.

There are, however, limits on what the Local Government Ombudsman can investigate. The Ombudsman cannot, for example (but not exclusively), investigate matters which have been known about for at least one year; matters which have already been the subject of an application to a court, tribunal or a government minister or are capable of so being; or the internal affairs of schools.[34]

The Ombudsman has investigated a number of complaints on behalf of children with special educational needs even though an application for judicial review had or would have had a good prospect of success. However, maladministration causing injustice to children with special educational needs could give rise to court proceedings and hence fall outside the Ombudsman's remit. For example, if the actions (or lack of them) of professionals employed by a local authority have resulted in negligence, the parents can bring a claim for damages.

In *X (Minors) v Bedfordshire County Council*,[35] for example, the House of Lords decided that where a local authority offered a service (such as an educational psychology service) it had a duty of care to those using the service to exercise care in its conduct. In addition, where a head teacher or advisory teacher gave advice to the

---

32 The Local Government Ombudsman was established by s 23 of the Local Government Act 1974 (c 7). His powers of investigation are conferred by s 26.

33 The leaflet is entitled 'How to complain to the Local Government Ombudsman' and is available from each of the four offices covering various parts of England and Wales. The address can be found in Appendix 8.

34 See s 26(6) of and para 5(2) of Sch 5 to the Local Government Act 1974.

35 [1995] 3 WLR 153, [1995] ELR 404.

parent of a child, that person had to exercise the skill and care of a reasonable teacher.

A complaint to the Local Government Ombudsman is not a short process. Once the complaint is received, if it cannot be investigated because it is excluded for whatever reason, the Ombudsman will explain why he cannot investigate the matter. If, however, it can be investigated, a copy of the complaint is sent to the local authority for its comments. In many cases that is the end of the matter, but some investigations can take several months and may result in a formal report being issued. Because the formal report will not use the complainant's real name, as it sets out in detail not only the legal basis of the complaint but also the factual background, a fictitious name will need to be used.

If a formal report is issued, the local authority has to make it available for public inspection and tell the Ombudsman what it intends to do about it. Usually, the grievance is remedied and may even include the payment of some level of compensation, although there is no power given to the Ombudsman to order payment. However, if the local authority does not tell the Ombudsman what it proposes to do in a reasonable time, or the Ombudsman is not satisfied with the authority's intended action, or the Ombudsman does not receive confirmation from the authority in a reasonable time that it has taken the proposed action, the Local Government Ombudsman will prepare a further report.

APPENDICES

Appendix 1

EDUCATION ACT 1993

PART III

CHILDREN WITH SPECIAL EDUCATIONAL NEEDS

Introductory

156 Meaning of 'special educational needs' and 'special educational provision' etc

(1) For the purposes of the Education Acts, a child has 'special educational needs' if he has a learning difficulty which calls for special educational provision to be made for him.

(2) For the purposes of this Act, subject to subsection (3) below, a child has a 'learning difficulty' if—

  (a) he has a significantly greater difficulty in learning than the majority of children of his age,

  (b) he has a disability which either prevents or hinders him from making use of educational facilities of a kind generally provided for children of his age in schools within the area of the local education authority, or

  (c) he is under the age of five years and is, or would be if special educational provision were not made for him, likely to fall within paragraph (a) or (b) when over that age.

(3) A child is not to be taken as having a learning difficulty solely because the language (or form of the language) in which he is, or will be, taught is different from a language (or form of a language) which has at any time been spoken in his home.

(4) In the Education Acts, 'special educational provision' means—

  (a) in relation to a child who has attained the age of two years, educational provision which is additional to, or otherwise different from, the educational provision made generally for children of his age in schools maintained by the local education authority (other than special schools) or grant-maintained schools in their area, and

  (b) in relation to a child under that age, educational provision of any kind.

(5) In this Part of this Act, 'child' includes any person who has not attained the age of nineteen years and is a registered pupil at a school.

Code of practice

157 Code of Practice

(1) The Secretary of State shall issue, and may from time to time revise, a code of practice giving practical guidance in respect of the discharge by local education authorities and the governing bodies of maintained or grant-maintained schools, or grant-maintained special schools, of their functions under this Part of this Act.

(2) It shall be the duty of—

(a) local education authorities, and such governing bodies, exercising functions under this Part of this Act, and

(b) any other person exercising any function for the purpose of the discharge by local education authorities, and such governing bodies, of functions under this Part of this Act,

to have regard to the provision of the code.

(3) On any appeal, the Tribunal shall have regard to any provision of the code which appears to the Tribunal to be relevant to any question arising on the appeal.

(4) The Secretary of State shall publish the code as for the time being in force.

158 Making and approval of code

(1) Where the Secretary of State proposes to issue or revise a code of practice, he shall prepare a draft of the code (or revised code).

(2) The Secretary of State shall consult such persons about the draft as he thinks fit and shall consider any representations made by them.

(3) If he determines to proceed with the draft (either in its original form or with such modifications as he thinks fit) he shall lay it before both Houses of Parliament.

(4) If the draft is approved by resolution of each House, the Secretary of State shall issue the code in the form of the draft and the code shall come into effect on such day as the Secretary of State may by order appoint.

Special educational provision: general

159 Review of arrangements

A local education authority shall keep under review the arrangements made by them for special educational provision and, in doing so, shall, to the extent that it appears necessary or desirable for the purpose of co-ordinating provision for children with special educational needs, consult the funding authority and the governing bodies of county, voluntary, maintained special and grant-maintained schools in their area.

160 Qualified duty to secure education of children with special educational needs in ordinary schools

(1) Any person exercising any functions under this Part of this Act in respect of a child with special educational needs who should be educated in a school shall secure that, if the conditions mentioned in subsection (2) below are satisfied, the child is educated in a school which is not a special school unless that is incompatible with the wishes of his parent.

(2) The conditions are that educating the child in a school which is not a special school is compatible with—

(a) his receiving the special educational provision which his learning difficulty calls for,

(b) the provision of efficient education for the children with whom he will be educated, and

(c) the efficient use of resources.

161 Duties of governing body etc in relation to pupils with special educational needs

(1) The governing body, in the case of a county, voluntary or grant-maintained school, and the local education authority, in the case of a maintained nursery school shall—

(a) use their best endeavours, in exercising their functions in relation to the school, to secure that if any registered pupil has special educational needs the special educational provision which his learning difficulty calls for is made,

(b) secure that, where the responsible person has been informed by the local education authority that a registered pupil has special educational needs, those needs are made known to all who are likely to teach him, and

(c) secure that the teachers in the school are aware of the importance of identifying, and providing for, those registered pupils who have special educational needs.

(2) In subsection (1)(b) above, 'the responsible person' means—

(a) in the case of a county, voluntary or grant-maintained school, the head teacher or the appropriate governer (that is, the chairman of the governing body or, where the governing body have designated another governor for the purposes of this paragraph, that other governor), and

(b) in the case of a nursery school, the head teacher.

(3) To the extent that it appears necessary or desirable for the purpose of co-ordinating provision for children with special educational needs—

(a) the governing bodies of county, voluntary and grant-maintained schools shall, in exercising functions relating to the provision for such children, consult the local education authority, the funding authority and the governing bodies of other such schools, and

(b) in relation to maintained nursery schools, the local education authority shall, in exercising those functions, consult the funding authority and the governing bodies of county, voluntary and grant-maintained schools.

(4) Where a child who has special educational needs is being educated in a county, voluntary or grant-maintained school or a maintained nursery school, those concerned with making special educational provision for the child shall secure, so far as is reasonably practicable and is compatible with—

(a) the child receiving the special educational provision which his learning difficulty calls for,

(b) the provision of efficient education for the children with whom he will be educated, and

(c) the efficient use of resources,

that the child engages in the activities of the school together with children who do not have special educational needs.

(5) The annual report for each county, voluntary, maintained special or grant-maintained school shall include a report containing such information as may be prescribed about the implementation of the governing body's policy for pupils with special educational needs; and in this subsection 'annual report' means the report prepared under the articles of government for the school in accordance with section 30 of the Education (No 2) Act 1986 or, as the case may be, paragraph 8 of Schedule 6 to this Act.

162 Provision of goods and services in connection with special educational needs

(1) A local education authority may for the purpose only of assisting—

(a) the governing bodies of county, voluntary or grant-maintained schools in their or any other area in the performance of the governing bodies' duties under section 161(1)(a) of this Act, or

(b) the governing bodies of maintained or grant-maintained special schools in their or any other area in the performance of the governing bodies' duties,

supply goods or services to them.

(2) The terms on which goods or services are supplied by local education authorities to the governing bodies of grant-maintained schools or grant-maintained special schools, or to the governing bodies of county, voluntary or maintained special schools in any other area, under this section may, in such circumstances as may be prescribed, include such terms as to payment as may be prescribed.

(3) This section is without prejudice to the generality of any other power of local education authorities to supply goods or services.

163 Special educational provision otherwise than in schools

(1) Where a local education authority are satisfied that it would be inappropriate for the special educational provision (or any part of the special educational provision) which a learning difficulty of a child in their area calls for to be made in a school, they may arrange for the provision (or, as the case may be, for that part of it) to be made otherwise than in a school.

(2) Before making an arrangement under this section, a local education authority shall consult the child's parent.

164 Provision outside England and Wales for certain children

(1) A local education authority may make such arrangements as they think fit to enable a child for whom they maintain a statement under section 168 of this Act to attend an institution outside England and Wales which specialises in providing for children with special needs.

(2) In subsection (1) above, 'children with special needs' means children who have particular needs which would be special educational needs if those children were in England and Wales.

(3) Where a local education authority make arrangements under this section in respect of a child, those arrangements may in particular include contributing to or paying—

(a) fees charged by the institution,

(b) expenses reasonably incurred in maintaining him while he is at the institution or travelling to or from it,

(c) his travelling expenses, and

(d) expenses reasonably incurred by any person accompanying him while he is travelling or staying at the institution.

(4) This section is without prejudice to any other powers of a local education authority.

Identification and assessment of children with special educational needs

165 General duty of local education authority towards children for whom they are responsible

(1) A local education authority shall exercise their powers with a view to securing that, of the children for whom they are responsible, they identify those to whom subsection (2) below applies.

(2) This subsection applies to a child if—

    (a)   he has special educational needs, and

    (b)   it is necessary for the authority to determine the special educational provision which any learning difficulty he may have calls for.

(3) For the purposes of this Part of this Act, a local education authority are responsible for a child if he is in their area and—

    (a)   he is a registered pupil at a maintained, grant-maintained or grant-maintained special school,

    (b)   education is provided for him at a school which is not a maintained, grant-maintained or grant-maintained special school at the expense of the authority or the funding authority,

    (c)   he does not come within paragraph (a) or (b) above but is a registered pupil at a school and has been brought to the authority's attention as having (or probably having) special educational needs, or

    (d)   he is not a registered pupil at a school, is not under the age of two years or over compulsory school age and has been been brought to their attention as having (or probably having) special educational needs.

166 Duty of Health Authority or local authority to help local education authority

(1) Where it appears to a local education authority that any Health Authority or local authority could, by taking any specified action, help in the exercise of any of their functions under this Part of this Act, they may request the help of the authority, specifying the action in question.

(2) An authority whose help is so requested shall comply with the request unless—

    (a)   they consider that the help requested is not necessary for the purpose of the exercise by the local education authority of those functions, or

    (b)   subsection (3) below applies.

(3) This subsection applies—

    (a)   in the case of a Health Authority, if that authority consider that, having regard to the resources available to them for the purpose of the exercise of their functions under the National Health Service Act 1977, it is not reasonable for them to comply with the request, or

    (b)   in the case of a local authority, if that authority consider that the request is not compatible with their own statutory or other duties and obligations or unduly prejudices the discharge of any of their functions.

(4) Regulations may provide that, where an authority are under a duty by virtue of subsection (2) above to comply with a request to help a local education authority in the making of an

assessment under section 167 of this Act or a statement under section 168 of this Act, they must, subject to prescribed exceptions, comply with the request within the prescribed period.

(5) In this section, 'local authority' means a county council, a metropolitan district council, a London borough council or the Common Council of the City of London.

### 167	Assessment of educational needs

(1) Where a local education authority are of the opinion that a child for whom they are responsible falls, or probably falls, within subsection (2) below, they shall serve a notice on the child's parent informing him—

(a)	that they propose to make an assessment of the child's educational needs,
(b)	of the procedure to be followed in making the assessment,
(c)	of the name of the officer of the authority from whom further information may be obtained, and
(d)	of the parent's right to make representations, and submit written evidence, to the authority within such period (which shall not be less than twenty-nine days beginning with the date on which the notice is served) as may be specified in the notice.

(2) A child falls within this subsection if—

(a)	he has special educational needs, and
(b)	it is necessary for the authority to determine the special educational provision which any learning difficulty he may have calls for.

(3) Where—

(a)	a local education authority have served a notice under subsection (1) above and the period specified in the notice in accordance with subsection (1)(d) above has expired, and
(b)	the authority remain of the opinion, after taking into account any representations made and any evidence submitted to them in response to the notice, that the child falls, or probably falls, within subsection (2) above,

they shall make an assessment of his educational needs.

(4) Where a local education authority decide to make an assessment under this section, they shall give notice in writing to the child's parent of that decision and of their reasons for making it.

(5) Schedule 9 to this Act (which makes provision in relation to the making of assessments under this section) shall have effect.

(6) Where, at any time after serving a notice under subsection (1) above, a local education authority decide not to assess the educational needs of the child concerned they shall give notice in writing to the child's parent of their decision.

### 168	Statement of special educational needs

(1) If, in the light of an assessment under section 167 of this Act of any child's educational needs and of any representations made by the child's parent in pursuance of Schedule 10 to this Act, it is necessary for the local education authority to determine the special educational provision which any learning difficulty he may have calls for, the authority shall make and maintain a statement of his special educational needs.

(2) The statement shall be in such form and contain such information as may be prescribed.

(3) In particular, the statement shall—

    (a)   give details of the authority's assessment of the child's special educational needs, and

    (b)   specify the special educational provision to be made for the purpose of meeting those needs, including the particulars required by subsection (4) below.

(4) The statement shall—

    (a)   specify the type of school or other institution which the local education authority consider would be appropriate for the child,

    (b)   if they are not required under Schedule 10 to this Act to specify the name of any school in the statement, specify the name of any school or institution (whether in the United Kingdom or elsewhere) which they consider would be appropriate for the child and should be specified in the statement, and

    (c)   specify any provision for the child for which they make arrangements under section 163 of this Act and which they consider should be specified in the statement.

(5) Where a local education authority maintain a statement under this section—

    (a)   unless the child's parent has made suitable arrangements, the authority—

        (i)   shall arrange that the special educational provision specified in the statement is made for the child, and

        (ii)   may arrange that any non-educational provision specified in the statement is made for him in such manner as they consider appropriate, and

    (b)   if the name of maintained, grant-maintained or grant-maintained special school is specified in the statement, the governing body of the school shall admit the child to the school.

(6) Subsection (5)(b) above does not affect any power to exclude from a school a pupil who is already a registered pupil there.

(7) Schedule 10 to this Act (which makes provision in relation to the making and maintenance of statements under this section) shall have effect.

169   Appeal against decision not to make statement

(1) If, after making an assessment under section 167 of this Act of the educational needs of any child for whom no statement is maintained under section 168 of this Act, the local educational authority do not propose to make such a statement, they shall give notice in writing of their decision, and of the effect of subsection (2) below, to the child's parent.

(2) In such a case, the child's parent may appeal to the Tribunal against the decision.

(3) On an appeal under this section, the Tribunal may—

    (a)   dismiss the appeal,

    (b)   order the local education authority to make and maintain such a statement, or

    (c)   remit the case to the authority for them to reconsider whether, having regard to any observations made by the Tribunal, it is necessary for the authority to determine the special educational provision which any learning difficulty the child may have calls for.

170   Appeal against contents of statement

(1) The parent of a child for whom a local education authority maintain a statement under section 168 of this Act may—

(a) when the statement is first made,

(b) where the description in the statement of the authority's assessment of the child's special educational needs, or the special educational provision specified in the statement, is amended, or

(c) where, after conducting an assessment of the educational needs of the child under section 167 of this Act, the local education authority determine not to amend the statement,

appeal to the Tribunal against the description in the statement of the authority's assessment of the child's special educational needs, the special educational provision specified in the statement or, if no school is named in the statement, that fact.

(2) Subsection (1)(b) above does not apply where the amendment is made in pursuance of paragraph 8 or 11(3)(b) of Schedule 10 to this Act or directions under section 197 of this Act; and subsection (1)(c) above does not apply to a determination made following the service of notice under paragraph 10 of Schedule 10 to this Act of a proposal to amend the statement.

(3) On appeal under this section, the Tribunal may—

(a) dismiss the appeal,

(b) order the authority to amend the statement, so far as it describes the authority's assessment of the child's special educational needs or specifies the special educational provision, and make such other consequential amendments to the statement as the Tribunal think fit, or

(c) order the authority to cease to maintain the statement.

(4) On an appeal under this section the Tribunal shall not order the local education authority to specify the name of any school in the statement (either in substitution for an existing name or in a case where no school is named) unless—

(a) the parent has expressed a preference for the school in pursuance of arrangements under paragaph 3 of Schedule 10 to this Act, or

(b) in the proceedings the parent, the local education authority or both have proposed the school.

(5) Before determining any appeal under this section the Tribunal may, with the agreement of the parties, correct any deficiency in the statement.

171 Access for local education authority to certain schools

(1) This section applies where—

(a) a local education authority maintain a statement for a child under section 168 of this Act, and

(b) in pursuance of the statement education is provided for the child at—

(i) a school maintained by another local education authority,

(ii) a grant-maintained school, or

(iii) a grant-maintained special school.

(2) Any person authorised by the local education authority shall be entitled to have access at any reasonable time to the premises of any such school for the purpose of monitoring the special educational provision made in pursuance of the statement for the child at the school.

172 Reviews of educational needs

(1) Regulations may prescribe the frequency with which assessments under section 167 of this Act are to be repeated in respect of children for whom statements are maintained under section 168 of this Act.

(2) Where—

- (a) the parent of a child for whom a statement is maintained under section 168 of this Act asks the local education authority to arrange for an assessment to be made in respect of the child under section 167 of this Act,
- (b) such an assessment has not been made within the period of six months ending with the date on which the request is made, and
- (c) it is necessary for the authority to make a further assessment under that section,

the authority shall comply with the request.

(3) If in any case where subsection (2)(a) and (b) above applies the authority determine not to comply with the request—

- (a) they shall give notice of that fact and of the effect of paragraph (b) below to the child's parent, and
- (b) the parent may appeal to the Tribunal against the determination.

(4) On an appeal under subsection (3) above the Tribunal may—

- (a) dismiss the appeal, or
- (b) order the authority to arrange for an assessment to be made in respect of the child under section 167 of this Act.

(5) A statement under section 168 of this Act shall be reviewed by the local education authority—

- (a) on the making of an assessment in respect of the child concerned under section 167 of this Act, and
- (b) in any event, within the period of twelve months beginning with the making of the statement or, as the case may be, with the previous review.

(6) Regulations may make provision—

- (a) as to the manner in which reviews of such statements are to be conducted,
- (b) as to the participation in such reviews of such persons as may be prescribed, and
- (c) in connection with such other matters relating to such reviews as the Secretary of State considers appropriate.

173 Assessment of educational needs at request of child's parent

(1) Where—

- (a) the parent of a child for whom a local education authority are responsible but for whom no statement is maintained under section 168 of this Act asks the authority to arrange for an assessment to be made in respect of the child under section 167 of this Act,
- (b) such an assessment has not been made within the period of six months ending with the date on which the request is made, and
- (c) it is necessary for the authority to make an assessment under that section,

the authority shall comply with the request.

(2) If in any case where subsection (1)(a) and (b) above applies the authority determine not to comply with the request—

(a)   they shall give notice of that fact and of the effect of paragraph (b) below to the child's parent, and

(b)   the parent may appeal to the Tribunal against the determination.

(3) On an appeal under subsection (2) above the Tribunal may—

(a)   dismiss the appeal, or

(b)   order the authority to arrange for an assessment to be made in respect of the child under section 167 of this Act.

174   Assessment of educational needs at request of governing body of grant-maintained school

(1) Where in the case of a child for whom a local education authority are responsible but for whom no statement is maintained under section 168 of this Act—

(a)   a grant-maintained school is specified in a direction in respect of the child under section 13 of this Act,

(b)   the governing body of the school ask the authority to arrange for an assessment to be made in respect of the child under section 167 of this Act, and

(c)   such an assessment has not been made within the period of six months ending with the date on which the request is made,

the local education authority shall serve a notice under subsection (2) below on the child's parent.

(2) The notice shall inform the child's parent—

(a)   that the local education authority propose to make an assessment of the child's educational needs,

(b)   of the procedure to be followed in making the assessment,

(c)   of the name of the officer of the authority from whom further information may be obtained, and

(d)   of the parent's right to make representations, and submit written evidence, to the authority within such period (which shall not be less than twenty-nine days beginning with the date on which the notice is served) as may be specified in the notice.

(3) Where—

(a)   a local education authority have served a notice under subsection (2) above and the period specified in the notice in accordance with subsection (2)(d) above has expired, and

(b)   the authority are of the opinion, after taking into account any representations made and any evidence submitted to them in response to the notice, that the child falls, or probably falls, within subsection (4) below,

they shall make an assessment of his educational needs under section 167 of this Act.

(4) A child falls within this subsection if—

(a)   he has special educational needs, and

(b)   it is necessary to determine the special educational provision which any learning difficulty he may have calls for.

(5) Where a local education authority decide in pursuance of this section to make an assessment under that section, they shall give notice in writing to the child's parent, and to the governing body of the grant-maintained school, of that decision and of their reasons for making it.

(6) Where, at any time after serving a notice under subsection (2) above, a local education authority decide not to assess the educational needs of the child concerned, they shall give notice in writing to the child's parent and to the governing body of the grant-maintained school of their decision.

175 Assessment of educational needs of children under two

(1) Where a local education authority are of the opinion that a child in their area who is under the age of two years falls, or probably falls, within subsection (2) below—

    (a)   they may, with the consent of his parent, make an assessment of the child's educational needs, and

    (b)   they shall make such an assessment at the request of his parent.

(2) A child falls within this subsection if—

    (a)   he has special educational needs, and

    (b)   it is necessary for the authority to determine the special educational provision which any learning difficulty he may have calls for.

(3) An assessment under this section shall be made in such manner as the authority consider appropriate.

(4) After making an assessment under this section, the authority—

    (a)   may make a statement of the child's special educational needs, and

    (b)   may maintain that statement,

in such manner as they consider appropriate.

176 Duty of Health Authority or National Health Service trust to notify parent etc

(1) This section applies where a Health Authority or a National Health Service trust, in the course of exercising any of their functions in relation to a child who is under the age of five years, form the opinion that he has (or probably has) special educational needs.

(2) The Health Authority or trust shall—

    (a)   inform the child's parent of their opinion and of their duty under this section, and

    (b)   after giving the parent an opportunity to discuss that opinion with an officer of the Health Authority or trust, bring it to the attention of the appropriate local education authority.

(3) If the Health Authority or trust are of the opinion that a particular voluntary organisation is likely to be able to give the parent advice or assistance in connection with any special educational needs that the child may have, they shall inform the parent accordingly.

Special Educational Needs Tribunal

177 Constitution of Tribunal

(1) There shall be established a tribunal, to be known as the Special Educational Needs Tribunal (referred to in this Part of this Act as 'the Tribunal'), to exercise the jurisdiction conferred on it by this Part of this Act.

(2) There shall be appointed—

    (a)   a President of the Tribunal (referred to in this Part of this Act as 'the President'),

    (b)   a panel of persons (referred to in this Part of this Act as 'the chairmen's panel') who may serve as chairman of the Tribunal, and

    (c)   a panel of persons (referred to in this Part of this Act as 'the lay panel') who may serve as the other two members of the Tribunal apart from the chairman.

(3) The President and the members of the chairmen's panel shall each be appointed by the Lord Chancellor.

(4) The members of the lay panel shall each be appointed by the Secretary of State.

(5) Regulations may—

    (a)   provide for the jurisdiction of the Tribunal to be exercised by such number of tribunals as may be determined from time to time by the President, and

    (b)   make such other provision in connection with the establishment and continuation of the Tribunal as the Secretary of State considers necessary or desirable.

(6) The Secretary of State may, with the consent of the Treasury, provide such staff and accommodation as the Tribunal may require.

178 The President and members of the panels

(1) No person may be appointed President or member of the chairmen's panel unless he has a seven year general qualification (within the meaning of section 71 of the Courts and Legal Services Act 1990).

(2) No person may be appointed member of the lay panel unless he satisfies such requirements as may be prescribed.

(3) If, in the opinion of the Lord Chancellor, the President is unfit to continue in office or is incapable of performing his duties, the Lord Chancellor may revoke his appointment.

(4) Each member of the chairmen's panel or lay panel shall hold and vacate office under the terms of the instrument under which he is appointed.

(5) The President or a member of the chairmen's panel or lay panel—

    (a)   may resign office by notice in writing to the Lord Chancellor or (as the case may be) the Secretary of State, and

    (b)   is eligible for re-appointment if he ceases to hold office.

179 Remuneration and expenses

(1) The Secretary of State may pay to the President, and to any other person in respect of his service as a member of the Tribunal, such remuneration and allowances as he may, with the consent of the Treasury, determine.

(2) The Secretary of State may defray the expenses of the Tribunal to such amount as he may, with the consent of the Treasury, determine.

180 Tribunal procedure

(1) Regulations may make provision about the proceedings of the Tribunal on an appeal under this Part of this Act and the initiation of such an appeal.

(2) The regulations may, in particular, include provision—

(a) as to the period within which, and the manner in which, appeals are to be instituted.
(b) where the jurisdiction of the Tribunal is being exercised by more than one tribunal—

    (i) for determining by which tribunal any appeal is to be heard, and
    (ii) for the transfer of proceedings from one tribunal to another,

(c) for enabling any functions which related to matters preliminary or incidental to an appeal to be performed by the President, or by the chairman,
(d) for the holding of hearings in private in prescribed circumstances,
(e) for hearings to be conducted in the absence of any member, other than the chairman,
(f) as to the persons who may appear on behalf of the parties,
(g) for granting any person such discovery or inspection of documents or right to further particulars as might be granted by a county court,
(h) requiring persons to attend to give evidence and produce documents,
(i) for authorising the administration of oaths to witnesses,
(j) for the determination of appeals without a hearing in prescribed circumstances,
(k) as to the withdrawal of appeals,
(l) for the award of costs or expenses,
(m) for taxing or otherwise settling any such costs or expenses (and, in particular, for enabling such costs to be taxed in the county court),
(n) for the registration and proof of decisions and orders, and
(o) for enabling the Tribunal to review its decisions, or revoke or vary its orders, in such circumstances as may be determined in accordance with the regulations.

(3) The Secretary of State may pay such allowances for the purpose of or in connection with the attendance of persons at the Tribunal as he may with the consent of the Treasury determine.

(4) The Arbitration Act 1950 shall not apply to any proceedings before the Tribunal but regulations may make provision corresponding to any provision of that Act.

(5) Any person who without reasonable excuse fails to comply with—

(a) any requirement in respect of the discovery or inspection of documents imposed by the regulations by virtue of subsection (2)(g) above, or
(b) any requirement imposed by the regulations by virtue of subsection (2)(h) above,

is guilty of an offence.

(6) A person guilty of an offence under subsection (5) above is liable on summary conviction to a fine not exceeding level 3 on the standard scale.

181 Supervision of and appeals from Tribunal

(1) In paragraph 15 of Part I of Schedule 1 to the Tribunals and Inquiries Act 1992 (tribunals under direct supervision of Council on Tribunals), after subparagraph (d) there is inserted—

'(e)   the Special Educational Needs Tribunal constituted under section 177 of the Education Act 1993'.

(2) In section 11(1) of that Act (appeals from certain tribunals), for '15(a) or (d)' there is substituted '15(a), (d) or (e)'.

Special schools and independent schools

182   Special schools

(1) A school which is specially organised to make special educational provision for pupils with special educational needs and is for the time being approved by the Secretary of State under section 188 of this Act shall be known as a special school.

(2) A special school maintained by a local education authority shall be known as a maintained special school.

(3) A special school conducted by a governing body incorporated in pursuance of proposals for the purpose—

(a)   made by the funding authority under section 183 of this Act, or
(b)   made under section 186 of this Act,

shall be known as a grant-maintained special school.

(4) Schedule 11 to this Act (which provides for the government and conduct of grant-maintained special schools) shall have effect.

183   Establishment, etc of maintained or grant-maintained special schools

(1) The funding authority may etablish in the area of any local education authority a school which is specially organised to make special educational provision for pupils with special educational needs if—

(a)   an order under section 12(1) of this Act applies to the area, and
(b)   the school is intended to provide relevant education for pupils in the area, whether or not it also provides other education or education for pupils from outside the area.

(2) Where a local education authority intend—

(a)   to establish a school which is specially organised to make special educational provision for pupils with special educational needs,
(b)   to make any prescribed alteration to a maintained special school, or
(c)   to discontinue such a school,

they shall serve under subsection (6) below notice of their proposals.

(3) Where the funding authority—

(a)   intend to establish a school which is specially organised to make special educational provision for pupils with special educational needs,
(b)   are of the opinion that any prescribed alteration should be made to a grant-maintained special school, or
(c)   are of the opinion that such a school should be discontinued,

and an order under section 12(1) of this Act applies to the area concerned, they shall serve under subsection (6) below notice of their proposals.

(4) Where the governing body of a grant-maintained special school intend—

    (a)   to make any prescribed alteration to the school, or

    (b)   to discontinue the school,

they shall serve under subsection (6) below notice of their proposals.

(5) Except in pursuance of proposals under this section approved under section 184 of this Act—

    (a)   a local education authority or the funding authority may not establish a school which is specially organised to make special educational provision for pupils with special educational needs,

    (b)   no prescribed alteration may be made to a maintained or grant-maintained special school, and

    (c)   a maintained or grant-maintained special school may not be discontinued.

(6) Notice for the purposes of subsections (2) to (4) above shall be served on—

    (a)   the Secretary of State, and

    (b)   such other persons as may be prescribed,

and shall give such information as may be prescribed.

(7) If the proposals are approved under section 184 of this Act, the body which served the notice or, in the case of proposals under subsection (3)(b) or (c) above, the governing body of the school shall implement them.

(8) If proposals under subsection (3)(a) above are so approved, a governing body of the school shall be incorporated on such date as may be specified in the proposals (referred to in this Part of this Act as the 'incorporation date').

(9) In relation to the establishment of a school in pursuance of proposals under subsection (3)(a) above, regulations may apply any provision of Chapter IV or V of Part II of this Act with or without modification.

(10) In this Part of this Act—

    (a)   references to the discontinuance of a maintained special school are to the local education authority ceasing to maintain it, and

    (b)   references to an alteration to a school include the transfer of the school to a new site.

184 Procedure for dealing with proposals

(1) Before a body serve notice of any proposals under section 183 of this Act they shall consult such persons as appear to them to be appropriate; and in discharging their duty under this subsection, the body shall have regard to any guidance given from time to time by the Secretary of State.

(2) Any person may, within such period (which shall not be less than two months beginning with the date on which the notice is served) as may be specified in the notice under that section, submit objections to the proposals to the body which served the notice.

(3) Within one month after the end of the period for making objections specified in the last notice to be served under that section, the body which served the notice shall transmit to the Secretary of State copies of all objections which have been duly made (and not withdrawn in writing), together with their observations on them.

(4) The Secretary of State may, after considering the proposals, any objections to the proposals and any observations on the objections, reject the proposals, approve them without modification or, after consulting the body which served notice of them and, in the case of proposals under section 183(3)(b) or (c) of this Act, the governing body, approve them with such modifications as he thinks desirable.

(5) The Secretary of State may modify any proposals required under section 183 of this Act to be implemented—

(a)   in the case of proposals under section 183(3)(b) or (c) of this Act—

    (i)   at the request of the governing body, or

    (ii)   at the request of the funding authority and after consulting the governing body, or

(b)   in any other case, at the request of the body which served notice of the proposals.

(6) References in this Part of this Act to proposals under section 183 of this Act, in any case where the Secretary of State has modified such proposals in pursuance of this section, are to the proposals as so modified.

(7) Service of a notice under that section which is sent by post in accordance with section 113 of the Education Act 1944 (notices) shall be taken to have been effected on the second day after the day on which the notice is posted.

185   Approval of premises of maintained or grant-maintained special schools

(1) Where a body serve under section 183(6) of this Act notice of proposals for the establishment of a school which is specially organised to make special educational provision for pupils with special educational needs, they shall submit to the Secretary of State the particulars in respect of the proposed premises of the school mentioned in subsection (3) below.

(2) Where a body serve under section 183(6) of this Act notice of proposals for making a prescribed alteration to a special school, they shall if the Secretary of State so directs submit to him the particulars in respect of the premises or proposed premises of the school mentioned in subsection (3) below.

(3) The particulars are—

(a)   particulars of the provision made or to be made in respect of the means of access to and within the premises or proposed premises of the school, and

(b)   such other particulars in respect of the premises or proposed premises of the school as the Secretary of State may require,

and they shall be submitted at such time and in such form and manner as the Secretary of State may direct.

(4) The particulars submitted under subsection (3)(a) above shall indicate the extent to which the provision referred to conforms with the minimum requirements, so far as they are relevant to school premises, of—

(a)   Design Note 18 'Access for Disabled People to Educational Buildings' published in 1984 on behalf of the Secretary of State, or

(b)   if that Note has been replaced by a document prescribed by regulations made or having effect as if made under the Town and Country Planning Act 1990, that document.

(5) Particulars submitted under this section in respect of the premises or proposed premises of the school require the approval of the Secretary of State.

(6) Where any proposals falling within subsection (1) or (2) above are required to be implemented, they shall be implemented in accordance with any particulars approved under this section.

186 Maintained special school becoming grant-maintained special school

(1) Regulations may make provision for maintained special schools, or any class or description of such schools, to cease to be maintained by the local education authority and become grant-maintained special schools.

(2) Regulations shall require, before a maintained special school becomes a grant-maintained special school in pursuance of the regulations—

- (a) the submission to the Secretary of State of proposals for the purpose by the governing body of the school, and
- (b) the approval of such proposals, as originally submitted or as modified by the Secretary of State (whether before or after they are approved).

(3) If the proposals are so approved, a governing body of the school shall be incorporated in accordance with Schedule 11 to this Act on the date of approval (referred to in this Part of this Act as the 'incorporation date').

(4) Regulations made for the purposes of this section may apply any provision of—

- (a) Chapter II, III or V of Part II of this Act,
- (b) section 184 of this Act, or
- (c) section 273 of this Act,

with or without modification.

187 Groups including grant-maintained special schools

(1) Regulations may modify the provisions of Chapter IX of Part II of this Act for the purpose of securing that—

- (a) two or more grant-maintained special schools, or one or more grant-maintained special schools together with one or more grant-maintained schools, may be conducted as a group by a single governing body,
- (b) a special school maintained by a local education authority may cease to be so maintained and may be conducted by a governing body incorporated under that Chapter, and
- (c) a grant-maintained special school may become a member of a group of schools conducted by such a governing body,

and that, were a group of schools including one or more special schools is conducted by such a governing body, the governing body are appropriately constituted.

(2) Regulations made for the purpose mentioned in subsection (1) above may modify sections 183 to 185 and 188 of this Act and Schedule 11 to this Act.

(3) Where that Chapter applies to special schools by virtue of regulations—

- (a) section 22(1) of this Act shall not be read as applying to such schools,
- (b) a special school conducted by a governing body incorporated under that Chapter shall be known as a grant-maintained special school, and

(c) references in Chapter I of Part V of this Act to a group of grant-maintained schools include a group of one or more grant-maintained special schools together with one or more grant-maintained schools.

188 Approval of special schools

(1) The Secretary of State may approve any school which is specially organised to make special educational provision for pupils with special educational needs, not being a maintained or grant-maintained school, and may give his approval before or after the school is established.

(2) Regulations may make provision as to the requirements which are to be complied with as a condition of approval under subsection (1) above.

(3) Any school which—

(a) is established in pursuance of proposals approved under section 184 of this Act, or
(b) immediately before the coming into force of this section, is a special school,

shall be treated, subject to subsection (4) below, as approved under this section.

(4) Regulations may make provision as to—

(a) the requirements which are to be complied with by a school while approved under this section, and
(b) the withdrawal of approval from a school (including approval treated as given under subsection (3) above) at the request of the proprietor or on the ground that there has been a failure to comply with any prescribed requirement.

(5) Without prejudice to the generality of subsections (2) and (4) above, the requirements which may be imposed by the regulations include requirements—

(a) which call for arrangements to be approved by the Secretary of State, or
(b) as to the organisation of any special school as a primary school or as a secondary school.

(6) Regulations shall make provision for securing that, so far as practicable, every pupil attending a special school—

(a) receives religious education and attends religious worship, or
(b) is withdrawn from receiving such education or from attendance at such worship in accordance with the wishes of his parent.

(7) Where approval is withdrawn from a maintained special school or grant-maintained special school, the local education authority or, as the case may be, the governing body shall serve under section 183 of this Act notice of their proposals to discontinue the school.

(8) For the purposes of proposals made under subsection (7) above—

(a) that section shall have effect as if the school had not ceased to be a special school on the withdrawal of the approval, and
(b) section 184 of this Act shall have effect as if subsections (1) to (3), and the reference in subsection (4) to the rejection of proposals, were omitted.

189 Approval of independent schools

(1) The Secretary of State may approve an independent school as suitable for the admission of children for whom statements are maintained under section 168 of this Act.

(2) Regulations may make provision as to—

(a) the requirements which are to be complied with by a school as a condition of its approval under this section,

(b) the requirements which are to be complied with by a school while an approval under this section is in force in respect of it, and

(c) the withdrawal of approval from a school at the request of the proprietor or on the ground that there has been a failure to comply with any prescribed requirement.

(3) An approval under this section may be given subject to such conditions (in addition to those prescribed) as the Secretary of State sees fit to impose.

(4) In any case where there is a failure to comply with such a condition imposed under subsection (3) above, the Secretary of State may withdraw his approval.

(5) No person shall so exercise his functions under this Part of this Act that a child with special educational needs is educated in an independent school unless—

(a) the school is for the time being approved by the Secretary of State as suitable for the admission of children for whom statements are maintained under section 168 of this Act, or

(b) the Secretary of State consents to the child being educated there.

190 Provision of education at non-maintained schools

(1) Subsection (2) below applies where—

(a) special educational provision in respect of a child with special educational needs is made at a school which is not a maintained school, and

(b) either the name of the school is specified in a statement in respect of the child under section 168 of this Act or the local education authority are satisfied that his interests require the necessary special educational provision to be made for him at a school which is not a maintained school and that it is appropriate for the child to be provided with education at the particular school.

(2) Where this subsection applies, the local education authority shall—

(a) pay the whole of the fees payable in respect of the education provided for him at the school, and

(b) if board and lodging are provided for the child at the school and the authority are satisfied that the necessary special educational provision cannot be provided for him at the school unless the board and lodging are also provided, pay the whole of the fees payable in respect of the board and lodging.

(3) In this section, 'maintained school' means—

(a) a school maintained by a local education authority,

(b) a grant-maintained school, and

(c) a grant-maintained special school.

Variation of deeds

191 Variation of trust deeds etc by order

(1) The Secretary of State may by order make such modifications of any trust deed or other instrument relating to a school as, after consultation with the governing body or other

proprietor of the school, appear to him to be necessary to enable the governing body or proprietor to meet any requirement imposed by regulations under section 188 or 189 of this Act.

(2) Any modification made by an order under this section may be made to have permanent effect or to have effect for such period as may be specified in the order.

SCHEDULE 9

MAKING OF ASSESSMENTS UNDER SECTION 167

Introductory

1. In this Schedule, 'assessment' means an assessment of a child's educational needs under section 167 of this Act.

Medical and other advice

2.—(1) Regulations shall make provision as to the advice which a local education authority are to seek in making assessments.

(2) Without prejudice to the generality of sub-paragraph (1) above, the regulations shall, except in such circumstances as may be prescribed, require the authority to seek medical, psychological and educational advice and such other advice as may be prescribed.

Manner, and timing, of assessments, etc

3.—(1) Regulations may make provision—

(a) as to the manner in which assessments are to be conducted,
(b) requiring the local education authority, where, after conducting an assessment under section 167 of this Act of the educational needs of a child for whom a statement is maintained under section 168 of this Act, they determine not to amend the statement, to serve on the parent of the child notice giving the prescribed information, and
(c) in connection with such other matters relating to the making of assessments as the Secretary of State considers appropriate.

(2) Sub-paragraph (1)(b) above does not apply to a determination made following the service of notice under paragraph 10 of Schedule 10 to this Act of a proposal to amend the statement.

(3) Regulations may provide that, where a local education authority are under a duty to make an assessment, the duty must, subject to prescribed exceptions, be performed within the prescribed period.

(4) Such provision shall not relieve the authority of the duty to make an assessment which has not been performed within that period.

Attendance at examinations

4.—(1) Where a local education authority propose to make an assessment, they may serve a notice on the parent of the child concerned requiring the child's attendance for examination in accordance with the provisions of the notice.

(2) The parent of a child examined under this paragraph may be present at the examination if he so desires.

(3) A notice under this paragraph shall—

    (a)   state the purpose of the examination,

    (b)   state the time and place at which the examination will be held,

    (c)   name an officer of the authority from whom further information may be obtained,

    (d)   inform the parent that he may submit such information to the authority as he may wish, and

    (e)   inform the parent of his right to be present at the examination.

Offence

5.—(1) Any parent who fails without reasonable excuse to comply with any requirements of a notice served on him under paragraph 4 above commits an offence if the notice relates to a child who is not over compulsory school age at the time stated in it as the time for holding the examination.

(2) A person guilty of an offence under this paragraph is liable on summary conviction to a fine not exceeding level 2 on the standard scale.

SCHEDULE 10

MAKING AND MAINTENANCE OF STATEMENTS UNDER SECTION 168

Introductory

1. In this Schedule, 'statement' means a statement of a child's special educational needs under section 168 of this Act.

Copy of proposed statement

2. Before making a statement, a local education authority shall serve on the parent of the child concerned—

    (a)   a copy of the proposed statement, and

    (b)   a written notice explaining the arrangements under paragraph 3 below, the effect of paragraph 4 below and the right to appeal under section 170 of this Act and containing such other information as may be prescribed,

but the copy of the proposed statement shall not specify any matter in pursuance of section 168(4) of this Act or any prescribed matter.

Choice of school

3.—(1) Every local education authority shall make arrangements for enabling a parent on whom a copy of a proposed statement has been served under paragraph 2 above to express a preference as to the maintained, grant-maintained or grant-maintained special school at which he wishes education to be provided for his child and to give reasons for his preference.

(2) Any such preference must be expressed or made within the period of fifteen days beginning—

    (a)   with the date on which the written notice mentioned in paragraph 2(b) above was served on the parent, or

    (b)   if a meeting has (or meetings have) been arranged under paragraph 4(1)(b) or (2) below, with the date fixed for that meeting (or the last of those meetings).

(3) Where a local education authority make a statement in a case where the parent of the child concerned has expressed a preference in pursuance of such arrangements as to the school at which he wishes education to be provided for his child, they shall specify the name of that school in the statement unless—

    (a)   the school is unsuitable to the child's age, ability or aptitude or to his special educational needs, or

    (b)   the attendance of the child at the school would be incompatible with the provision of efficient education for the children with whom he would be educated or the efficient use of resources.

(4) A local education authority shall, before specifying the name of any maintained, grant-maintained or grant-maintained special school in a statement, consult the governing body of the school and, if the school is maintained by another local education authority, that authority.

Representations

4.—(1) A parent on whom a copy of a proposed statement has been served under paragraph 2 above may—

    (a)   make representations (or further representations) to the local education authority about the content of the statement, and

    (b)   require the authority to arrange a meeting between him and an officer of the authority at which the statement can be discussed.

(2) Where a parent, having attended a meeting arranged by a local education authority under sub-paragaph (1)(b) above, disagrees with any part of the assessment in question, he may require the authority to arrange such meeting or meetings as they consider will enable him to discuss the relevant advice with the appropriate person or persons.

(3) In this paragraph—

    'relevant advice' means such of the advice given to the authority in connection with the assessment as they consider to be relevant to that part of the assessment with which the parent disagrees, and

    'appropriate person' means the person who gave the relevant advice or any other person who, in the opinion of the authority, is the appropriate person to discuss it with the parent.

(4) Any repesentations under sub-paragraph (1)(a) above must be made within the period of fifteen days beginning—

    (a)   with the date on which the written notice mentioned in paragraph 2(b) above was served on the parent, or

    (b)   if a meeting has (or meetings have) been arranged under sub-paragraph (1)(b) or (2) above, with the date fixed for that meeting (or the last of those meetings).

(5) A requirement under sub-paragraph (1)(b) above must be made within the period of fifteen days beginning with the date on which the written notice mentioned in paragraph 2(b) above was served on the parent.

(6) A requirement under sub-paragraph (2) above must be made within the period of fifteen days beginning with the date fixed for the meeting arranged under sub-paragraph (1)(b) above.

Making the statement

5.—(1) Where representations are made to a local education authority under paragraph 4(1)(a) above, the authority shall not make the statement until they have considered the representations and the period of the last of the periods allowed by paragraph 4 above for making requirements or further representations has expired.

(2) The statement may be in the form originally proposed (except as to the matters required to be excluded from the copy of the proposed statement) or in a form modified in the light of the representations.

(3) Regulations may provide that, where a local education authority are under a duty (subject to compliance with the preceding requirements of this Schedule) to make a statement, the duty, or any step required to be taken for performance of the duty, must, subject to prescribed exceptions, be performed within the prescribed period.

(4) Such provision shall not relieve the authority of the duty to make a statement, or take any step, which has not been performed or taken within that period.

Service of statement

6. Where a local education authority make a statement they shall serve a copy of the statement on the parent of the child concerned and shall give notice in writing to him—

(a) of his right under section 170(1) of this Act to appeal against the description in the statement of the authority's assessment of the child's special educational needs, the special educational provision specified in the statement or, if no school is named in the statement, that fact, and

(b) of the name of the person to whom he may apply for information and advice about the child's special educational needs.

Keeping, disclosure and transfer of statements

7.—(1) Regulations may make provision as to the keeping and disclosure of statements.

(2) Regulations may make provision, where a local education authority become responsible for a child for whom a statement is maintained by another authority, for the transfer of the statement to them and for Part III of this Act to have effect as if the duty to maintain the transferred statement were their duty.

Change of named school

8.—(1) Sub-paragraph (2) below applies where—

(a) the parent of a child for whom a statement is maintained which specifies the name of a school or institution asks the local education authority to substitute for that name the name of a maintained, grant-maintained or grant-maintained special school specified by the parent, and

(b) the request is not made less than twelve months after—

(i) a request under this paragraph,

(ii) the service of a copy of the statement under paragraph 6 above,

(iii) if the statement has been amended, the date when notice of the amendment is given under paragraph 10(3)(b) below, or

(iv) if the parent has appealed to the Tribunal under section 170 of this Act or this paragraph, the date when the appeal is concluded,

whichever is the later.

(2) The local education authority shall comply with the request unless—

(a) the school is unsuitable to the child's age, ability or aptitude or to his special educational needs, or

(b) the attendance of the child at the school would be incompatible with the provision of efficient education for the children with whom he would be educated or the efficient use of resources.

(3) Where the local education authority determine not to comply with the request—

(a) they shall give notice of that fact and of the effect of paragraph (b) below to the parent of the child, and

(b) the parent of the child may appeal to the Tribunal against the determination.

(4) On the appeal the Tribunal may—

(a) dismiss the appeal, or

(b) order the local education authority to substitute for the name of the school or other institution specified in the statement the name of the school specified by the parent.

(5) Regulations may provide that, where a local education authority are under a duty to comply with a request under this paragraph, the duty must, subject to prescribed exceptions, be performed within the prescribed period.

(6) Such provision shall not relieve the authority of the duty to comply with such a request which has not been complied with within that period.

Procedure for amending or ceasing to maintain a statement

9.—(1) A local education authority may not amend, or cease to maintain, a statement except in accordance with paragraph 10 or 11 below.

(2) Sub-paragraph (1) above does not apply where the local education authority—

(a) cease to maintain a statement of a child who has ceased to be a child for whom they are responsible,

(b) amend a statement in pursuance of paragraph 8 above,

(c) are ordered to cease to maintain a statement under section 170(3)(c) of this Act, or

(d) amend a statement in pursuance of directions under section 197 of this Act.

10.—(1) Before amending a statement, a local education authority shall serve on the parent of the child concerned a notice informing him—

(a) of their proposal, and

(b) of his right to make representations under sub-paragraph (2) below.

(2) A parent on whom a notice has been served under sub-paragraph (1) above may, within the period of fifteen days beginning with the date on which the notice is served, make representations to the local education authority about their proposal.

(3) The local education authority—

(a)   shall consider any representations made to them under sub-paragraph (2) above, and

(b)   on taking a decision on the proposal to which the representations relate, shall give notice in writing to the parent of their decision.

(4) Where a local education authority make an amendment under this paragraph to the description in a statement of the authority's assessment of a child's special educational needs or to the special educational provision specified in a statement, they shall give notice in writing to the parent of his right under section 170(1) of this Act to appeal against the description in the statement of the authority's assessment of the child's special educational needs, the special educational provision specified in the statement or, if no school is named in the statement, that fact.

(5) A local education authority may only amend a statement under this paragraph within the prescribed period beginning with the service of the notice under sub-paragraph (1) above.

11.—(1) A local education authority may cease to maintain a statement only if it is no longer necessary to maintain it.

(2) Where the local education authority determine to cease to maintain a statement—

(a)   they shall give notice of that fact and of the effect of paragraph (b) below to the parent of the child, and

(b)   the parent of the child may appeal to the Tribunal against the determination.

(3) On an appeal under this paragraph the Tribunal may—

(a)   dismiss the appeal, or

(b)   order the local education authority to continue to maintain the statement in its existing form or with such amendments of the description in the statement of the authority's assessment of the child's special educational needs or the special educational provision specified in the statement, and such other consequential amendments, as the Tribunal may determine.

(4) Except where the parent of the child appeals to the Tribunal under this paragraph, a local education authority may only cease to maintain a statement under this paragraph within the prescribed period beginning with the service of the notice under sub-paragraph (2) above.

Appendix 2

SPECIAL EDUCATIONAL NEEDS TRIBUNAL REGULATIONS 1995 (SI 1995/3113)

ARRANGEMENT OF REGULATIONS

PART 1

GENERAL

PART 2

MAKING AN APPEAL TO THE TRIBUNAL AND REPLY BY THE AUTHORITY

(A) THE PARENT

(B) THE REPLY BY THE AUTHORITY

PART 3

PREPARATION FOR A HEARING

PART 4

THE DETERMINATION OF APPEALS

PART 5

ADDITIONAL POWERS OF AND PROVISIONS RELATING TO THE TRIBUNAL

The Secretary of State for Education and Employment, in respect of England, and the Secretary of State for Wales, in exercise of the powers conferred by sections 177(5), 178(2), 180(1) and (2), 301(6) and 305(1) of the Education Act 1993, and after consultation with the Council on Tribunals in accordance with section 8 of the Tribunals and Inquiries Act 1992, hereby make the following Regulations:

PART 1

GENERAL

1 Citation and commencement

These Regulations may be cited as the Special Educational Needs Tribunal Regulations 1995 and shall come into force on 1st January 1996.

2 Interpretation

In these Regulations, unless the context otherwise requires—

'the 1993 Act' means the Education Act 1993;
'the authority' means the local education authority which made the disputed decision;
'child' means the child in respect of whom the appeal is brought;

'disputed decision' means the decision or determination in respect of which the appeal is brought;

'the clerk to the tribunal' means the person appointed by the Secretary of the Tribunal to act in that capacity at one or more hearings;

'hearing' means a sitting of the tribunal duly constituted for the purpose of receiving evidence, hearing addresses and witnesses or doing anything lawfully requisite to enable the tribunal to reach a decision on any question;

'parent' means a parent who has made an appeal to the Special Educational Needs Tribunal under the 1993 Act;

'records' means the records of the Special Educational Needs Tribunal;

'the Secretary of the Tribunal' means the person for the time being acting as the Secretary of the office of the Special Educational Needs Tribunal;

'the tribunal' means the Special Educational Needs Tribunal but where the President has determined pursuant to regulation 4(1) that the jurisdiction of the Special Educational Needs Tribunal is to be exercised by more than one tribunal, it means, in relation to any proceedings, the tribunal to which the proceedings have been referred by the President;

'working day', except in regulation 24, means any day other than—

(a) a Saturday, a Sunday, Christmas Day, Good Friday or a day which is a bank holiday within the meaning of the Banking and Financial Dealings Act 1971; or

(b) a day in August.

3 Members of lay panel

No person may be appointed as a member of the lay panel unless the Secretary of State is satisfied that he has knowledge and experience in respect of—

(a) children with special educational needs; or

(b) local government.

4 Establishment of tribunals

(1) Such number of tribunals shall be established to exercise the jurisdiction of the Special Educational Needs Tribunal as the President may from time to time determine.

(2) The tribunals shall sit at such times and in such places as may from time to time be determined by the President.

5 Membership of tribunal

(1) Subject to the provisions of regulation 28(5), the tribunal shall consist of a chairman and two other members.

(2) For each hearing—

(a) the chairman shall be the President or a person selected from the chairman's panel by the President; and

(b) the two other members of the tribunal other than the chairman shall be selected from the lay panel by the President.

6 Proof of documents and certification of decisions

(1) A document purporting to be a document issued by the Secretary of the Tribunal on behalf of the Special Educational Needs Tribunal shall, unless the contrary is proved, be deemed to be a document so issued.

(2) A document purporting to be certified by the Secretary of the Tribunal to be a true copy of a document containing a decision of the tribunal shall, unless the contrary is proved, be sufficient evidence of matters contained therein.

PART 2

MAKING AN APPEAL TO THE TRIBUNAL AND REPLY BY THE AUTHORITY

(A) THE PARENT

7 Notice of appeal

(1) An appeal to the Special Educational Needs Tribunal shall be made by notice which—

    (a)   shall state—
- (i) the name and address of the parent making the appeal and if more than one address is given, the address to which the tribunal should send replies or notices concerning the appeal;
- (ii) the name of the child;
- (iii) that the notice is a notice of appeal;
- (iv) the name of the authority which made the disputed decision and the date on which the parent was notified of it;
- (v) the grounds of the appeal;
- (vi) if the parent seeks an order that a school (other than one already named in the statement of special educational needs relating to the child) be named in the child's statement, the name and address of that school;

    (b)   shall be accompanied by—
- (i) a copy of the notice of the disputed decision;
- (ii) where the appeal is made under section 170 of, or paragraph 8 of Schedule 10 to, the 1993 Act, a copy of the statement of special educational needs relating to the child; and

    (c)   may state the name, address and profession of any representative of the parent to whom the tribunal should (subject to any notice under regulation 42(2)(a)) send replies or notices concerning the appeal instead of the parent.

(2) The parent shall sign the notice of appeal.

(3) The parent must deliver the notice of appeal to the Secretary of the Tribunal so that it is received no later than the first working day after the expiry of 2 months from the date on which the authority gave him notice, under Part III of the 1993 Act, that he had a right of appeal.

8 Response, and supplementary provisions

(1) If the authority delivers a reply under regulation 12 the parent may deliver a written response to it.

(2) A response under paragraph (1) above must be delivered to the Secretary of the Tribunal no later than 15 working days from the date on which the parent receives a copy of the authority's written reply from the Secretary of the Tribunal.

(3) Subject to paragraph (5) below a response under paragraph (1) shall include all written evidence which the parent wishes to submit to the tribunal (unless such evidence was delivered with the notice of appeal);

(4) The parent may in exceptional cases (in addition to delivering a response under paragraph (1) above)—

(a)   with the permission of the President, at any time before the hearing; or
(b)   with the permission of the tribunal at the hearing itself—

amend the notice of appeal or any response, deliver a supplementary statement of grounds of appeal or amend a supplementary statement of grounds of appeal.

(5) The parent may in exceptional cases—

(a)   with the permission of the President at any time within 15 working days from the date on which a response under paragraph (2) above could have been delivered, or
(b)   with the permission of the tribunal at the hearing itself—

deliver written evidence (if he has not previously done so) or further written evidence.

(6) The parent shall deliver a copy of every amendment and supplementary statement made under paragraph (4)(a) above and any written evidence delivered under paragraph (5)(a) above to the Secretary of the Tribunal.

9 Withdrawal of appeal

The parent may

(a)   at any time before the hearing of the appeal withdraw his appeal by sending to the Secretary of the Tribunal a notice signed by him stating that he withdraws his appeal;
(b)   at the hearing of the appeal, withdraw his appeal.

10 Further action by parent

(1) The parent shall supply the Secretary of the Tribunal with the information requested in the enquiry made under regulation 17.

(2) If the parent does not intend to attend or be represented at the hearing, he may, not less than 5 working days before the hearing, send to the Secretary of the Tribunal additional written representations in support of his appeal.

11 Representatives of the parent: further provisions

(1) Where a parent has not stated the name of a representative in the notice of appeal pursuant to regulation 7(1)(c) he may at any time before the hearing notify the Secretary of the Tribunal in writing of the name, address and profession of a representative to whom the tribunal should (subject to any notice under regulation 42(2)(a)) send any subsequent documents or notices concerning the appeal instead of to the parent;

(2) Where a parent has stated the name of a representative, whether in the notice of appeal pursuant to regulation 7(1)(c) or pursuant to paragraph (1) above, he may at any time notify the Secretary of the Tribunal in writing—

(a)   of the name, address and profession of a new representative of the parent to whom the tribunal should send documents or notices concerning the appeal instead of to the representative previously notified; or

(b)   that no person is acting as a representative of the parent and accordingly any subsequent documents or notices concerning the appeal should be sent to the parent himself.

(3) If the person named by the parent as a representative under regulation 7(1)(c) or paragraphs (1) or (2)(a) above notifies the Secretary of the Tribunal in writing that he is not prepared, or is no longer prepared, to act in that capacity—

(a)   the Secretary of the Tribunal shall notify the parent, and
(b)   any subsequent documents or notices concerning the appeal shall be sent to the parent himself.

(4) At a hearing, the parent may conduct his case himself (with assistance from one person if he wishes) or may appear and be represented by one person whether or not legally qualified:

Provided that, if the President gives permission before the hearing or the tribunal gives permission at the hearing, the parent may obtain assistance or be represented by more than one person.

(B) THE REPLY BY THE AUTHORITY

12 Action by the authority on receipt of a notice of appeal

(1) An authority which receives a copy of a notice of appeal shall deliver to the Secretary of the Tribunal a written reply acknowledging service upon it of the notice of appeal and stating—

(a)   whether or not the authority intends to oppose the appeal and, if it does intend to oppose the appeal, the grounds on which it relies; and
(b)   the name and profession of the representative of the authority and the address for service of the authority for the purposes of the appeal.

(2) The authority's reply shall include—

(a)   a statement summarising the facts relating to the disputed decision;
(b)   if they are not part of the decision, the reasons for the disputed decision; and
(c)   subject to regulation 13(3) all written evidence which the authority wishes to submit to the tribunal.

(3) Every such reply shall be signed by an officer of the authority who is authorised to sign such documents and shall be delivered to the Secretary of the Tribunal not later than 20 working days after the date on which the copy of the notice of appeal was received by the authority from the Secretary of the Tribunal.

13 Amendment of reply by the authority

(1) The authority, if it has delivered a reply pursuant to regulation 12, may, in exceptional cases—

(a)   with the permission of the President at any time before the hearing; or
(b)   with the permission of the tribunal at the hearing itself

amend its reply, deliver a supplementary reply or amend a supplementary reply.

(2) The President or, as the case may be, the tribunal may give permission under paragraph (1) above on such terms as he or it thinks fit including the payment of costs or expenses.

(3) The authority may, in exceptional cases—

(a)   with the permission of the President at any time within 15 working days from the date on which the parent could have delivered a response under regulation 8(1); or

(b)   with the permission of the tribunal at the hearing itself

deliver written evidence (if it has not previously done so) or further written evidence.

(4)   The authority shall send a copy of every amendment and supplementary statement made before the hearing to the Secretary of the Tribunal.

14   Failure to reply and absence of opposition

If no reply is received by the Secretary of the Tribunal within the time appointed by regulation 12(3) or if the authority states in writing that it does not resist the appeal, or withdraws its opposition to the appeal the tribunal shall—

(a)   determine the appeal on the basis of the notice of appeal without a hearing; or

(b)   without notifying the authority hold a hearing at which the authority is not represented.

15   Representation at hearing and further action by the authority

(1)   At a hearing or part of a hearing the authority may be represented by one person whether or not legally qualified:

Provided that if the President gives permission before the hearing or the tribunal gives permission at the hearing the authority may be represented by more than one person.

(2)   The authority shall supply the Secretary of the Tribunal with the information requested in the enquiry made under Regulation 17.

(3)   If the authority does not intend to attend or be represented at the hearing it may, not less than 5 working days before the hearing, send to the Secretary of the Tribunal additional written representations in support of its reply.

PART 3

PREPARATION FOR A HEARING

16   Acknowledgement of appeal and service of documents by the Secretary of the Tribunal

(1)   Upon receiving a notice of appeal the Secretary of the Tribunal shall—

(a)   enter particulars of it in the records;

(b)   send to the parent—
   (i)   an acknowledgement of its receipt and a note of the case number entered in the records;
   (ii)   a note of the address to which notices and communications to the Special Educational Needs Tribunal or to the Secretary of the Tribunal should be sent; and
   (iii) notification that advice about the appeal procedure may be obtained from the office of the Special Educational Needs Tribunal;

(c)   subject to paragraph (6) below, send to the authority—
   (i)   a copy of the notice of appeal and any accompanying papers;

    (ii)   a note of the address to which notices and communications to the Special Educational Needs Tribunal or to the Secretary of the Tribunal should be sent, and

    (iii)   a notice stating the time for replying and the consequences of failure to do so.

(2) Where the Secretary of the Tribunal is of the opinion that, on the basis of the notice of appeal, the parent is asking the Special Educational Needs Tribunal to do something which it cannot, he may give notice to that effect to the parent stating the reasons for his opinion and informing him that the notice of appeal will not be entered in the records unless the parent notifies the Secretary of the Tribunal that he wishes to proceed with it.

(3) Where the Secretary of the Tribunal is of the opinion that there is an obvious error in the notice of appeal—

    (a)   he may correct that error and if he does so shall notify the parent accordingly and such notification shall state the effect of sub-paragraph (b) below; and

    (b)   unless within 5 working days the parent notifies the Secretary of the Tribunal that he objects to the correction, the notice of appeal as so corrected shall be treated as the notice of appeal for the purposes of these Regulations.

(4) An appeal, as respects which a notice has been given under paragraph (2) above, shall only be treated as having been received for the purposes of paragraph (1) when the parent notifies the Secretary of the Tribunal that he wishes to proceed with it.

(5) Subject to paragraph (6) below, the Secretary of the Tribunal shall forthwith send a copy of a reply by the authority under regulation 12 and of a response under regulation 8 together with any amendments or supplementary statements, written representations, written evidence or other documents received from a party, to the other party to the proceedings.

(6) If a notice of appeal, reply by the authority under regulation 12 or response by the parent under regulation 8 is delivered to the Secretary of the Tribunal after the time prescribed by these Regulations, the Secretary of the Tribunal shall defer the sending of the copies referred to in paragraph (1)(c) or (5) above pending a decision by the President as to an extension of the time limit pursuant to regulation 41.

17 Enquiries by the Secretary of the Tribunal

The Secretary of the Tribunal shall, at any time after he has received the notice of appeal—

    (a)   enquire of each party—
        (i)   whether or not the party intends to attend the hearing;
        (ii)   whether the party wishes to be represented at the hearing in accordance with regulation 11(4) or 15(1) and if so the name of the representative;
        (iii)   whether the party wishes the hearing to be in public;
        (iv)   whether the party intends to call witnesses and if so the names of the proposed witnesses; and
        (v)   whether the party or a witness will require the assistance of an interpreter; and
    (b)   enquire of the parent whether he wishes any persons (other than a person who will represent him or any witness which he proposes to call) to attend the hearing if the hearing is to be in private and if so the names of such persons.

18 Directions in preparation for a hearing

(1) The President may at any time before the hearing give such directions (including the issue of a witness summons) as are provided in this Part of these Regulations to enable the parties to prepare for the hearing or to assist the tribunal to determine the issues.

(2) Directions given pursuant to regulations 20 and 21 may be given on the application of a party or of the President's own motion.

(3) A witness summons issued pursuant to regulation 22 may only be issued on the application of a party.

(4) An application by a party for directions shall be made in writing to the Secretary of the Tribunal and, unless it is accompanied by the written consent of the other party, shall be served by the Secretary of the Tribunal on that other party. If the other party objects to the directions sought, the President shall consider the objection and, if he considers it necessary for the determination of the application, shall give the parties an opportunity of appearing before him.

(5) Directions containing a requirement under this Part of these Regulations shall, as appropriate—

(a) include a statement of the possible consequences for the appeal, as provided by regulation 23, of a party's failure to comply with the requirement within the time allowed by the President; and

(b) contain a reference to the fact that, under section 180(5) of the 1993 Act, any person who without reasonable excuse fails to comply with requirements regarding discovery or inspection of documents, or regarding attendance to give evidence and produce documents, shall be liable on summary conviction to a fine not exceeding level 3 on the standard scale and shall, unless the person to whom the direction is addressed had an opportunity of objecting to the direction, contain a statement to the effect that that person may apply to the President under regulation 19 to vary or set aside the direction.

19 Varying or setting aside of directions

Where a person to whom a direction (including any summons) given under this Part of these Regulations is addressed had no opportunity to object to the giving of such direction, he may apply to the President, by notice to the Secretary of the Tribunal, to vary it or set it aside, but the President shall not so do without first notifying the person who applied for the direction and considering any representations made by him.

20 Particulars and supplementary statements

The President may give directions requiring any party to provide such particulars or supplementary statements as may be reasonably required for the determination of the appeal.

21 Disclosure of documents and other material

(1) The President may give directions requiring a party to deliver to the tribunal any document or other material which the tribunal may require and which it is in the power of that party to deliver. The President shall make such provision as he thinks necessary to supply copies of any document obtained under this paragraph to the other party to the proceedings, and it shall be a condition of such supply that that party shall use such a document only for the purposes of the appeal.

(2) The President may grant to a party such discovery or inspection of documents (including the taking of copies) as might be granted by a county court.

22 Summoning of witnesses

The President may by summons require any person in England and Wales to attend as a witness at a hearing of an appeal at such time and place as may be specified in the summons and at the hearing to answer any questions or produce any documents or other material in his custody or under his control which relate to any matter in question in the appeal:

Provided that—
(a) no person shall be compelled to give any evidence or produce any document or other material that he could not be compelled to give or produce at a trial of an action in a Court of law;
(b) in exercising the powers conferred by this regulation, the President shall take into account the need to protect any matter that relates to intimate personal or financial circumstances or consists of information communicated or obtained in confidence;
(c) no person shall be required to attend in obedience to such a summons unless he has been given at least 5 working days' notice of the hearing or, if less than 5 working days, he has informed the President that he accepts such notice as he has been given; and
(d) no person shall be required in obedience to such a summons to attend and give evidence or to produce any document unless the necessary expenses of his attendance are paid or tendered to him.

23 Failure to comply with directions

(1) If a party has not complied with a direction to it under this Part of these Regulations within the time specified in the direction the tribunal may—

(a) where the party in default is the parent, dismiss the appeal without a hearing;
(b) where the party in default is the authority, determine the appeal without a hearing; or
(c) hold a hearing (without notifying the party in default) at which the party in default is not represented or, where the parties have been notified of the hearing under regulation 24, direct that neither the party in default nor any person whom he intends should represent him be entitled to attend the hearing;

(2) In this regulation 'the party in default' means the party which has failed to comply with the direction.

24 Notice of place and time of hearing and adjournments

(1) Subject to the provisions of regulation 25, the Secretary of the Tribunal shall, after consultation with the parties, fix the time and place of the hearing and send to each party a notice that the hearing is to be at such time and place.

(2) The notice referred to in paragraph (1) above shall be sent—

(a) not less than 5 working days before the date fixed for the hearing where the hearing is held under regulation 14, 31 or 36;
(b) not less than 10 working days before the date fixed for the hearing in any other case

or within such shorter period before the date fixed for the hearing as the parties may agree.

(3) The Secretary of the Tribunal shall include in or with the notice of hearing—

(a) information and guidance, in a form approved by the President, as to attendance at the hearing of the parties and witnesses, the bringing of documents, and the right of representation or assistance as provided by regulation 11(4) or 15(1); and

(b) a statement explaining the possible consequences of non-attendance and of the right of—

    (i) a parent; and

    (ii) the authority, if it has presented a reply,

who does not attend and is not represented, to make representations in writing.

(4) The tribunal may alter the time and place of any hearing and the Secretary of the Tribunal shall give the parties not less than 5 working days (or such shorter time as the parties agree) notice of the altered hearing date:

Provided that any altered hearing date shall not (unless the parties agree) be before the date notified under paragraph (1).

(5) The tribunal may from time to time adjourn the hearing and, if the time and place of the adjourned hearing are announced before the adjournment, no further notice shall be required.

(6) Nothing in paragraphs (1) or (4) above shall oblige the Secretary of the Tribunal to consult, or send a notice to any party who by virtue of any provision of these Regulations is not entitled to be represented at the hearing.

(7) In this regulation 'working day' means any day other than a Saturday, a Sunday, Christmas Day, Good Friday or a day which is a bank holiday within the meaning of the Banking and Financial Dealings Act 1971.

PART 4

DETERMINATION OF APPEALS

25 Power to determine an appeal without a hearing

(1) The tribunal may—

    (a) if the parties so agree in writing; or

    (b) in the circumstances described in regulations 14 and 23,

determine an appeal or any particular issue without a hearing.

(2) The provisions of regulation 27(2) shall apply in respect of the determination of an appeal, or any particular issue, under this regulation.

26 Hearings to be in private: exceptions

(1) A hearing by the tribunal shall be in private unless—

    (a) both the parent and the authority request that the hearing be in public; or

    (b) the President, at any time before the hearing, or the tribunal at the hearing, orders that the hearing should be in public.

(2) The following persons (as well as the parties and their representatives and witnesses) shall be entitled to attend the hearing of an appeal, even though it is in private—

    (a) subject to the provisions of paragraph (8), below, any person named by the parent in response to the enquiry under regulation 17(b) unless the President has determined that any such person should not be entitled to attend the hearing and notified the parent accordingly;

(b) a parent of the child who is not a party to the appeal;

(c) the clerk to the tribunal and the Secretary of the Tribunal;

(d) the President and any member of the chairmen's or lay panel (when not sitting as members of the tribunal);

(e) a member of the Council on Tribunals;

(f) any person undergoing training as a member of the chairmen's or lay panel or as a clerk to the tribunal;

(g) any person acting on behalf of the President in the training or supervision of clerks to tribunals;

(h) an interpreter.

(3) The tribunal, with the consent of the parties or their representatives actually present, may permit any other person to attend the hearing of an appeal which is held in private.

(4) Without prejudice to any other powers it may have, the tribunal may exclude from the hearing, or part of it, any person whose conduct has disrupted or is likely, in the opinion of the tribunal, to disrupt the hearing.

(5) For the purposes of arriving at its decision a tribunal shall, and for the purposes of discussing any question of procedure may, notwithstanding anything contained in these Regulations, order all persons to withdraw from the sitting of the tribunal other than the members of the tribunal or any of the persons mentioned in paragraph (2)(c) to (f) above.

(6) Except as provided in paragraph (7) below none of the persons mentioned in paragraphs (2) or (3) above shall, save in the case of the clerk to the tribunal or an interpreter as their respective duties require, take any part in the hearing or (where entitled or permitted to remain) in the deliberations of the tribunal.

(7) The tribunal may permit a parent of the child who is not a party to the appeal to address the tribunal on the subject matter of the appeal.

(8) Where the parent has named more than two persons in response to the enquiry under regulation 17(b) only two persons shall be entitled to attend the hearing unless the President has given permission before the hearing or the tribunal gives permission at the hearing for a greater number to attend.

27 Failure of parties to attend hearing

(1) If a party fails to attend or be represented at a hearing of which he has been duly notified, the tribunal may—

(a) unless it is satisfied that there is sufficient reason for such absence, hear and determine the appeal in the party's absence; or

(b) adjourn the hearing.

(2) Before disposing of an appeal in the absence of a party, the tribunal shall consider any representations in writing submitted by that party in response to the notice of hearing and, for the purpose of this regulation the notice of appeal, any reply by the authority under regulations 12 or 13 and any response by the parent under regulation 8 shall be treated as representations in writing.

28 Procedure at hearing

(1) At the beginning of the hearing the chairman shall explain the order of proceeding which the tribunal proposes to adopt.

(2) The tribunal shall conduct the hearing in such manner as it considers most suitable to the clarification of the issues and generally to the just handling of the proceedings; it shall, so far as appears to it appropriate, seek to avoid formality in its proceedings.

(3) The tribunal shall determine the order in which the parties are heard and the issues determined.

(4) The tribunal may, if it is satisfied that it is just and reasonable to do so, permit a party to rely on grounds not stated in his notice of appeal or, as the case may be, his reply or response and to adduce any evidence not presented to the authority before or at the time it took the disputed decision.

(5) If at or after the commencement of any hearing a member of the tribunal other than the chairman is absent, the hearing may, with the consent of the parties, be conducted by the other two members and in that event the tribunal shall be deemed to be properly constituted and the decision of the tribunal shall be taken by those two members.

29 Evidence at hearing

(1) In the course of the hearing the parties shall be entitled to give evidence, to call witnesses, to question any witnesses and to address the tribunal both on the evidence and generally on the subject matter of the appeal:

Provided that neither party shall be entitled to call more than two witnesses to give evidence orally (in addition to any witnesses whose attendance is required pursuant to paragraph (2) below) unless the President has given permission before the hearing or the tribunal gives permission at the hearing.

(2) Evidence before the tribunal may be given orally or by written statement, but the tribunal may at any stage of the proceedings require the personal attendance of any maker of any written statement:

Provided that neither party shall be entitled to give evidence by written statement if such evidence was not submitted with the notice of appeal or submitted in accordance with regulation 8 or (as appropriate) regulations 12 or 13.

(3) The tribunal may receive evidence of any fact which appears to the tribunal to be relevant.

(4) The tribunal may require any witness to give evidence on oath or affirmation, and for that purpose there may be administered an oath or affirmation in due form, or may require any evidence given by written statement to be given by affidavit.

30 Decision of the tribunal

(1) A decision of the tribunal may be taken by a majority and where the tribunal is constituted by two members only under regulation 28(5) the chairman shall have a second or casting vote.

(2) The decision of the tribunal may be given orally at the end of the hearing or reserved and, in any event, whether there has been a hearing or not shall be recorded forthwith in a document which, save in the case of a decision by consent, shall also contain, or have annexed to it, a statement of the reasons (in summary form) for the tribunal's decision, and each such document shall be signed and dated by the chairman.

(3) Neither a decision given orally nor the document referred to in paragraph (2) above shall contain any reference to the decision being by majority (if that be the case) or to any opinion of a minority.

(4) Every decision of the tribunal shall be entered in the records.

(5) As soon as may be the Secretary of the Tribunal shall send a copy of the document referred to in paragraph (2) above to each party, accompanied by guidance, in a form approved by the President, about the circumstances in which there is a right to appeal against a tribunal decision and the procedure to be followed.

(6) Where, under regulations 7(1)(c), or 11(1) or (2)(a) a parent has stated the name of a representative the Secretary of the Tribunal shall (notwithstanding regulation 42) send a copy of the documents referred to in paragraph (5) above to the parent as well as to the representative.

(7) Every decision shall be treated as having been made on the date on which a copy of the document recording it is sent to the parent (whether or not the decision has been previously announced at the end of the hearing).

31 Review of the tribunal's decision

(1) Any party may apply to the Secretary of the Tribunal for the decision of the tribunal to be reviewed on the grounds that—

(a)   its decision was wrongly made as a result of an error on the part of the tribunal staff;
(b)   a party, who was entitled to be heard at a hearing but failed to appear or to be represented, had good and sufficient reason for failing to appear;
(c)   there was an obvious error in the decision of the tribunal which decided the case; or
(d)   the interests of justice require.

(2) An application for the purposes of paragraph (1) above shall be made not later than 10 working days after the date on which the decision was sent to the parties and shall be in writing stating the grounds in full.

(3) An application for the purposes of paragraph (1) above may be refused by the President, or by the chairman of the tribunal which decided the case, if in his opinion it has no reasonable prospect of success, but if such an application is not refused—

(a)   the parties shall have an opportunity to be heard on the application for review; and
(b)   the review shall be determined by the tribunal which decided the case or, where it is not practicable for it to be heard by that tribunal, by a tribunal appointed by the President.

(4) The tribunal may of its own motion review its decision on any of the grounds referred to in sub-paragraphs (a) to (d) of paragraph (1) above, and if it proposes to do so—

(a)   it shall serve notice on the parties not later than ten working days after the date on which the decision was sent to the parties; and
(b)   the parties shall have an opportunity to be heard on the proposal for review.

(5) If, on the application of a party under paragraphs (1) to (3) above or of its own motion under paragraph (4) above the tribunal is satsified as to any of the grounds referred to in sub-paragraphs (a) to (d) of paragraph (1) above, the tribunal may review and, by certificate under the chairman's hand, set aside or vary the relevant decision.

(6) If, having reviewed the decision, the decision is set aside, the tribunal shall substitute such decision as it thinks fit or order a rehearing before either the same or a differently constituted tribunal.

(7) If any decision is set aside or varied under this regulation or altered in any way by order of a superior court, the Secretary of the Tribunal shall alter the entry in the records to conform with the chairman's certificate or order of a superior court and shall notify the parties accordingly.

32 Review of the President's decision

(1) If, on the application of a party to the Secretary of the Tribunal or of his own motion the President is satisfied that—

(a) a decision by him was wrongly made as a result of an error on the part of the tribunal staff;

(b) there was an obvious error in his decision; or

(c) the interests of justice require,

the President may review and set aside or vary the relevant decision of his.

(2) An application for the purposes of paragraph (1) above shall be made not later than 10 working days after the date on which the party making the application was notified of the decision and shall be in writing stating the grounds in full. Where the President proposes to review his decision of his own motion he shall serve notice of that proposal on the parties within the same period.

(3) The parties shall have an opportunity to be heard on any application or proposal for review under this regulation and the review shall be determined by the President.

(4) If any decision is set aside or varied under this regulation the Secretary of the Tribunal shall alter the entry in the records and shall notify the parties accordingly.

33 Orders for costs and expenses

(1) The tribunal shall not normally make an order in respect of costs and expenses, but may, subject to paragraph (2) below, make such an order—

(a) against a party (including any party who has withdrawn his appeal or reply) if it is of the opinion that the party has acted frivolously or vexatiously or that his conduct in making, pursuing or resisting an appeal was wholly unreasonable;

(b) against a party which has failed to attend or be represented at a hearing of which he has been duly notified;

(c) against the authority where it has not delivered a written reply under regulation 12; or

(d) against the authority, where it considers that the disputed decision was wholly unreasonable.

(2) Any order in respect of costs and expenses may be made—

(a) as respects any costs or expenses incurred, or any allowances paid; or

(b) as respects the whole, or any part, of any allowance (other than allowances paid to members of tribunals) paid by the Secretary of State under section 180(3) of the 1993 Act to any person for the purposes of, or in connection with, his attendance at the tribunal.

(3) No order shall be made under paragraph (1) above against a party without first giving that party an opportunity of making representations against the making of the order.

(4) An order under paragraph (1) above may require the party against whom it is made to pay the other party either a specified sum in respect of the costs and expenses incurred by that other party in connection with the proceedings or the whole or part of such costs as taxed (if not otherwise agreed).

(5) Any costs required by an order under this regulation to be taxed in the county court according to such of the scales prescribed by the county court rules for proceedings in the county court as shall be directed in the order.

PART 5

ADDITIONAL POWERS OF AND PROVISIONS RELATING TO THE TRIBUNAL

34 Transfer of proceedings

Where it appears to the President that an appeal pending before a tribunal could be determined more conveniently in another tribunal he may at any time, upon the application of a party or of his own motion, direct that the said proceedings be transferred so as to be determined in that other tribunal:

Provided that no such direction shall be given unless notice has been sent to all parties concerned giving them an opportunity to show cause why such a direction should not be given.

35 Miscellaneous powers of the tribunal

(1) Subject to the provisions of the 1993 Act and these Regulations, a tribunal may regulate its own procedure.

(2) A tribunal may, if it thinks fit, if both parties agree in writing upon the terms of a decision to be made by the tribunal, decide accordingly.

36 Power to strike out

(1) The Secretary of the Tribunal shall, at any stage of the proceedings if the authority applies or the President so directs serve a notice on the parent stating that it appears that the appeal should be struck out on one or both of the grounds specified in paragraph (2) below or for want of prosecution.

(2) The grounds referred to in paragraph (1) above are that—

    (a)   the appeal is not, or is no longer, within the jurisdiction of the Special Educational Needs Tribunal;

    (b)   the notice of the appeal is, or the appeal is or has become, scandalous, frivolous or vexatious.

(3) The notice under paragraph (1) above shall state that the parent may make representations in accordance with paragraph (8) below.

(4) The tribunal, after considering any representations duly made, may order that the appeal should be struck out on one or both of the grounds specified in paragraph (2) above or for want of prosecution.

(5) The tribunal may make such an order without holding a hearing unless either party requests the opportunity to make oral representations, and if the tribunal holds a hearing it may be held at the beginning of the hearing of the substantive appeal.

(6) The President may, if he thinks fit, at any stage of the proceedings order that a reply, response or statement should be struck out or amended on the grounds that it is scandalous, frivolous or vexatious.

(7) Before making an order under paragraph (6) above, the President shall give to the party against whom he proposes to make the order a notice inviting representations and shall consider any representations duly made.

(8) For the purposes of this regulation—

(a) a notice inviting representations must inform the recipient that he may, within a period (not being less than 5 working days) specified in the notice, either make written representations or request an opportunity to make oral representations;

(b) representations are duly made if—

(i) in the case of written representations, they are made within the period so specified; and

(ii) in the case of oral representations, the party proposing to make them has requested an opportunity to do so within the period so specified.

37 Power to exercise powers of President and Chairman

(1) An act required or authorised by these Regulations to be done by the President may be done by a member of the chairman's panel authorised by the President.

(2) Where, pursuant to paragraph (1) above, a member of the chairman's panel carries out the function under regulation 5(2) of selecting the chairman of a tribunal, he may select himself.

(3) Where, pursuant to paragraph (1) above a member of the chairman's panel makes a decision, regulation 32 shall apply in relation to that decision taking the reference in that regulation to the President as a reference to the member of the chairman's panel by whom the decision was taken.

(4) Subject to regulation 39(6) in the event of the death or incapacity of the chairman following the decision of the tribunal in any matter, the functions of the chairman for the completion of the proceedings, including any review of the decision, may be exercised by the President or any member of the chairman's panel.

38 The Secretary of the Tribunal

A function of the Secretary of the Tribunal may be performed by another member of the staff of the Tribunal authorised for the purpose of carrying out that function by the President.

39 Irregularities

(1) An irregularity resulting from failure to comply with any provisions of these Regulations or of any direction of the tribunal before the tribunal has reached its decision shall not of itself render the proceedings void.

(2) Where any such irregularity comes to the attention of the tribunal, the tribunal may, and shall, if it considers that any person may have been prejudiced by the irregularity, give such directions as it thinks just before reaching its decision to cure or waive the irregularity.

(3) Clerical mistakes in any document recording a decision of the tribunal or a direction or decision of the President produced by or on behalf of the tribunal or errors arising in such documents from accidental slips or omissions may at any time be corrected by the chairman or the President (as the case may be) by certificate under his hand.

(4) The Secretary of the Tribunal shall as soon as may be send a copy of any corrected document containing reasons for the tribunal's decision, to each party.

(5) Where under regulations 7(1)(c) or 11(1) or (2)(a) a parent has stated the name of a representative the Secretary of the Tribunal shall (notwithstanding regulation 42) send a copy of the document referred to in paragraph (4) above to the parent as well as to the representative.

(6) Where by these Regulations a document is required to be signed by the chairman but by reason of death or incapacity the chairman is unable to sign such a document, it shall be signed by the other members of the tribunal, who shall certify that the chairman is unable to sign.

40 Method of sending, delivering or serving notices and documents

(1) A notice given under these Regulations shall be in writing and where under these Regulations provision is made for a party to notify the Secretary of the Tribunal of any matter he shall do so in writing.

(2) All notices and documents required by these Regulations to be sent or delivered to the Secretary of the Tribunal or the tribunal may be sent by post or by facsimile or delivered to or at the office of the Special Educational Needs Tribunal or such other office as may be notified by the Secretary of the Tribunal to the parties.

(3) All notices and documents required or authorised by these Regulations to be sent or given to any person mentioned in sub-paragraph (a) or (b) below may (subject to paragraph (5) below) either be sent by first class post or by facsimile or delivered to or at—

    (a)   in the case of a notice or document directed to a party—
        (i)   his address for service specified in the notice of appeal or in a written reply or in a notice under paragraph (4) below, or
        (ii) if no address for service has been so specified his last known address; and
    (b)   in the case of a notice or document directed to any person other than a party, his address or place of business or if such a person is a corporation, the corporation's registered or principal office and if sent or given to the authorised representative of a party shall be deemed to have been sent or given to that party.

(4) A party may at any time by notice to the Secretary of the Tribunal change his address for service under these Regulations.

(5) The recorded delivery service shall be used instead of the first class post for service of a summons issued under regulation 22 requiring the attendance of a witness.

(6) A notice or document sent by the Secretary of the Tribunal by post in accordance with these Regulations, and not returned, shall be taken to have been delivered to the addressee on the second working day after it was posted.

(7) A notice or document sent by facsimile shall be taken to have been delivered when it is received in legible form.

(8) Where for any sufficient reason service of any document or notice cannot be effected in the manner prescribed under this regulation, the President may dispense with service or make

an order for substituted service in such manner as he may deem fit and such service shall have the same effect as service in the manner prescribed under this regulation.

41 Extensions of time

(1) Where, pursuant to any provision of these Regulations anything is required to be done by a party within a period of time the President may, on the application of the party in question or of his own motion, in exceptional circumstances extend any period of time.

(2) Where a period of time has been extended pursuant to paragraph (1) above any reference in these Regulations to that period of time shall be construed as a reference to the period of time as so extended.

42 Parent's representative

(1) Subject to paragraph (2) below where, pursuant to regulations 7(1)(c) or 11(1) or (2)(a) a parent has stated the name of a representative, any reference in Parts 3, 4 or 5 of these Regulations (however expressed) to sending documents to, or giving notice to, the parent shall be construed as a reference to sending documents to or giving notice to the representative and any such reference to sending documents to or giving notice to a party or the parties shall in the context of the parent be likewise construed as a reference to sending documents to, or giving notice to the representative.

(2) Paragraph (1) above does not apply if—

   (a)   the parent has notified the Secretary of the Tribunal that he does not wish it to apply;

   (b)   the parent has notified the Secretary of the Tribunal under regulation 11(2)(b) that no person is acting as a representative; or

   (c)   the representative named has notified the Secretary of the Tribunal under regulation 11(3) that he is not prepared or no longer prepared to act in that capacity.

43 Revocation and Transitional Provisions

(1) The Special Educational Needs Tribunal Regulations 1994 (in this regulation referred to as 'the 1994 Regulations') are hereby revoked.

(2) Notwithstanding paragraph (1) above—

   (a)   any notice of appeal received before 1st March 1996 may comply either with regulation 7 of the 1994 Regulations or with regulation 7 of these Regulations; and

   (b)   the 1994 Regulations shall continue to apply in relation to any appeal where the notice of appeal was entered in the records under regulation 17(2) of the 1994 Regulations before 1st January 1996.

Appendix 3

SUMMARY CHART OF THE STEPS LEADING TO A STATUTORY ASSESSMENT

School-based stages: Stage 3

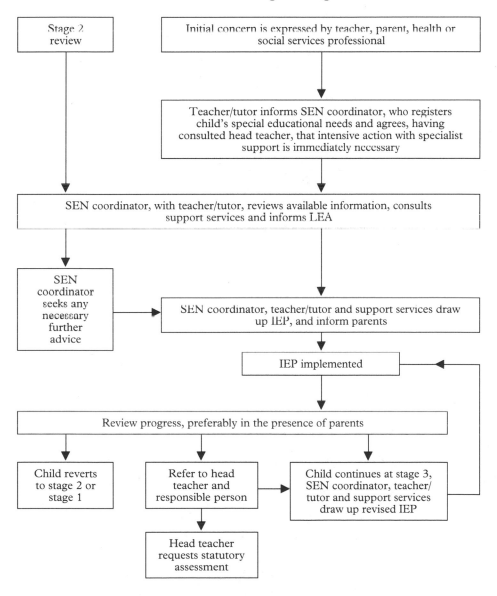

Source: *Code of Practice on the Identification and Assessment of Special Educational Needs* (DFE, 1994) (Crown copyright: reproduced with the permission of the Controller of HMSO).

Appendix 4

SUMMARY CHART OF TIME-LIMITS FOR MAKING ASSESSMENTS, STATEMENTS AND APPEALS TO THE TRIBUNAL

Time-limits for making assessments, statements and appeals to the Tribunal are as follows:

Consideration of whether a statutory assessment is necessary

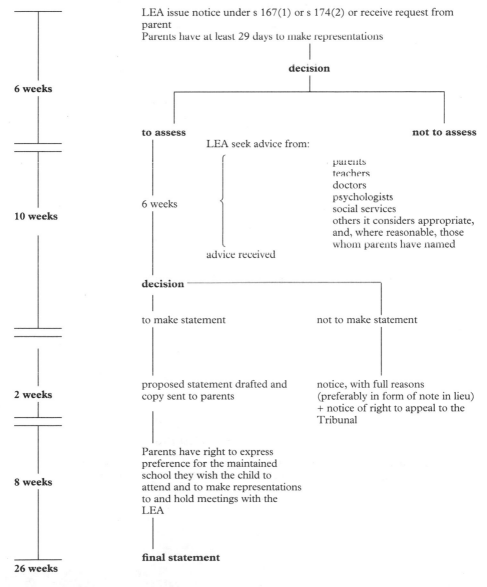

LEA issue notice under s 167(1) or s 174(2) or receive request from parent
Parents have at least 29 days to make representations

decision

6 weeks

to assess   not to assess

LEA seek advice from:

parents
teachers
doctors
psychologists
social services
others it considers appropriate, and, where reasonable, those whom parents have named

6 weeks

advice received

10 weeks

decision

to make statement   not to make statement

proposed statement drafted and copy sent to parents

notice, with full reasons (preferably in form of note in lieu) + notice of right to appeal to the Tribunal

2 weeks

Parents have right to express preference for the maintained school they wish the child to attend and to make representations to and hold meetings with the LEA

8 weeks

final statement

26 weeks

Appeals to the Tribunal

Notice of the right to appeal to the Tribunal

**2 months
(unless expires in
August when 1st
September)**

Notice of Appeal must be received by Secretary of Tribunal

10 working days   Copy Notice of Appeal sent to LEA

20 working days   LEA must deliver to Tribunal a written Reply signed by an authorised
                             officer
                             Copy Reply sent to parents by Tribunal

15 working days   Parents can deliver a written Response to the Secretary of the Tribunal

Unless appeal determined without a hearing, Secretary of Tribunal sends Notice of time and place of hearing to each party together with information and guidance.

**Not less than 10
working days
unless under
Regulation 14, 31
or 36, when not
less than 5
working days**   Any additional written representations by either party should be sent to
                               the Secretary of the Tribunal not less than 5 working days before the
                               hearing

——————— **HEARING** ———————

Source: Adapted from *Code of Practice on the Identification and Assessment of Special Educational Needs* (DFE, 1994) (Crown copyright: reproduced with the permission of the Controller of HMSO).

Appendix 5

EDUCATION (SPECIAL EDUCATIONAL NEEDS) REGULATIONS 1994 (SI 1994/1047)

SCHEDULE
PART A
NOTICE TO PARENT

To: [*name and address of parent*]

1. Accompanying this notice is a copy of a statement of the special educational needs of [*name of child*] which [*name of authority*] ('the authority') propose to make under the Education Act 1993.

2. You may express a preference for the maintained, grant maintained or grant-maintained special school you wish your child to attend and may give reasons for your preference.

3. If you wish to express such a preference you must do so not later than 15 days from the date on which you receive this notice and the copy of the statement or 15 days from the date on which you last attend a meeting in accordance with paragraph 10 or 11 below, whichever is later. If the 15th day falls on a weekend or a bank holiday you must do so not later than the following working day.

4. If you express a preference in accordance with paragraphs 2 and 3 above the authority are required to specify the name of the school you prefer in the statement, and accordingly to arrange special educational provision at that school, unless—

   (a) the school is unsuitable to your child's age, ability or aptitude or to his/her special educational needs, or

   (b) the attendance of your child at the school would be incompatible with the provision of efficient education for the children with whom he/she would be educated or the efficient use of resources.

5. The authority will normally arrange special educational provision in a maintained, grant-maintained or grant-maintained special school. However, if you believe that the authority should arrange special educational provision for your child at a non-maintained special school or an independent school you may make representations to that effect.

6. The following maintained, grant-maintained and grant-maintained special schools provide [*primary/secondary*] education in the area of the authority:

[Here list all maintained, grant-maintained, and grant-maintained special schools in the authority's area which provide primary education, or list all such schools which provide secondary education, depending on whether the child requires primary or secondary education. Alternatively, list the required information in a list attached to this notice.]

7. A list of the non-maintained special schools which make special educational provision for pupils with special educational needs in England and Wales and are approved by the Secretary of State for Education or the Secretary of State for Wales is attached to this notice.

8. A list of the independent schools in England and Wales which are approved by the Secretary of State for Education or the Secretary of State for Wales as suitable for the admission of children for whom statements of special educational needs are maintained is attached to this notice.

9. You are entitled to make representations to the authority about the content of the statement. If you wish to make such representations you must do so not later than 15 days from the date on which you receive this notice, or 15 days from the date on which you last attended a meeting in accordance with the next paragraph, whichever is the later date.

10. You are entitled, not later than 15 days from the date on which you receive this notice, to require the authority to arrange a meeting between you and an officer of the authority at which any part of the statement, or all of it, may be discussed. In particular, any advice on which the statement is based may be discussed.

11. If having attended a meeting in accordance with paragraph 10 above you still disagree with any part of the assessment in question, you may within 15 days of the date of the meeting require the authority to arrange a meeting or meetings to discuss the advice which they consider relevant to the part of the assessment you disagree with. They will arrange for the person who gave the advice, or some other person whom they think appropriate, to attend the meeting.

12. If at the conclusion of the procedure referred to above the authority serve on you a statement with which you disagree you may appeal to the Special Educational Needs Tribunal against the description of your child's special educational needs, against the special educational provision specified including the school named, or, if no school is named, against that fact.

13. All correspondence with the authority should be addressed to the officer responsible for this case:

    [Here set out name, address and telephone number of case officer, and any reference number which should be quoted.]

_____   _____

[Date]   *[Signature of officer responsible]*

PART B

STATEMENT OF SPECIAL EDUCATIONAL NEEDS

Part 1: Introduction

1. In accordance with section 168 of the Education Act 1993 ('the Act') and the Education (Special Educational Needs) Regulations 1994 ('the Regulations'), the following statement is made by [**here set out name of authority**] ('the authority') in respect of the child whose name and other particulars are mentioned below.

Child	
Surname	Other names ....
Home address	....
....	Sex ....
....	Religion ....
Date of Birth	Home language ....
Child's parent or person responsible	
Surname	Other names ....
Home address	....
....	Relationship to child ....
....	....
Telephone No	

2. When assessing the child's special educational needs the authority took into consideration, in accordance with regulation 10 of the Regulations, the representations, evidence and advice set out in the Appendices to this statement.

Part 2: Special educational needs

[*Here set out the child's special educational needs, in terms of the child's learning difficulties which call for special educational provision, as assessed by the authority.*]

Part 3: Special educational provision

Objectives

[*Here specify the objectives which the special educational provision for the child should aim to meet.*]

Educational provision to meet needs and objectives

[*Here specify the special educational provision which the authority consider appropriate to meet the needs specified in Part 2 and to meet the objectives in this Part, and in particular specify—*

(a)   *any appropriate facilities and equipment, staffing arrangements and curriculum,*
(b)   *any appropriate modifications to the application of the National Curriculum,*
(c)   *any appropriate exclusions from the application of the National Curriculum, in detail, and the provision which it is proposed to substitute for any such exclusions in order to maintain a balanced and broadly based curriculum; and*
(d)   *where residential accommodation is appropriate, that fact.*]

Monitoring

[*Here specify the arrangements to be made for—*

(a)   *regularly monitoring progress in meeting the objectives specified in this Part,*
(b)   *establishing targets in furtherance of those objectives,*
(c)   *regularly monitoring the targets referred to in (b),*
(d)   *regularly monitoring the appropriateness of any modifications to the application of the National Curriculum, and*
(e)   *regularly monitoring the appropriateness of any provision substituted for exclusions from the application of the National Curriculum.*

Here also specify any special arrangements for reviewing this statement.]

Part 4: Placement

[*Here specify—*

(a)   *the type of school which the authority consider appropriate for the child and the name of the school for which the parent has expressed a preference or, where the authority are required to specify the name of a school, the name of the school which they consider would be appropriate for the child and should be specified, or*
(b)   *the provision for his education otherwise than at a school which the authority consider appropriate.*]

Part 5: Non-educational needs

[*Here specify the non-educational needs of the child for which the authority consider provision is appropriate if the child is to properly benefit from the special educational provision specified in Part 3.*]

Part 6: Non-educational provision

[*Here specify any non-educational provision which the authority propose to make available or which they are satisfied will be made available by a district health authority, a social services authority or some other body, including the arrangements for its provision. Also specify the objectives of the provision, and the arrangements for monitoring progress in meeting those objectives.*]

_____   _____

Date   *A duly authorised officer of the authority*

Appendix A: Parental representations

[Here set out any written representations made by the parent of the child under section 167(1)(d) of or paragraph 4(1) of Schedule 10 to the Act and a summary which the parent has accepted as accurate of any oral representations so made or record that no such representations were made.]

Appendix B: Parental evidence

[Here set out any written evidence either submitted by the parent of the child under section 167(1)(d) of the Act or record that no such evidence was submitted.]

Appendix C: Advice from the child's parent

[Here set out the advice obtained under regulation 6(1)(a).]

Appendix D: Educational advice

[Here set out the advice obtained under regulation 6(1)(b).]

Appendix E: Medical advice

[Here set out the advice obtained under regulation 6(1)(c).]

Appendix F: Psychological advice

[Here set out the advice obtained under regulation 6(1)(d).]

Appendix G: Advice from the social services authority

[Here set out the advice obtained under regulation 6(1)(e).]

Appendix H: Other advice obtained by the authority

[Here set out the advice obtained under regulation 6(1)(f).]

Appendix 6

SUMMARY CHART OF APPEAL PROCEDURE AND TIMETABLE

Timetable from making an appeal to getting the tribunal's decision

The timetable below shows the number of working days an action takes. Working days do not include Saturdays, Sundays, Bank Holidays or any day in August.

- Parents make an appeal and the tribunal office decides whether the tribunal can deal with the appeal.

- If the tribunal cannot deal with the appeal, the tribunal office tells parents in writing **within 10 working days**.

- If the tribunal can deal with the appeal, the tribunal office sends the LEA a copy of the appeal **within 10 working days**.

- The LEA replies **within 20 working days**.

- As soon as the LEA's reply arrives, the tribunal office sends a copy of the reply to parents. If parents want to give their views on the LEA's reply, they send them to the tribunal office **within 15 working days**.

- When the tribunal office sends parents a copy of the LEA reply, it also sends a form asking them for details of who they want to attend the hearing. At the same time, it sends the LEA a form asking for details of who they will be sending to the hearing.

- Parents and the LEA return forms to the tribunal office **within 30 working days**.

- The tribunal office tells the parties the date and location of the hearing **at least 10 working days beforehand**.

- The tribunal office sends a written decision to parents and the LEA **within 10 working days after the hearing**.

Source: *How to Appeal* (DFE, 1995) (Crown copyright: reproduced with the permission of the Controller of HMSO).

Appendix 7

MODEL NOTICE OF APPEAL

Notice of Appeal to the Special Educational Needs Tribunal

Please use this form if you want to send a notice of appeal to the Special Educational Needs Tribunal. You must send in this form so that it arrives in the tribunal office no later than the first working day, two months after the LEA told you that you could appeal. If the end of the two month period is in August, you will have until 1 September to make your appeal.

● *Please fill in the boxes below. This form has to be photocopied, so please use black ink and capital letters.*

● *If there is not enough space for your answer, please continue on a separate sheet and attach it to this form.*

Section 1

Please give below the details of the child, for whom the appeal is being made:

Child's surname ....

Child's first names ....

Child's date of birth ....

Child's gender M/F ....

It will help us if you tick one of the boxes below. You do not have to, but the information will give the tribunal useful statistics. All information is kept in the strictest confidence. The tribunal is registered under the Data Protection Act.

Child's ethnic origin:

☐ Black African ☐ Bangladeshi ☐ Chinese

☐ Black Caribbean ☐ Indian ☐ White

☐ Black Other* ☐ Pakistani ☐ Other*

* If you have ticked other, please give details:..................................

....

....

Section 2

Please give your details below. Parents can appeal jointly but if you live at different addresses we will only send papers to the address you give first.

Your name   Mr ☐ Mrs ☐ Miss ☐ Ms ☐ Other ☐

Your surname ....

First names. ....

Your relationship to the child, for example, father, mother, guardian, and so on ....

Your address ....

....

....

.... Postcode ....

Your telephone number, if any..

Your name   Mr ☐ Mrs ☐ Miss ☐ Ms ☐ Other ☐

Your surname ....

First names. ....

Your relationship to the child, for example, father, mother, guardian, and so on ....

Your address ....

....

....

.... Postcode ....

Your telephone number, if any..

Section 3

If it would help you for us to send tribunal papers to someone else instead of you, please give the following details:

Name: ....

Address ....

....

....

.... Postcode ....

Telephone number: ....

Section 4

Please give the name of the local education authority whose decision you are appealing against:

....

Please give the date you received the letter from the LEA telling you that you could appeal to the tribunal:

....

Please tick the boxes below that apply to your appeal. **Please include a separate sheet of paper explaining briefly why you disagree with the LEA.**

I am appealing to the SEN tribunal because:

1 I have asked the LEA to assess, or re-assess my child, but they have refused. ☐

2 The LEA have assessed my child but refused to provide a statement. ☐

3 The LEA have provided a statement, but I disagree with part 2 or part 3 of it, or both parts. ☐

4 The LEA have provided a statement, but I disagree with the school they have named in part 4. ☐

5 The LEA have provided a statement, but they have not named a school in it. ☐

6 I have asked the LEA to change the school named in the statement, but they have refused. ☐

7 The LEA have decided not to maintain my child's statement. ☐

The school I would prefer my child to go to is: (Please give the name and address of the school if you have ticked the box in 4, 5 or 6.)

....

....

Section 5

If you live in Wales, do you want the hearing to be in Welsh?

☐ Yes ☐ No

Section 6

Please make sure you send the following documents with this appeal form. **We cannot register your appeal without them.**

- A copy of your child's statement of special educational needs (if he or she has one), **even if the LEA have refused to maintain it.**

- The other documents attached to the statement (appendices). **If they were not attached to the final statement, send the ones attached to the proposed (draft) statement.**

- A copy of the letter (notice) from the LEA which sets out the decision you are appealing against.

- If you have ticked box 1 in section 4, send a copy of your letter to the LEA asking them to make an assessment.

You will be able to send further documents at a later date if you want.

Your signatures ....
....
Date ....

This form should be returned to London even if the appeal will be processed by the Darlington office.

Please return this form together with any supporting documents to the address below:

> **Special Educational Needs Tribunal**
> **Secretariat**
> **71 Victoria Street**
> **LONDON SW1H OHW**
> **Telephone: 0171-925 6935 Facsimile: 0171-925 6926**

Source: *How to Appeal* (DFE, 1995) (Crown copyright: reproduced with the permission of the Controller of HMSO).

Appendix 8

TRIBUNAL ADDRESSES AND CONTACTS

ADDRESSES

Special Educational Needs Tribunal
71 Victoria Street
London
SW1H 0HW

Telephone: 0171 925 6925
Fax: 0171 925 6926

Special Educational Needs Tribunal
Mowden Hall
Staindrop Road
Darlington
County Durham
DL3 9BG

Telephone: 01325 391046
Fax: 01325 391045 (The Secretary)

Council on Tribunals
7th Floor
22 Kingsway
London
WC2B 6LE

SPECIAL EDUCATIONAL NEEDS TRIBUNAL

CONTACT NAMES, TELEPHONE NUMBERS AND LOCAL EDUCATION AUTHORITY DIVISIONS

London

Team 1

Bruce Barton, tel: 0171 925 6127
Shelley Stewart-Fleming, tel: 0171 925 6910
Bernice Cayenne, tel: 0171 925 6910
Denese Newell, tel: 0171 925 6811

Initial contact for:

Bath and NE Somerset	Gloucestershire	South Gloucestershire
Berkshire	Isles of Scilly	Surrey

Bexley	Kent	Wandsworth
City of Bristol	Kingston	Westminster
Cornwall	North Somerset	Wiltshire
Devon	Richmond	
Dorset	Somerset	

Team 2

Sue Collins, tel: 0171 925 6904
Bill Willoughby, tel: 0171 925 6905
Lorne Campbell, tel: 0171 925 6108

Initial contact for:

Bedfordshire	Hammersmith and Fulham	Northamptonshire
Birmingham	Harrow	Sandwell
Cambridgeshire	Hillingdon	Solihull
Coventry	Islington	Suffolk
Dudley	Kensington and Chelsea	Tower Hamlets
East Sussex	Lambeth	West Sussex
Greenwich	Leicestershire	
Hackney	Norfolk	

Team 3

Alison Henry, tel: 0171 925 6903
Neil Manning, tel: 0171 925 6906
Matthew Chase, tel: 0171 925 6159

Initial contact for:

Barking	Enfield	Oxfordshire
Barnet	Essex	Staffordshire
Bromley	Haringey	Sutton
Camden	Havering	Walsall
City of London	Hounslow	Waltham Forest
Croydon	Lincolnshire	Wolverhampton
Derbyshire	Nottinghamshire	

Team 3 – Appeals in Wales

Alison Henry, tel: 0171 925 6903
Brigid Hamilton, tel: 0171 925 6161
Mala Harinath, tel: 0171 925 6160

Initial contact for:

Aberconwy and Colwyn	Carmarthenshire	Powys
Anglesey	Denbighshire	Rhondda Cynon Taff
Bridgend	Flintshire	Swansea
Blaenau Gwent	Merthyr Tydfil	Torfaen
Caernarfonshire	Monmouthshire	Vale of Glamorgan
Caerphilly	Neath and Port Talbot	Wrexham
Cardiff	Newport	
Cardiganshire	Pembrokeshire	

Team 4

Melanie Hooper, tel: 0171 925 6130
Brenda Fitzgerald, tel: 0171 925 6912
Joanna Driscoll, tel: 0171 925 6920
Louise Turner, tel: 0171 925 6920

Initial contact for:

Brent	Hereford and Worcester	Newham
Buckinghamshire	Hertfordshire	Redbridge
Cheshire	Isle of Wight	Shropshire
Ealing	Lewisham	Southwark
Hampshire	Merton	Warwickshire

Darlington

Mark Sawyer, tel: 01325 391046
Martin Rackham, tel: 01325 391043
Dawn Wayman, tel: 01325 391042
Sue Wilson, tel: 01325 391044

Initial contact for:

Barnsley	Leeds	Sefton
Bolton	Liverpool	Sheffield
Bradford	Manchester	South Tyneside
Bury	Middlesborough	St Helens
Calderdale	Newcastle	Stockport
Cumbria	NE Lincolnshire	Stockton-on-Tees
Doncaster	North Lincolnshire	Sunderland
Durham	North Tyneside	Tameside
East Riding of Yorkshire	Northumberland	Trafford
Gateshead	North Yorkshire	Wakefield
Hartlepool	Oldham	Wigan
Kingston-upon-Hull (City)	Redcar and Cleveland	Wirral
Kirklees	Rochdale	City of York
Knowsley	Rotherham	
Lancashire	Salford	

Appendix 9

OTHER USEFUL ADDRESSES

1. GENERAL

Action for ME
PO Box 1302
Wells BA5 2WE

Tel: 01749 670799

Action for Sick Children
Argyle House
29–31 Euston Road
London NW1 2SD

Tel: 0171 833 2041

Advisory Centre for Education
Unir 1B
Aberdeen Studios
22 Highbury Grove
London N5 2EA

Tel: 0171 354 8321
(advice line 2–5 pm)

AFASIC – Overcoming Speech
Impairments
347 Central Markets
Smithfield
London EC1A 9NII

Tel: 0171 236 3632/6487

Albino Fellowship
9 Burnley Road
Hapton
Burnley
Lancashire BB11 5QR

Tel: 01282 776145

Anaphylaxis Campaign
PO Box 149
Fleet
Hampshire GU13 9XU

Tel: 01252 318723

The Arthritic Association
Hill House
1 Little New Street
London EC4A 3TR

Tel: 0171 491 0233

Arthritis Care
18 Stephenson Way
London NW1 2HD

Tel: 0171 916 1500

Association for Brain Damaged Children
47 Northumberland Road
Coventry CV1 3AP

Tel: 01203 25617

Association for Spina Bifida and
Hydrocephalus (ASBAH)
ASBAH House
42 Park Road
Peterborough
Cambridgeshire PE1 2UQ

Tel: 01733 555988

Association of Parents of
Vaccine-Damaged Children
2 Church Street
Shipston-on-Stour
Warwickshire CV36 4AP

Tel: 01608 61595

Barnardos
Tanners Lane
Barkingside
Ilford
Essex IG6 1QG

Tel: 0181 550 8822

Brain Research Trust
1 Wakefield Street
London WC1N 1PJ

Tel: 0171 278 5051

British Association for Early Childhood
Education
11 City View House
463 Bethnal Green Road
London E2 9QY

Tel: 0171 739 7594

British Deaf Association
39 Victoria Place
Carlisle CA1 1HU

Tel: 01228 48844

British Diabetic Association
10 Queen Anne Street
London W1M 0BD

Tel: 0171 323 1531

British Dyslexia Association
98 London Road
Reading
Berkshire RG1 5AU

Tel: 0118 966 8271

British Epilepsy Association
Anstey House
40 Hanover Square
Leeds LS3 1BE

Tel: 0113 2439393

British Institute for Brain Injured Children
(BIBIC)
Knowle Hall
Knowle
Bridgwater
Somerset TA7 8PJ

Tel: 01278 684060

British Medical Association
BMA House
Tavistock Square
London WC1H 9JP

Tel: 0171 387 4499

British Migraine Association
178A High Road
West Byfleet
Surrey KT14 7ED

Tel: 01932 352468

British Paediatric Association
5 St Andrew's Place
Regent's Park
London NW1 4LB

British Sports Association for the Disabled
Hayward House
Barnard Crescent
Aylesbury
Buckinghamshire HP21 0PG

Tel: 01296 27889

British Wireless for the Blind Fund
Gabriel House
34 New Road
Chatham
Kent ME4 4QR

Tel: 01634 832501

Brittle Bone Society
Ward 8
Strathmartine Hospital
Strathmartine
Dundee DD3 0PG

Tel: 01382 817771

Camden Parent Advocacy Service
St Margaret's
Leighton Road
London NW5 2QD

Tel: 0171 482 2593/0171 267 1089

Camphill Village Trust
19 South Road
Stourbridge
West Midlands DY8 3YA

Tel: 01384 372122

Catholic Children's Society
49 Russell Hill Road
Purley
Surrey CR8 2XB

Tel: 0181 668 2181

Cellmark Diagnostics
Blacklands Way
Abingdon Business Park
Abingdon
Oxfordshire OX14 1DY

Tel: 01235 528609

Centre for Studies on Integration in
Education
4th Floor
415 Edgware Road
London NW2 6NB

Tel: 0181 452 8642

Child Growth Foundation
2 Mayfield Avenue
Chiswick
London W4 1PW

Tel: 0181 995 0257

Children Nationwide
Nicholas House
181 Union Street
London SE1 0LN

Tel: 0171 928 2425

Children's Legal Centre
20 Compton Terrace
London N1 2UN

Tel: 0171 359 6251
(helpline 2–5 pm)

CLIC UK
(Cancer and Leukaemia in Childhood)
12–13 King Square
Bristol BS2 8JH

Tel: 0117 924 8844

Contact-a-Family
170 Tottenham Court Road
London W1P 0HA

Tel: 0171 383 3555

Council for Disabled Children
c/o National Children's Bureau
8 Wakley Street
London EC1V 7QE

Tel: 0171 843 6000

CRYSIS Support Group
BM CRY-SIS
London WC1N 3XX

Tel: 0171 404 5011

Cystic Fibrosis Research Trust
Alexandra House
5 Blyth Road
Bromley
Kent DR1 3RS

Tel: 0181 464 7211

Dial UK
Park Lodge
St Catherine's Hospital
Tickhill Road
Doncaster DN4 8QN

Tel: 01302 310123

Disability Information Service
10 Warwick Row
London SW1E 5EP

Tel: 0171 630 5994

Disability Alliance, ERA
1st Floor East
Universal House
88–94 Wentworth Street
London E1 7SA

Tel: 0171 247 8763

Disability Law Service
Room 241
2nd Floor
49–51 Bedford Row
London WC1R 4LR

Tel: 0171 831 8031

Disabled Living Foundation
380–384 Harrow Road
London W9 2HU

Tel: 0171 289 6111

Down's Syndrome Association
153–155 Mitcham Road
London SW17 9PG

Tel: 0181 682 4001

Dyslexia Institute
133 Gresham Road
Staines
Middlesex TW18 2AJ

Tel: 01784 463935

Education Advisor
Association for Spina Bifida and
Hydrocephalus
Asbah House
42 Park Road
Peterborough PE1 2UQ

Tel: 01733 555988

Education Otherwise
PO Box 7420
London N9 9SG

Family Fund
Joseph Rowntree Memorial Trust
PO Box 50
York YO1 1UY

Tel: 01904 621115

Foundation for Nephrology
14 Park Grove
Cardiff CF1 3BN

Tel: 01222 388353

Friedreich's Ataxia Group
The Common
Cranley
Surrey GU8 8SB

Tel: 01483 27274

Friends of Cheyne Centre for Children
with Cerebral Palsy
63 Cheyne Walk
London SW3 5LT

Tel: 0171 352 6740

Gifted Children's Information Centre
Hampton Grange
21 Hampton Lane
Solihull
West Midlands BN1 2QJ

Tel: 0121 705 4547

Greater London Association for Disabled
People (GLAD)
336 Brixton Road
London SW9 7AA

Tel: 0171 274 0107

Haemophilia Society
123 Westminster Bridge Road
London SE1 7HR

Tel: 0171 928 2020

HAPA
(formerly Handicapped Adventure
Playground Association)
Fulham Palace
Bishop's Avenue
London SW6 6EA

Tel: 0171 731 1435

Hearing Dogs for the Deaf
HDFD Training Centre
London Road
Lewknor
Oxfordshire OX9 5RY

Tel: 01844 353898

Home Start Consultancy
140 New Walk
Leicester LE1 7JL

Tel: 01533 554988

Huntington's Disease Association
108 Battersea High Street
London SW11 3HP

Tel: 0171 223 7000

Hyperactive Children's Support Group
71 Whyke Lane
Chichester
Sussex PO19 2LD

Tel: 01903 725182

I Can
Barbican City Gate
1–3 Dufferin Street
London EC1Y 8NA

Tel: 0171 374 4422

In Touch
10 Norman Road
Sale
Cheshire M33 3DF

Tel: 0161 962 4441
(information and contacts for rare
handicapping conditions)

IPSEA (Independent Panel for Special
Educational Advice)
22 Warren Hill Road
Woodbridge
Suffolk IP12 4DU

Tel: 01394 382814 (Enquiries)
    01394 380518 (Administration)

KIDS
80 Waynflete Square
London W10 6UD

Tel: 0181 969 2817

Lady Hoare Trust for Physically Disabled
Children
Mitre House
44–46 Fleet Street
London EC4Y 1BN

Tel: 0171 583 1951

Leukaemia Care Society
14 Kingfisher Court
Venney Bridge
Pinhoe
Exeter
Devon EX4 8JN

Tel: 01392 464848

Make-A-Wish Foundation
Rossmore House
26 Park Street
Camberley
Surrey GU15 3PL

Tel: 0125 24127

Medic Alert Foundation
12 Bridge Wharf
156 Caledonian Road
London N1 9UU

Tel: 0800 58420

MENCAP (Royal Society for Mentally
Handicapped Children and Adults)
Early Years Project
117–123 Golden Lane
London EC1Y 0RT

Tel: 0171 454 0454

MIND (National Association for Mental
Health)
Granta House
15–19 Broadway
Stratford
London E15 4BQ

Tel: 0181 519 2122

Motability
Gate House
West Gate
The High
Harlow
Essex CM10 1HR

Tel: 01279 635666

Multiple Sclerosis Society
25 Effie Road
London SW6 1EE

Tel: 0171 610 7171

Muscular Dystrophy Group of Great
Britain
7–11 Prescott Place
London SW4 6BS

Tel: 0171 720 8055

Myasthenia Gravis Association
Keynes House
Chester Park
Alfreton Road
Derby DE21 4AS

Tel: 01332 290219

National Association for the Education of
Sick Children
Open School
18 Victoria Park Square
Bethnal Green
London E2 9PF

Tel: 0181 980 6263/8523

National Association for Gifted Children
Park Campus
Boughton Green Road
Northampton NN2 7AL

Tel: 01604 792300

National Association of Citizens' Advice
Bureaux
115–123 Pentonville Road
London N1 9LZ

Tel: 0171 833 2181

National Association of Special
Educational Needs (NASEN)
York House
Exhall Grange
Wheelwright Lane
Coventry
Warwickshire CV7 9HP

Tel: 01203 362414

National Asthma Campaign
300 Upper Street
London N1 2XX

Tel: 0171 226 2260

National Autistic Society
276 Willesden Lane
London NW2 5RB

Tel: 0181 451 1114

National Childcare Campaign/Daycare
Trust
Wesley House
4 Wild Court
London WC2B 5AU

Tel: 0171 405 5617

National Deaf Children's Society
Family Services Centre
Carlton House
24 Wakefield Road
Rothwell Haigh
Leeds LS26 0SF

Tel: 0113 2823458
Freephone: 0800 252380

National Eczema Society
163 Eversholt Street
London NW1 1BU

Tel: 0171 388 4097

National Federation of the Blind of the UK
Unity House
Smyth Street
Westgate
Wakefield
West Yorkshire WF1 1ER

Tel: 01924 291313

National Library for the Handicapped
Child
Ash Court
Rose Street
Wokingham
Berkshire RG11 1XS

Tel: 0118 989 1101

National Meningitis Trust
Fern House
Bath Road
Stroud
Gloucestershire GL5 3TJ

Tel: 01453 751738

National Physically Handicapped and Able
Bodied (PHAB)
Padholme Road East
Peterborough
Cambridgeshire PE1 5UL

Tel: 01733 54117

National Portage Association
4 Clifton Road
Winchester
Hampshire

Tel: 01962 60148
(work with parents of young handicapped
children)

National Rathbone Society
1st Floor
Princess House
105–107 Princess Street
Manchester M1 6DD

Tel: 0161 236 5358

National Society for Epilepsy
Chalfont St Peter
Buckinghamshire SL9 0RJ

Tel: 01494 873991

National Toy Libraries Association
68 Churchway
London NW1 1LT

Tel: 0171 387 9592

NCH Action for Children
85 Highbury Park
London N5 1UD

Tel: 0171 226 2033

Network 81
1–7 Woodfield Terrace
Chapel Hill
Stansted
Essex CM24 8AJ

Tel: 01279 647415

Network
16 Princeton Street
London WC1R 4BB

Tel: 0171 831 8031/7740
(advice service)

Network for the Handicapped
16 Princeton Street
London WC1R 4BB

Tel: 0171 831 8031/7740
(advice service)

NORCAP
3 New High Street
Headington
Oxford OX3 7AJ

Tel: 01865 750554

Norwood Child Care
221 Golders Green Road
London NW11 9DL

Tel: 0181 458 3282

OAASIS
(Autism and Asperger Syndrome Support
Service)
Southlands School
Vicar's Hill
Boldre
Lymington
Hampshire SO4 5QB

Tel: 01590 677237

Parent Network (England)
44–46 Caversham Road
London NW5 2DS

Tel: 0171 485 85345

Parents in Partnership
Unit 2, Ground Floor
70 South Lambeth Road
London SW8 1RL

Tel: 0171 735 7735

Partially Sighted Society
Queen's Road
Doncaster DN1 2NX

Tel: 01302 323132

Portland College
Nottingham Road
Mansfield
Nottinghamshire NG18 4TJ

Tel: 01623 792141

Pre-School Group Association
61–63 Kings Cross Road
London WC1X 9LL

Tel: 0171 833 0991

Reach
(Association for Children with Hand or
Arm Deficiency)
12 Wilson Way
Earls Barton
Northamptonshire NN6 0NZ

Tel: 01604 811041

Research Trust for Metabolic Diseases in
Children (RTMDC)
53 Beam Street
Nantwich
Cheshire CW5 5NF

Tel: 01270 629782

Riding for the Disabled Association
National Agricultural Centre
Kenilworth
Warwickshire CV8 2LY

Tel: 01203 676510

Royal Association for Disability and
Rehabilitation (RADAR)
12 City Forum
250 City Road
London EC1V 8AF

Tel: 0171 250 3222

Royal National Institute for the Blind
224 Great Portland Street
London W1N 6AA

Tel: 0171 388 1266

Royal National Institute for the Deaf
105 Gower Street
London WC1E 6AH

Tel: 0171 387 8033

SCOPE (former Spastics Society)
12 Park Crescent
London W1N 4EQ

Tel: 0171 737 5020
Freephone: 0800 626216
(helpline 1 pm–10 pm)

SEEABILITY
56–66 Highlands Road
Leatherhead
Surrey KT22 8NR

Tel: 01372 373086

SENSE
11–13 Clifton Terrace
Finsbury Park
London N4 3SR

Tel: 0171 272 7774

Sickle Cell Society
54 Station Road
London NW10 4UA

Tel: 0181 961 7795

SKILL
(formerly National Bureau for
Handicapped Students)
336 Brixton Road
London SW9 7AA

Tel: 0171 274 0565

Slade Centre
Sidmouth
Devon EX10 0NU

Tel: 01395 578222

Special Education Consortium
c/o Council for Disabled Children
8 Wakley Street
London EC1V 7QE

Tel: 0171 278 9441

Spinal Injuries Association
Newpoint House
76 St James Lane
London N10 3DF

Tel: 0181 444 2121

Steps
(National Association for Children with
Lower Limb Abnormalities)
15 Statham Close
Lymm
Cheshire WA13 9NN

Tel: 01925 757525

Stroke Association
CHSA House
Whitecross Street
London EC1Y 8JJ

Tel: 0171 490 7999

Supportive Parents
c/o HFT
Merchants House
Wapping Road
Bristol BS1 4RW

Tel: 0117 9772225

The Children's Society
Edward Rudolph House
Margery Street
London WC1X 0JL

Tel: 0171 837 4299

Treloar Trust
Froyle
Alton
Hampshire GU34 4JX

Tel: 01420 22442

Tuberous Sclerosis Association of Great
Britain
Little Barnsley Farm
Catshill
Bromsgrove
Worcestershire B61 0NQ

Tel: 01527 781898

Voluntary Council for Handicapped
Children
8 Wakley Street
Islington
London EC1V 7QE

Tel: 0171 278 9441

Young Minds
22a Boston Place
London NW1 6ER

Tel: 0171 724 7262

2. LEGAL

High Court of Justice
Royal Courts of Justice
Strand, London WC2A 2LL

Tel: 0171 936 6000

Crown Office of the Supreme Court
Royal Courts of Justice
Strand, London WC2A 2LL

Tel: 0171 936 6205

Principal Registry of the Family Division
Somerset House
Strand, London WC2R 1LP

Tel: 0171 936 6000

Judicial Office of the House of Lords
London SW1A 0PW

Tel: 0171 219 3111

Court of Appeal Civil Division
Royal Courts of Justice
Room 246, Strand
London WC2A 2LL

General Office: 0171 936 6409
Listings Office: 0171 936 6195

Legal Aid Board
29–37 Red Lion Street
London WC1R 4PP

Tel: 0171 831 4209

Legal Aid Board
Cardiff Area No 5
Marland House
Central Square
Cardiff CF1 1PF

Tel: 01222 388971

The Law Society
113 Chancery Lane
London WC2A 1PL

Tel: 0171 242 1222

3. GOVERNMENT AND OTHERS

Pupils and Parents Branch
Department for Education and
Employment
Sanctuary Buildings
Great Smith Street
Westminster
London SW1P 3BT

Tel: 0171 925 5000
Fax: 0171 925 6000

DfEE Publications Centre
PO Box 6927
London E3 3NZ

Tel: 0171 510 0150

Welsh Office Education Department
Government Buildings
Ty Glas Road
Llanishen
Cardiff CF4 5WE

Tel: 01222 761456

Local Government Ombudsman
21 Queen Anne's Gate
London SW1H 9BU

Tel: 0171 222 5622

Local Ombudsman
Derwen House
Court Road
Bridgend
Mid Glamorgan CF31 1BN

Tel: 01656 661325

Government Department of Health
Community Services Division (CS3)
Alexander Fleming House
Elephant and Castle
London SE1 6BY

Tel: 0171 972 4083

Home Office
C2 Division (Family)
Queen Anne's Gate
London SW1H 9AT

Tel: 0171 273 3617

Registered Homes Tribunal
Community Services Division
Department of Health
Alexander Fleming House
Elephant and Castle
London SE1 6BY

Tel: 0171 407 5522

Welsh Office
Public Health and Family Division
(Child and Family Service Issues)
Cathays Park
Cardiff CF1 3NQ

Tel: 01222 823145

4. INTERNET WEB SITES

British Dyslexia Association Computer Committee:

http://www.dur.ac.uk/dot7da/home.html

Careers Advisory Network on Disability Opportunities:

http://www.comp.lancs.ac.uk/uni-services/careers/cando

Deaf UK:

http://www.wlv.ac.uk/www/depts/sles/deafuk/

Deaf World Web:

http://deafworldweb.org/deafworld/

Dyslexia Archive:

http://www.hensa.ac.uk/dyslexia.html

Multimedia Enabling Technologies Group:

http://met.open.ac.uk/

National Council for Education Technology:

http://ncet.csv.warwick.ac.uk/

RNIB:

http://www.rnib.org.uk

Mailbase (has a number of special needs mailing lists):

http://www.mailbase.ac.uk/

Appendix 10

DRAFT LETTER FROM SOLICITORS TO PARENTS

Dear

I write further to our meeting to explain what you need to do next in your appeal to the Special Educational Needs Tribunal. I enclose two blank copies of the Notice of Appeal which should be completed by you. You only need to send one to the Tribunal, but it is sensible to keep a copy for your own records – as you should do with every document from now on. You will see that the grounds of appeal are set out in Section 4 of the Notice of Appeal. You will need to tick ground .... As I am not acting for you, your names and address should be the only ones given. DO NOT put my name or address in Section 3.

As the decision against which you are appealing was made in the letter sent to you dated .... and there is a limit of 2 months in which to appeal, you MUST send the Notice of Appeal to the Tribunal not later than .... As I mentioned to you, the Tribunal will send you an acknowledgement of your appeal and then contact the Council to ask for their views. If they do not agree with your appeal they will let the Tribunal know and there will have to be a hearing. There is a timetable for this and I enclose a copy to show you what should happen then.

As the members of the Tribunal will read the papers before the hearing, it is important that you send to the Tribunal all the information you want to rely on as soon as possible. The rules actually say that you must do this either when you submit your appeal or within 2 weeks of any reply by the Council. It is much better to give the Tribunal the documents when you send the notice of appeal, however.

It is important to keep in mind that you will need to make all the points you want to make on paper and that every point needs to be backed up with evidence. As you are appealing against .... the documents you will need to send to the Tribunal are [*insert here those documents listed in Appendix 11*].

It is possible that there are reports which are produced after you have sent those documents listed above to the Tribunal. You have two options. First, you may write to the President of the Tribunal asking for permission to use the new report, or secondly you may ask the permission of the Tribunal at the hearing. If there is sufficient time, it is better to ask permission beforehand.

The Council will also produce documents that they want to use. Many of them will be the same as yours but there could be some which are different. You need to read those you have not seen before as they may be of importance.

At the hearing (which will be made as informal as possible) it is important that you express your point of view. The Chairman of the Tribunal may suggest that different aspects of ....'s case are dealt with one at a time, rather than dealing with them all at once. By taking each aspect of the case in turn, everyone will be given the opportunity to concentrate on points as they come up.

On each point to be considered (which will be identified by the Chairman at the start of the hearing) the Council's representative will be asked to explain the local education authority's point of view first. If the Council has a witness to give this point of view both you and the members of the Tribunal will be able to ask questions. You should not expect or rely upon the members of the Tribunal to ask the questions for you.

Once the local education authority's view has been expressed and any questions that need to be asked finished, you will be asked to explain your point of view. If you have a witness to explain it, you should ask questions of the witness and, as with the Council's case, you and your witness will be asked questions by the Council and the members of the Tribunal.

Just because the Chairman has raised a number of issues to discuss, the hearing will not be limited to those matters alone. You will be asked if you wish to add anything else and perhaps the best way to make sure you say all you want to is to write out a list before the hearing of what you want to cover and tell the Tribunal. If you tick the points off as you raise them you will then make sure that nothing is left out.

As we discussed when I met you, you are able to put facts in writing or they can be given by a witness at the hearing. You are entitled to bring only two witnesses. If you want to have more you will need to ask permission of the President well before the hearing. It is important to make sure that if you are going to call a witness that that person is fully familiar with the facts they are going to talk about.

You will not be given a decision on the day of the hearing. It will be sent to you in writing and should arrive within 2 weeks of the hearing.

If I can be of any more help, please contact me.

Yours sincerely

A. Solicitor & Co

Appendix 11

POTENTIAL DOCUMENT BUNDLE

It will be of considerable help to the members of the Tribunal if all documents sent in by the parties are consecutively numbered. It makes it much easier for everyone to find the right page quickly at the hearing. It will also ensure that the same document is not reproduced three times!

1. Failure to assess and failure to make a statement
Index
Notice of Appeal
Refusal letter
Any individual education plan that has been produced
Any professional reports to be relied upon
From the local authority: financial information about delegation of budget in the school
Any correspondence, oldest first, in consecutive order

2. Contents of the statement and refusal to reassess and ceasing to maintain
Index
Notice of Appeal
Letter from local authority
Statement
Reports appended to statement
If appealing against the name of a school, school prospectuses
If appealing against the need/provision, any reports obtained by the parents
From the local authority: financial information about additional cost, etc, if relying on that ground
Any correspondence, oldest first, in consecutive order

INDEX